A STORY OF PASSION, COMMITMENT AND
A SEARCH FOR JUSTICE AND FREEDOM

KOBAD GHANDY

a prison memoir

LOTUS COLLECTION
ROLI BOOKS

Lotus Collection

© Kobad Ghandy, 2021

First published in March 2021
Second impression April 2021

The Lotus Collection
An imprint of
Roli Books Pvt. Ltd
M-75, Greater Kailash II Market, New Delhi 110 048
Phone: +91 (011) 40682000
E-mail: info@rolibooks.com
Website: www.rolibooks.com
Also at Bengaluru, Chennai & Mumbai

Photographs courtesy: Kobad Ghandy
Cover Design: Pallavi Agarwala
Layout Design: Bhagirath Kumar
Production: Lavinia Rao

ISBN: 978-81-949691-6-7

Typeset in ITC Galliard Std by Roli Books Pvt. Ltd
Printed at Saurabh Printers Pvt. Ltd., India

This book is dedicated to my late wife Anuradha, fondly called Anu, in whom I saw all that was good in society. Her commitment to truth and justice and her idealism could dispel the darkness of a benighted world. Anu's courage of conviction, simplicity, straightforwardness, her intelligence and honesty, made her the ideal social activist.

Contents

SECTION III
REFLECTIONS and RELEVANCE

Preface

17 September 2009. A day I shall never forget. It was four in the afternoon when I was standing at a bus stop below Bhikaji Cama Place in Delhi. I had gone to the bustling business district with a friend to purchase computer material. I was waiting at the bus stop for a few minutes when a SUV pulled up and about half a dozen toughs pounced on me, pushing me to the ground as I struggled to free myself. They seized everything on me, dragged me into their car and sped away.

Little did I know that this marked the beginning of a ten-year-long journey, as an undertrial, through seven jails in five states across the country. I was sixty-two years old and had come to Delhi from Mumbai for urgent medical attention, for a serious prostrate/urinary problem, as well as orthopaedic and hypertension issues.

The abduction was in fact an arrest. The charge? That I was a member of the banned Communist Party of India (Maoist), with the media widely propagating that I was supposedly one of its top leaders. This needs to be put in context, as, at that time, the Maoist sweep was being referred to as the Red Corridor, stretching from Nepal (the bulk of which was under Maoist control) and West Bengal (the famous Lalgarh movement) in the north and east, down to

Bihar, Jharkhand, Orissa, Chhattisgarh (and two districts of Maharashtra), Andhra Pradesh/Telangana, Karnataka, and finally the tri-junction of Tamil Nadu, Karnataka and Kerala. It then, (though no longer) comprised a huge swathe of the country making the government nervous. Together with this, the entire Northeast and Kashmir were in ferment. At that time nearly half the country and the bulk of Nepal was being swept by upheaval and insurgencies.

What then is this 'dangerous' party, of which merely being a member invites a life sentence, and even bail is not possible? The Maoist party belonged to that trend of communism which was initiated by the Naxalbari Uprising in 1967 in West Bengal. It distinguished itself from the parliamentary Left by its belief in armed agrarian revolution and adoption of the Chinese model. It was then called the Communist Party of India (Marxist–Leninist), but by 1972 it had been decimated in its place of origin, West Bengal. Later, it revived in many parts of the country, particularly Andhra Pradesh and Bihar under the respective banners of the PWG (People's War Group) and the MCC (Maoist Communist Centre). Later, in 2004, these (together with some others) merged to form the CPI (Maoist). The then prime minister, Manmohan Singh, had defined this party as the single greatest threat to internal security, more so than the threat posed by Islamic fundamentalists. Though the party was only put on the banned list in June 2009, its separate constituents, PWG and MCC, had been banned much earlier, together with many of their purported 'front' organizations. Besides which, various state governments had banned them at different times. About that time the government had unleashed the horrific Salwa Judum in Bastar where villages were burnt, houses destroyed, women raped and youth disappeared, which was finally disbanded under instructions from the Supreme Court.

Coming back to that fateful afternoon, after purchasing

some computer material, I descended to the side lane to catch a bus when I was accosted. Inside the car they were speaking Telugu amongst themselves, while one questioned me in broken Hindi. From four that afternoon to three o'clock the next morning, I was driven around the city with the occupants consistently talking to their bosses in Telugu on the phone, a language I didn't understand. The word 'airport', though, kept cropping up. The Andhra Pradesh Intelligence Bureau (IB) were known to fly people in helicopters to jungles in their state and bump them off, and report that they'd been 'killed in encounter'. I assumed this was the end.

But, at three in the morning, we reached a 'safe house' with high walls where I was finally allowed a few hours of sleep. The next morning, intelligence people from a number of states had gathered at the safe house but the main questioning was by the men from Andhra Pradesh. They claimed I was a politburo member of the CPI (Maoist) and wanted details of other members of the Central Committee and Politburo of the party – details which they seemed to already have; certainly more than what I knew. When they could not elicit any additional details from me, they used threats, but did no direct physical harm, probably given my age, and the fact that I was already ill and had just come from a hospital check-up. They were particularly keen on getting to the place I was staying in Delhi, in the working-class locality of Badarpur, where my friend Rajender Kumar (and later co-accused) had a rented accommodation, to get my computer and any other written 'incriminating' material.

They tried all the standard techniques, stopping short of using physical force, to extract information from me; they'd raise the same questions again and again, quote others as having confessed, issue various threats and enticements of not putting cases, and so on. As the entire procedure was illegal (IB does not have the powers to arrest, I later learnt), they would not openly go to the room where I had been staying in Delhi though they tried to reach the room by other means.

By 20 September it appeared that news was leaked to the press that I had 'disappeared'. I gathered this because in the morning there was a great flurry to urgently produce me before the Special Cell of the Delhi Police. On the way to the Special Cell office I was instructed to not mention that I had been picked up three days ago, and instead say it had just been a few hours. That afternoon, I was deposited at the first floor of the Special Cell office.

There was a bit of black comedy to the whole situation, as this was the first time a 'Naxalite' had been brought to their office. Having been used to Islamic terrorists, they knew little about what we creatures were.

They went through the standard routine of recording my details and then off we went to Rajender Kumar's house, where I stayed when I came to Delhi. Rajender was not at home when we reached, and the police found nothing of importance. They gathered books, mostly Hindi progressive literature bought from bookshops which my associate who lived there was interested in. The CDs too were mostly ordinary films. This is when the inspector who accompanied me became suspicious and asked me when I had actually been picked up, thinking that the key material had been already taken by the Andhra Pradesh IB. Despite the earlier warning, I decided to tell them the truth: that it had been three days since I was detained. This confirmed to them the feeling (incorrect) that the Andhra Pradesh IB had already visited the site and confiscated all important material. Of course, I did not clarify, nor did they ask. It's possible they later found out the truth from the landlord.

When we returned to the Special Cell office with all the material, I found the senior inspector on the computer googling exactly what Naxalites were. Though they may not have known much, the media, by then, had whipped up the notion that I was a prime catch, worthy of big dividends.

When I was produced the next day in the magistrate court, the lady magistrate (a good soul by the name of Kaveri Baweja) saw the condition of my health and refused immediate police custody. She ordered that I be medically examined at once at the nearby government hospital and brought back. After that, when I was reproduced with the doctor's report, she ordered I be sent to jail.

My arrest had apparently got a lot of publicity. At the court was my sister-in-law, Reetha Balsavar, who handed me a sling bag with some toiletries. The human rights organization representative, Rona Wilson, had already made arrangements for senior advocate Rebecca John to appear for me. The sling bag that Reetha gave me then was so sturdy that even though it accompanied me around seven jails it never broke in spite of the weight it carried. I use it to this day.

I was driven to jail amidst high security (which was to become the norm during my entire stay in Delhi). There were four commandos with bullet-proof jackets, an inspector, a few sub-inspectors, some fifteen AK-47 wielding commandos and a few others who accompanied me.

During this two-hour journey from Tis Hazari Court to jail, I did not know what to expect and I began reflecting on what had transpired these last few days and how suddenly my life had been upturned. Though one expects arrest in our line of activity, given that I had not been arrested in the past forty years, it did come as a shock. Certainly, it was nothing compared to the suddenness and shock of my beloved wife

Anu's death at the age of fifty-four, barely eighteen months earlier. That was a hundred times worse. So, in comparison, this shock was numbed.

The horror of that night, waiting in the hospital lobby as Anu was on a ventilator, kept flashing in the mind. Those thoughts sort of blunted my reaction to the arrest; after all, I thought, what could be worse? I was deep in such thoughts when the police van rolled into the Tihar complex. I had entered an Indian prison for the first time.

It was 21 September 2009.

SECTION I

AN INITIATION: RESPONSES AND REACTIONS

What was it that initiated me into the line of work that led to my arrest on that day in September 2009 and resulted in me spending nearly 15 per cent of my life in Indian jails, that too after being repeatedly acquitted in all the Maoist-related charges?

In this section I trace the background to the path my wife Anu and I chose. Our families were like any other upper middle-class ones. Prior to awakening to consciousness, I was totally ignorant of society in general, like any privileged Parsi youth. Although Anu's family had communist leanings and the liberal atmosphere at her home was reflected in a sharp intellect, she too had a carefree childhood and was the typical fun-loving college girl. What changed us, and that too so radically? What led us to this line of politics?

During the entire period of my incarceration, I had no intention of writing a jail diary but in the last lap of my imprisonment in the solitude of Surat jail, where I spent a month-and-a-half, I began reflecting on the past. I made some notes. And interestingly the very first memory that came to my mind was my arrest in London in 1971 when I was only twenty-four years old.

London 1972:
A Beginning and an End

It was April 1972 and the third and final day of my court hearing at a London courthouse. I was finally asked by the honourable judge if I had anything to say in my defence. During that time in India the Naxalites had called for the boycott of 'bourgeois courts'. I remember feeling that it was more pertinent to make a political point.

Although I cannot recall the exact words, I remember the essence of what I said when I walked up to witness box:

'Your Honour, we were holding a corner meeting a year back, in this working-class locality, against racism. As I was speaking, we were suddenly attacked by white racist skinheads. The Bobbies (police) present, instead of restraining them, arrested three of us. I, being the only non-white amongst the three, was segregated by the police and soundly thrashed in the lock-up amidst racist abuse. Your Honour, the British rulers (I have nothing against the ordinary British people) robbed and looted our country for over two centuries as a result of which millions of my countrymen perished. Except for a handful of collaborators, we were treated like dogs. A rich country that contributed 25 per cent of the world's yearly income before the entry of the British, was reduced to penury – a mere 3 per cent at the time the British left. Your Honour, the colonial era is long since over but imperial colonial attitudes continue in the form of racism. But, in this post-colonial age we will no longer tolerate this false sense of superiority. We will stand erect as self-respecting citizens, proud of our Indian origins. Your Honour, we have been wrongly framed. The real culprits are the British rulers who whip up such crude hatred to perpetuate their neo-colonial order and ideas. It is they who should be put on trial. That is all I have to say.'

Barely had I sat down when the judge, whose face had long-since turned red with anger, shouted, 'Lock this man up, he is dangerous! I will pronounce the verdict tomorrow.' I was led off to Brixton prison. The next day when we were produced in court, he sentenced two of us to three months' hard labour in prison while the third, a woman, was let off with a fine.

~

But how did I find myself behind bars in London?

I had come to the UK in 1968 to do my Chartered Accountancy (CA), after graduating in BSc (Chemistry) from St. Xavier's College, Bombay (present-day Mumbai). I was probably the only student to come to do CA with a science degree, all the others were either economics or commerce graduates. I had taken up science in college partly due to my excellent organic chemistry teacher, Prof Nadkarni. Besides, I did not find studying an unrelated field to CA a handicap.

I was received at Heathrow Airport by another student from India, Homi Khusrokhan, who was then studying at the London School of Economics and was introduced to me by my father. He helped me settle into the YMCA hostel at Warren Street, where I stayed for the first six months. Homi returned to India in 1972 and joined the pharmaceutical giant

4

GlaxoSmithKline and stayed with them for twenty-nine years, much of that time as managing director. He has since retired, and has been for many years the president of Bombay's Willingdon Club.

In order to become a certified chartered accountant one has to work (article) with a firm of auditors for the entire four-year period of study at a nominal stipend and, through a correspondence course, sit for the three exams. Passing is exceedingly difficult (the pass rate used to be something like 1-2 per cent) and most people repeatedly sit for the exams. Without the articleship one cannot sign up for studying Chartered Accountancy. I was articled to the auditing firm Jackson and Pixley, in the city of London.

During my schooling at the Doon School, Dehra Dun, and later college in Mumbai, I was – like most of my peers – devoid of social consciousness or for that matter any knowledge of the social environment beyond my immediate world. In school it was studies and sports, both of which I cruised through with mediocrity; and at college it was studies, and passing time with friends, like Adi Irani (a compulsive card player, chess player and boxer), and at the Willingdon Club playing golf, badminton and swimming. When I came to the UK, it was like any other promising young man on the precipice of building a successful career, which in my case, being a London-returned CA would guarantee. For example, my closest friend and classmate from Doon School, Ishaat Hussain, who was also in the UK doing CA at the same time, went on to become finance director of Tata Sons for over a decade.

Within a few months, while staying at the Indian YMCA at Warren Street, I began to notice the racism directed at Indians and others of colour. The derogatory term WOGs (Western Oriental Gentlemen) was one of the abuses often hurled at us. This made me think. The docility of the Indians first angered me, but I later realized their need to stay in the UK for jobs or education, compelled them to accept the abuse. They swallowed the humiliation and/or even pretended it didn't exist.

One had read about Mahatma Gandhi fighting racism in South Africa (where it manifested in the crude and aggressive form of apartheid) but not in the UK. I remember witnessing one incident in particular. While travelling on the underground to work, I saw an Indian being pushed around by white youngsters. He quietly accepted the humiliation. I felt terrible. Although I did not experience overt racism of this kind, at work I did notice a condescending attitude during audits, and the occasional smirk from white colleagues. I too pretended not to notice, but internally I was furious and decided to do something, however small, to raise my voice. I naively brought out an anonymous handbill asking all Indians to not suffer the humiliation in a foreign land and to return home to build their country. It did not get much of a response, given that most of its target audience had come to seek better fortunes not available in their own country.

I began to think, were we really inferior to the British? I personally did not feel so, as in my auditing work I was better than most of my British colleagues, a fact soon recognized by the company, which began assigning the more difficult audits to me. Meanwhile, the Left movement was reaching its peak in London in the form of huge rallies against the US war in Vietnam. These protests and the discussions around them opened my eyes and I started looking at the world more critically.

I decided to research the reasons for racism. During the day I would be sent to companies to carry out audits, while the evenings were spent studying for the correspondence course for the CA exam. I began visiting the British Museum Library in the only free time I had – weekends. I began to research India's colonial legacy, of which, until then, I knew very little. I came across the books of B.C. Dutt, Dadabhai Naoroji and others, who had laid the ideological basis for the freedom struggle and had explained the methods of colonial loot. These books also delved into the underlying racism of colonial rule.

I learnt from these studies that the levels of racism the British adopted in India were extreme with clubs, hotels and restaurants, top administrative jobs, railway jobs and jobs in all important institutions being reserved strictly for the British. 'Dogs and Indians not allowed', was a common notice in elite public places. This racism was reflected in every aspect of the Empire. Racism was central to the colonial project; it was widespread, crude and deeply insulting. The discrimination was also in salaries, with British being paid by European standards. The colonialists openly declared that 'we do not want generals, statesmen and legislators. We want industrious husbandmen.' At the height of the Bengal famine which took 4 million lives in 1943, Churchill famously said 'the famine was their own fault, for "breeding like rabbits".' He diverted food from starving Indians to British soldiers. Malthus's theories were already widely promoted. And towards the end of World War II, during the disastrous retreat from Burma, even Gandhiji noted 'thousands perished without food or drink, and the wretched discrimination stared even these miserable people in the face – one route for whites, another for blacks! India is being ground down into the dust even before the Japanese advent.' And this at a time when Indian soldiers were giving their lives for the British war. To add fuel to the fire, that rabidly racist author, Rudyard Kipling, was rewarded with the Nobel Prize. It was he who hailed the butcher General Dyer as 'The Man who Saved India'. They did not even spare the rajas. For example, though the family of Mughal emperor, Bahadhur Shah Zafar, surrendered peacefully, they were cruelly

7

decimated. Of the 16 sons, most were hung while others were shot in cold blood. Of course, their jewellery was looted and their entire wealth robbed.

The apologists of colonialism, inculcated a deeply racist approach in the British population through their education system and cultural promoters like Rudyard Kipling, Malthus, Macaulay and others. This resulted in the racism I and other Indians faced in Britain even decades later. Of course, their racist project, I discovered, through my studies, was intrinsically linked to the devastation they wrecked on what was then the richest country in the world. With that they had the pretext of being called a 'civilizing' nation out to enlighten the backward natives. If fact, the situation was quite the reverse: India was far more advanced than Britain when the East India Company (EIC) began their exploits. They were reduced to rubble by the ravages of two centuries of loot and de-industrialization.

In fact, in 1 CE India accounted for 33 per cent of world GDP, while UK, France and Germany combined had a mere 3 per cent. Even as late as 1700, on the eve of British rule in India, India produced 25 per cent of world GDP while Britain was just over 2 per cent. By the time the British left in 1947, India was reduced to barely 3 per cent of world GDP while a tiny country like Britain had increased to 10 per cent. As early as the twelfth century, India produced the best quality of steel and its swords were in demand all over the world. An American minister J.T. Sunderland wrote

Nearly every kind of manufacture or product known to the civilised world – prized either for its utility or beauty – had long been produced in India. India was a far greater industrial and manufacturing nation than any in Europe and Asia. Her textile goods – the fine products of her looms in cotton, wool, linen and

8

silk – were famous over the civilised world; so were her exquisite jewellery and her precious stones cut in every lovely form; so were her pottery, porcelains, ceramics of every kind, quality, colour and beautiful shape; so were her works of metal – iron, steel, silver and gold. She had great architecture – equal in beauty to any in the world. She had great engineering works. She had great merchants. Not only was she the greatest shipbuilding nation, but she had great commerce and trade by land and sea which extended to all known civilised countries. Such was India which the British found when they came.

After realizing the wealth India earlier possessed, I was shocked on reading the level of the devastation the British wrecked on our country in their two centuries of rule. The difference between the British and all earlier foreign rulers was that the latter stayed in India and the wealth stayed here, while the British siphoned it all off to their home country and the elite rulers. Britain's Industrial Revolution was built on the destruction of India's thriving manufacturing industries. Textiles were smashed, substituting for British manufactures; Indian industry was destroyed, as was Indian trade, shipping and shipbuilding.

Indian weavers were destroyed in vast numbers and the recalcitrant had their thumbs cut off and their looms physically destroyed. Huge shipbuilding existed in Bengal, Surat, Calicut and Quilon. The Bengal fleet alone at the end of the seventeenth century had 5,000 ships of 500 tonnes each. After 1756, the EIC and the British ships that they contracted were given a monopoly on trade routes. Duties were imposed on Indian ships making them unviable and killing the industry and trade. Similarly, India's steel industry was strangled and in fact, the entire railways was built with British steel at a huge cost paid by the Indian taxpayer to British steel companies amounting to £18,000 per mile compared to £2,000 in the US. Diamonds and other precious metals were looted, no fine ethics here; the currency rates were manipulated to India's disadvantage as a result of which agricultural prices collapsed but British tax demands did not.

The worst aspects of the British raj were the exorbitant tax collections from the land and the forcible growing of opium, which gave the British their huge revenues and profits and was the major cause of famines in the country which claimed roughly 35 million lives in the two centuries of British rule. In 1901, William Digby calculated the net amount extracted by the economic drain from India in the nineteenth century at £ 4,187,922,732 (in today's terms it would be £419 billion). But this was not all. The Indian taxpayer had to pay the huge salaries of the British civil service and their army in India. As also the massive pensions of those retired living in the lap of luxury in Britain. We veritably paid for our own oppression. Further there was also massive and outright loot of gold, diamonds and other precious metals as also the treasury of the maharajas, while crores were extracted through corruption from the ordinary citizen. So, for example, on his first return to England, Robert Clive took with him £2,34,000 (equivalent to £23 million in today's money); he came back in 1765 and returned two years later with £4 lakhs (£40 million in today's terms). In 1702, Thomas Pitt acquired what was said to be the biggest diamond in the world. He was then governor of Madras and later his family gave two British prime ministers. Till today the famous Kohinoor is lodged in the crown of the Queen. This was seized from Maharaja Ranjit Singh, but our servile rulers say it was gifted and refuse to demand its return. The list could go on and on.

Paul Baran estimated that 8 per cent of India's Gross National Product (GNP) went to Britain each year and it was Dadabhai Naoroji who presented his famous drain theory which lit the fire of India's freedom struggle.

Last but not least it was the blood of Indians that not only built the vast British empire but was spilt to fight British wars of conquest including the two world wars.

India's indentured labour worked the British sugar cane plantations and mines throughout the world. This was virtual slave labour working in inhuman conditions. Just to Mauritius some five lakh labour was transferred and about 2.5 million were transported to the Caribbean toiling on sugar plantations, building roads, clearing forests. The inhuman conditions on the ships where they were packed like sardines resulted in the death of 12 per cent of all males, 18 per cent of the women, 28 per cent of the boys, 36 per cent of the girls and 55 per cent of the infants. The dead were merely tossed into the sea as fodder for the fish.

What is even worse, to spread the Empire, Indians were used as cannon fodder with troops being sent to China, Ethiopia, Malaya, Malta, Egypt, Sudan, Burma, East Africa and Ceylon. In the Burmese war alone, six of every seven soldiers died. In the First World War, 1,215,318 Indian soldiers participated and over one lakh were killed. Over and above that, in the last stages of the war many contracted the Spanish flu in the trenches, which finally resulted in the death of 12 million Indians in 1918. For this service, India was rewarded with the fraudulent Montagu-Chelmsford Reform of 1918, the draconian Rowlatt Act of 1919 and the Jallianwala Bagh massacre of civilians (including women and children) – 1,500 killed and 1,137 injured. In the Second World War, 1.5 lakh Indian soldiers gave their lives with about two million taking part in the British war effort.

And to maintain their rule the British resorted to a type of terror rarely seen. For example, the suppression of the 1857 mutiny was conducted by extreme brutality, with hundreds of rebels being blown up from the mouth of canons or hanged publicly, and over one lakh losing their lives. Similar was the fate of those in the Vellore mutiny of 1806. Casual murder was common and the British killed Indians at will. Beatings, flogging, racial abuse, were a daily phenomenon of the white rulers. During the 1942 Quit India movement women were raped to terrorize the satyagrahis while prisoners were forced to sleep on blocks of ice until they lost consciousness.

The list of atrocities and of the loot could go on and on; suffice it to say it was British rule that reduced a great country to rubble from which we are unable to rise even 75 years after independence.

It was after getting to know all these facts that I could understand the root cause for the racism we faced and its interconnection with the destruction of my country and its people. With this knowledge my anger towards the British rulers increased manifold and was the main reason to change my orientation from doing a CA and joining some big corporate to serving the oppressed of our country.

Simultaneously, communism/socialism was sweeping the entire world. The Naxalite movement had just begun in India and the Great Proletarian Cultural Revolution (GPCR) was gathering momentum in China. The impact of these movements was felt by youth all over the world, as India and China were the two largest countries and had both been victims of colonial loot. The literature of the Naxalites and the GPCR was freely available in London at a bookshop called Banner Books. Besides, it was only the communists (of various shades) who were opposing racism in the UK. As also the continuing capitalist system in India with many of the British laws and structures continuing could not pull India out of the British-created mess. Quite naturally I veered towards communism and began reading all its associated literature voraciously, particularly Western writers' accounts of the Chinese revolution, like those of Edgar Snow, William Hinton, Jack Belden, and numerous others. I particularly remember the book *The Scalpel, the Sword* on the life of Dr. Norman Bethune, the dedicated Canadian doctor who worked and died of septicaemia (no antibiotics then) while treating Chinese communists fighting the Japanese aggressors. This book had an enormous impact on me. I regularly attended meetings of both the Maoist and the Trotskyites, mostly held at small halls on varied current and sometimes theoretical issues. At that time Maoism was the rage, though the Trotskyites were far more in number (till today, they have a strong presence in the Labour Party).

But my life as a CA and these 'extracurricular activities' were veritably two different worlds with no overlap whatsoever. At my auditing firm and at audits my colleagues had no inkling of my other life and interests. I worked hard and did my best, which kept my employers happy. No one could even dream that in the City of London, the very heart of bourgeois and colonial power, anything progressive could ever be discerned within it. My associates in the Left were mostly from white working-class backgrounds, while my work colleagues mostly had aristocratic or semi-aristocratic backgrounds – surprisingly few, in either sphere, were students or those with an intellectual bent of mind.

It was finally the book *India Today* by R.P. Dutt (former general-secretary of the British Communist Party), on the history of the Indian freedom struggle which confirmed my Marxist orientation. In the beginning I had veered towards Gandhism, as he too had fought racism, but I found no significant answers there – neither to the question of racism

13

nor to that of the economic progress of our country. I then joined one of the Maoist circles. Though this consolidated my inclination towards Maoist ideology, being impressionable in those early years, I now feel that it also inculcated in me the same rigidity that encompassed the Maoist groups there. This was reflected in my earlier intolerance of any opinion that was different, even within the Left circles, let alone others, and not giving credit to another point of view. This unyielding attitude would have its negative impact once I started working in India, but more on that later.

Meanwhile, my CA study also continued, and of the three exams, I passed the first (the intermediate) in 1970, in the very first attempt. My employers were not only happy with my auditing work but were doubly impressed by my exam results: the fact that I'd cleared in my first attempt was itself an achievement but I also received a high rank. As I mentioned, the stipend is very low in articleship (in India there was then no stipend paid at all), so to augment my income I began working at the famous department store Selfridges on the weekends. It was manual labour – I was carrying items from the storeroom in the basement and filling the shelves upstairs – but I was paid by the hour. After six months, the maximum period students were allowed to stay at the Indian YMCA, I moved to a small room in Belsize Park near the beautiful Hampstead Heath, where I would often take long walks. During these walks I would contemplate and deliberate on whatever I happened to be reading – whether on Indian history or communism. The serene atmosphere and greenery all around were ideally suited for new ideas to crystallize.

While I continued my auditing, my involvement in political activities gradually intensified and I began attending meetings and enlisting in study circles, alongside my continued study of both Marxism and Indian history in greater detail.

14

I increasingly felt that following the CA profession was incompatible with my new Marxist beliefs. The former entailed joining some corporate job, while the latter meant working with the poor. The inherent conflict in these potential pursuits found its way to the detailed letters I wrote to my father at this time. He was understanding, but worried about my future. In our letters (now unfortunately lost), we exchanged ideas and debates on communism, the meaning of life itself and the future of society. He made the usual arguments about communism being autocratic, that in theory it may be good but in practice it was not viable; human nature does not change and people are basically selfish and greedy, there is no democracy and all news is propaganda, that power corrupts whatever the system, etc. On my part I tried to show that much of these ills existed in capitalist countries under the façade of democracy; that the capitalist system had proved unviable for the wretched of the earth. I also introduced him to the writings on Norman Bethune, and the work of people like Edgar Snow, William Hinton and others on the Chinese revolution, which showed that people do change if given a chance.[1]

For a man who, until recently, had been finance director at Glaxo, my father was very democratic and in no way didactic. In the end he admitted he was convinced by my views. This gave me further confidence to pursue a different path; until then, I had felt somewhat guilty of having wasted the limited money my father had earned and also damaging his goodwill with the auditing firm.

It was against this backdrop and with these debates coursing through my mind, that I was arrested in 1971 – an event that sealed my lifelong affiliation with left politics. Of course, I wrote to my father about it and he too was horrified at the behaviour of the London police and seemed to support my decision. In Britain, after arrest one is granted bail. The owner of the far-left bookstall Banner Books provided the bail. Hyde Park was famous for groups of people making protest speeches from platforms. It was a place most tourists and intellectuals came to witness protests. But we felt we needed to reach out to the working class. That is why we held a street corner meeting in a working-class locality giving speeches against racism and the capitalist system. It was then that we were attacked as already mentioned in my court speech. Though there was no obstruction or blockage of the road it was surprising that in a democratic country we were arrested and charged and finally imprisoned for a mere street-corner speech.

While waiting for the trial, I made the final decision that CA was not my vocation and that I needed to get back to India to work for the oppressed of our country. Now, equipped with a better understanding, I used the two months' study leave one gets for the exam, to delve deeper into learning about Indian history and Marxism at the British Museum Library. The job at Selfridges, plus my stipend, which continued during the study leave, was more than sufficient to cover my limited expenditure. I formally sat for the exam and then resigned from Jackson and Pixley, with one exam remaining, but continued the job at Selfridges.

I waited for the trial as I did not want to leave the country with the case still pending, for it would seem that I was afraid to face the court. The case came up after a year and was held on a daily basis until the conviction and sentence of hard labour in Brixton prison. The hard labour entailed carrying sacks of potatoes from the godown to the kitchen. The warder in-charge soon became quite friendly when he realized that the nature of my case was political. In the UK one had to serve only two-thirds of the sentence. Being an Indian citizen, the judge had asked whether I would like to contact the Indian consulate; I declined, having heard rumours of the then Congress government, particularly in Calcutta, lining up radical students of Presidency College and Jadavpur University against a wall, and shooting them point blank. It was rumoured that nearly every middle-class house in Calcutta lost a child to this terror.

The jail conditions at Brixton were not too bad compared to what I faced in India decades later. Most of the day went in work and my main interaction was with the warder in-charge. I was too exhausted at the end of the day to socialize with the other inmates. The food was mediocre. I quietly served my sentence and the two months passed quickly. Having developed an understanding of India's freedom struggle and Marxism while in London, after serving my three-month prison sentence at Brixton, there was no reason to stay on in the UK, though I could have if I wanted, as there was no deportation order on me. I flew back to Bombay as soon as I could.

Here are some thoughts and a brief account of what I learnt and taught myself about Marxism in London.

A Turn to the Revolutionary Cause

There were two aspects of my study that moved me to the revolutionary cause. First was the issue of racism and the history of the colonial loot of our country that destroyed one of the wealthiest nations in the world and devastated a rich civilization. The second was to seek the cause for such an occurrence – the reasons why colonialism arose – and the search for the lack of growth in the two decades since independence – both answers to which I found in Marxism, historical materialism and the very nature of capitalism/imperialism. In the earlier section we witnessed in brief the

17

history of the British colonial impact; here I will turn to the result of my studies on Marxism and its resulting impact on my future life.

To put it in perspective, communism was introduced to the world by its originators, Marx and Engels, particularly Marx who wrote the famous *Das Kapital*, a scientific analysis of the capitalist system as it evolved from feudalism. He wrote the *Communist Manifesto* in 1848 picturing a future, just order. In my view, as of today I have not found a better scientific analysis of the inner workings of the capitalist system. Not surprisingly, during the 2008 financial crisis, reports came in that people in the West were re-reading Marx to try and get a better understanding of the nature of the crisis.[2]

The Marxist ideology, in its varied avatars, is basically for a changing society to build a more egalitarian economy, which capitalism has never been able to engender. They stand for the interests of the most oppressed of society. I will not go into the pros and cons of this alternative at present; suffice to say, that the existing international system is becoming more and more unjust and also unsustainable, requiring a major alternative. To take just one example, the growing level of inequality worldwide: after the 2008 economic crisis, in 2010, just 388 billionaires – the majority in the US – had as much wealth as the bottom 50 per cent of the world population. By 2012 this came down to 159 billionaires having as much wealth as the bottom 50 per cent of the world population; by 2014 it was down to 80 billionaires; by 2016 it was further down to 8 billionaires and in 2019 it was just 5 billionaires. In other words, today merely five billionaires have as much wealth as nearly 4 billion of the poorest people worldwide. How is this sustainable, and what does this entail for the lives of those at the bottom rung? With the present economic crisis, together with the pandemic, one does not know the horrors

18

awaiting us; we have already witnessed heart-wrenching stories of millions of our migrants, never seen before in independent India. Worse horrors probably await us.

In the late 1960s, while I was studying Chartered Accountancy in London, at first I did not see this entire picture. The thoughts were just confined to the humiliations our Indians faced in the UK as a result of racism. It was only later, through study that I began to understand the bigger picture of the ravages of capitalism and its impact on our country through two centuries of British colonial rule. What I realized was that the root cause of both – racism and the mass impoverization of our people – was the same; the capitalist/colonial system. It was this realization that turned me towards communism, which at that time encompassed nearly half the world.

In India, in those days, the bulk of the idealist youth were attracted to the Naxalite trend with the parliamentary communists no longer having much appeal. The reason being that the former were more radical and the entire world at that time was witnessing similar upsurges. An aspect in the eyes of the youth was that the traditional communists had lost their idealism and many had got corrupted and instutionalized. One felt that the world was on the brink of change and revolution. I too felt the same way in the 1970s, as it was with Anuradha and other students of that time. When they arrested me in 2009, three decades had passed since then, yet they accused me of being a Maoist party member – that too at a time when the prime minister, Manmohan Singh, kept saying that the Naxal danger was the single biggest threat to our country. Imagine the hysteria in the media, against me at such a time, adding fuel to the fire of portraying me as one of the top leaders of the party.

But they had no evidence except fake confession statements purportedly taken in police custody and not even signed by me.

In fact, in the Delhi case they made up the story that I had come to Delhi to recce the place for bomb blasts. No one believed that, and no evidence was provided, and all know such wanton acts of terror are only the handiwork of fundamentalists, and strongly opposed by communists of all types. No wonder I was acquitted everywhere of all Maoist charges, yet faced over ten years of incarceration. Such is the fate of all those sincerely working for the oppressed of the country.

Many ask me that while people from my background, in their youth, often turn communist, but as they grow up they settle down with family and jobs, leaving their idealism behind – why did you and Anu not follow this norm and trend? Well, I don't really know; with the comforts we had been used to, it was no doubt difficult living a frugal existence, travelling in crowded buses and trains and eating simple food. It would have been far easier to settle down with all the inherited wealth. But then, when I think again, would that have given us happiness? Anu was such a natural, honest person she could never have compromised with her convictions. And I would never have been comfortable in the corporate world of greed. So, communism seemed the answer for both of us.

Oscar Wilde once said, 'To live is the rarest thing in the world. Most people exist, that is all.' But if we were to truly 'live' we cannot but be sensitive to our surroundings, where now, not only our people but also nature, our land, forests, water, and even air, are being destroyed. To merely 'exist' could be convenient for oneself, but tends to turn people into robots; at the most enjoying sensual and material pleasures with little sensitivity of love, affection, warmth in their relations with others or empathy for the sufferings of others. Yet one is so caught up in one's own struggle for survival, that our emotions tend to get numbed.

The excruciating poverty, the demeaning humiliations

(particularly Dalits, Adivasis and women), the vicious discrimination (especially of Muslims), the unbelievable levels of suffering particularly of our children, the horrifying conditions of health care and the extent of disease, one of the worst levels of patriarchal oppression in the world, the poor levels of education and large amounts of illiteracy – even after decades of independence and so-called freedom – was enough to shake me out of my stupor. If not to action, at least, to find the cause of the ailment. How could one stay unmoved when one sees millions perishing before our very eyes through deaths far more agonizing than those that are 'natural'. Fortunately, we are saved from actually viewing the corpses, otherwise it would be difficult to countenance. Besides, for every unnatural death there are at least a thousand living-dead – due to disease, poverty, casteism, patriarchy, and often a combination of these afflicting the victim. Can one remain a silent spectator? No doubt one can act in varied ways and it need not be revolutionary. After all, drops fill the ocean of dissent.

But to remain silent, after all, means consent. As Einstein once said, 'The world will not be destroyed by those who do evil, but those who watch without doing anything.'

Unfortunately, in this society, particularly post-1990, there is a vicious struggle not only to survive, but to get 'ahead', by cutting others down; a perpetual game of one-upmanship, to be seen also in organizations working for the oppressed. In this, much of our sensitivity is lost to pragmatic existence of survival and to power games. In such an environment only the most unscrupulous can flourish, few have the Anuradha-like values which encourage others to flower along with oneself.

Thus began my journey of an entire decade as a criminal, which finally ended on 16 October 2019 when I was released from Surat jail on bail. But that does not mean that the harassment is over. Ten cases are still pending, many consciously kept so. What was worse, in a case like mine, there was no clarity whether one would be ever released, whether new charges would keep being fabricated against me, or whether at this late age one would ever come out alive and if one did, would one be a cripple for ever, in every sense of the word. Even as I now pen these thoughts into words, constructive, long-term reflection was very difficult while within the jail. The act of writing seemed a futile activity when one cannot know where the end will be. Yet, at other times, it doesn't seem entirely futile. Thoughts, words, memories bring solace; a kind of release and a kind of faith in the future.

Besides, I drew courage from people like Kenyan writer Ngugi wa Thiong'o, Che, Bhagat Singh and Subhas Chandra Bose. Their lives and their work helped me at that time, and help me today as well. It though was a long journey starting off as a typical normal Parsi youth aspiring for some top corporate job, to life in UK witnessing a gigantic churning within and three months in a British jail, then to four decades of grassroots activism, and finally a decade in Indian jails and the torturous procedures of the courts. It has been a veritable half century of revolutionary life, rich in experiences, with many ups and down. Though tough, it has been an extremely rich experience, with many a lessons learned along the way. And, though free, the harassment is not yet over with ten cases still pending on me all over the country and the Delhi Police having challenged my acquittal in the high court.

The Road Not Taken

If I now turn to my past, I cannot remember much of my school days at the St. Mary's School, Bombay, where I studied until class five. I remember being studious and being dropped to school in my parents' car. In the evenings, as little children, we would often go for swimming lessons to the Willingdon Club. Because of this early training my brother Farrokh became quite a good swimmer and participated in the Doon School swimming competitions. I vaguely recall Farrokh being a classmate of Rajiv Gandhi whom he met once after the latter became prime minister.

At the age of eleven I shifted to the boarding school, Doon School at Dehra Dun. My classmates at Doon included Sanjay Gandhi, Kamal Nath and Naveen Patnaik; not to mention my close friends from Hyderabad House in school, Ishaat Hussain and Gautam Vohra. The latter has been a continuous source of support from day one of my arrest. Doon School was divided into four 'Houses' – Hyderabad, Kashmir, Jaipur and Tata – to accommodate all the students. I am told that the names of the Houses were given on the basis of large donations from the respective princely states and the Tatas. Doon School focussed on all-round development and sports was just as important as studies. I recollect playing nearly every sport – hockey, football, tennis, badminton, table-tennis, swimming, boxing – but not really excelling at any. Our morning would start off with Physical Training (PT) and there would be the novel mid-term trek in the nearby mountains every year.

I was mediocre at both studies and sports, having won only one sports prize, in chess. Recently, my classmate (Class of '63) Alok Jayal (of Tata House), who later served thirty-five years in the army, was reflecting on those days when our teachers were completely dedicated to their work, not only the subject they taught but also to sports and extra-curricular activities. About our Headmaster John Martyn, he reminisced: 'Once when Nehru came to see his grandkids, Rajiv and Sanjay, Martyn asked Panchu, Nehru's aide, whether he had come as the prime minister or as a grandfather. When told that Nehru had come

23

as a grandfather Martyn asked him to wait, since he was busy playing football with the boys.' And regarding our history teacher, Holdsworth, Jayal said, 'Holdy would teach you about primulas, jungle foods, boxing, soccer, cricket and good custom; i.e anything but his subject....' And then of course there was our geography teacher, the legendary Gurdial Singh (Guru), who, as Jayal says, 'knows the Himalayas like the back of his hand' – a brilliant mountaineer, now over ninety, he lives in Chandigarh. He also made his subject exceedingly interesting; in fact, his classes are the only ones that I can still remember.

Ishaat and I, from the same class and House, had a similar temperament and became close friends. After graduating from St. Stephen's, Delhi he too went on to do CA in the UK where we met a number of times. As I cannot recall much from that time, I asked him to write a short piece on what he remembered of our days together in school. He was kind enough to send the following account:

Kobad (Koby) and I joined the Doon School in the autumn term of 1958. We were both in Hyderabad House but spent our first term in "Holding House" and we were also both in E Form. Koby was from Bombay and I was from Patna – to say the least our worldviews at that time were slightly different. I was quite in awe of Koby's Bombay pedigree and his being a Parsi only enhanced his mystique in my mind. It is against this background that over the years in school, Koby became my closest and dearest friend. On reflection our personalities, temperament, and academic attainments could have not been more similar. We probably signed the honours book roughly the same number of times. He never broke bounds (i.e. secretly going out of the school premises), while I was punished just once for

24

this indiscretion on technical grounds and was given my one and only yellow card. If my memory serves me right, he was never given a yellow card and both of us never got a blue card and neither of us was dumb enough to get a red card. A final point about our similarity was that the end of term Headmaster's report, which we compared on returning to school the following term was, no surprise, also very similar.

Koby and I were lucky to have had wonderful classmates; the batch of '63 was a relatively small one. The batch of '63 in Hyderabad House was a tightly-knit group and I remember all of them with fondness.

After leaving school in 1963, I went to study economics at St Stephen's College, Delhi and Koby studied chemistry at Bombay University. Both of us graduated in 1967. I did meet Koby during those years, perhaps a couple of times, on my infrequent trips to Bombay. It was during this time one was considering career options and it is here that Koby played a critical role in helping me decide on the career I finally chose. Koby's father was a CA and was at that time the finance director of Glaxo, the giant pharmaceutical company. Koby had decided to follow his father's profession. As is quite evident from the description I gave of our general disposition, Koby and I were ideally suited to become CAs, and it took little persuasion for me to follow my dear friend's advice.

So, after college both of us ended up in London becoming articled clerks with the aim to become CAs. We were once again in the same city and we used to meet over the weekends for lunch. Koby lived at the Indian YMCA and there were some Indian restaurants in its vicinity which Koby and I would patronise. London of the 1960s was a heady place full of opportunities but pitfalls as well. Our finances were meagre and the chance to partake in the ritz and glitz on offer was very constrained. Also, the late '60s saw a surge in left wing activism in many parts of Europe including the UK, but the country also saw a resurgence of racism against immigrants from UK's former colonies.

Unknown to me at that time these developments had a life changing impact on Koby as suddenly in the latter half of 1969 I lost all contact with him.

I next met Koby after 50 years in November 2019. In the intervening years our respective lives could not have been more different. I went on to qualify as a chartered accountant and was very much a part of the corporate world for 45 years from which I finally retired in 2017. My career evolved along the lines which could have been predicted when I left school; Koby's is of course a very different story which no doubt you will read about in this book.

Over the years I made several enquiries to locate Koby but to no avail. Around 1990 I met a person, who himself had been an activist and knew of Koby. It is from him that I learnt of Koby's activism, however, he had no information of his whereabouts. Then of course many years later he resurfaced in 2009 under the most unfortunate circumstances and spent the next ten years in jails in various states fighting protracted legal battles for his release. I, like all his friends, was delighted to hear of his release in 2019 and to learn that he was in Mumbai. I must admit I was not quite sure if Koby was up to meeting old friends and checked with Gautam Vohra, who had been in touch with him over the entire period of his incarceration whether it would be appropriate for me to call Koby. Gautam responded that of course Koby would be delighted. So that's how we got in touch again and very soon thereafter we met at my flat for lunch.

It was a very emotional moment for me to meet my old friend. Memories of the past came flooding back and as we chatted through the afternoon and the evening, he eventually conceded that I had a better memory than he did. Since then we have been meeting often and speak regularly, hoping to make up for all the lost years. I am fascinated with his stories and amazed by the absence of any rancour in him. He has a deep insight into the complexities of our caste system and its pervasive influence on the politics of the country.

I told Koby how intrigued I was by his sudden disappearance in London and to discover later that he had taken the path of leftist activism in such earnestness. How did our paths diverge so dramatically after the summer of June 1969? From the various conversations that I have had with Koby, I sense he was deeply troubled by the racism he saw around him which also sensitized him to the myriad of other injustices heaped on common people. This possibly attracted him to left-wing activism, which he eventually embraced. I too was exposed to similar influences but I suppose I lacked his idealism and continued on my chosen path. Ironically, though we progressed in two very different worlds, some of the broad conclusions that we have drawn about life in general and on economics and politics are very similar. For both of us Humanism, broadly defined as the well-being of all of human kind, has to be at the centre of every endeavour. Only "isms" which fulfil this criterion are worthy of consideration.

Alas, the world has not found an enduring one so far but the search must go on. I look forward to engaging with Koby on this deeply philosophical issue. I am delighted to have rediscovered Koby!

With such a background, the life that awaited me on return from the UK was some top corporate job which all my contemporaries in Doon got. Doon School educated, a first class in graduation at Xavier's and a CA qualification was a sure formula to success up any corporate ladder in India. But life in Bombay on my return, took me down a completely different path amongst the slum dwellers, Dalit youth and working class of the city. Fired by the revolutionary knowledge and experience, my focus now was on the poor and middle classes, who comprise over 90 per cent of our people. It makes me wonder about the nationalist credentials of those who are steeped in corruption, amassing huge wealth for themselves at the expense of the poor as also resulting in sub-standard development projects. Astonishingly, much of this is, in addition, siphoned abroad to tax havens, draining the wealth of our country just as the British did. In fact, the single major factor of our country languishing in poverty even 75 years after independence, is precisely this drain of wealth, generated in the country, into the hands of a miniscule 0.1 per cent of the elite, big corporate houses, and particularly US digital moguls together with the foreign sharks (FIIs, FDIs, PEs, VCs, etc). A true nationalist/patriot, whatever their ideology, would seek to put an end to this rapacious loot and see that the wealth generated goes to promote agriculture, education, health and hygiene, as also indigenous entrepreneurship, and local research and development. It was, in fact, a nationalist zeal aroused through witnessing racism of Indians in the UK that finally pushed me on this path to serve our people and country.

Introduction to Radical Politics in Mumbai

My parents came to the airport to receive me upon my return in May 1972 from London. Coming to Mumbai was like entering a desert as I knew no one in the entire city who belonged to progressive circles; no one with whom I could share my views.

I decided to start locally and began doing social work in the slum at Mayanagar, Worli Naka, about a kilometre from our home at Worli Sea Face. Here, in the heart of Mumbai, were sprawling slums with absolutely no infrastructure or facilities like water or electricity, let alone proper latrines. It would be an understatement to say that the drainage system was primitive. Slum dwellers were forced to pay for everything, right down to a bucket of water, as their lives were controlled by the slum mafia.

I began organizing the youth, demanding basic facilities and speaking out against the loot of the slumlord. I still remember a young Dalit man named Rajesh Bhalerao who was very intelligent, and one Arul Francis who was good at sports and knew a smattering of English as also Ramesh Sakpal; together with others like Bhimrao Gavande, Bhagwan Nile who took the lead in organizing the local youth against local slum-lords and for free water.

We then began focusing on the government to implement their much-touted resettlement programme in the slum which would bring them all the facilities, reorganize the hutments and introduce a proper drainage system. When I visited Mayanagar after my release I found that the slum had completely changed into four high rise buildings as part of the government's rehabilitation scheme. This was possible as the entire process of resettlement was initiated by an active slum dwellers committee which demanded from the government that the resettlement plan be implemented. In fact, the very neighbouring slum, Premnagar, continues to languish in the same condition for lack of such an active committee. Around 180 families have been housed in these buildings being given an area of 225 sq. ft. each, with an independent toilet and regular water supply. Though this took place around 2000, well before this the local committee also campaigned for electricity. In 1977, the first street lights were brought to the slum, then electrification. It indicates when people are awakened to their rights, they can themselves take the initiative to improve their lives. Prior to this the Dalit Panther movement peaked in 1974 where Mayanagar became an important centre not only for retaliation against the goons but refuge for Dalits from the neighbouring BDD (Bombay Development Directorate) chawls. They also agitated against the rape of a girl in Jijamatanagar in 1973. I also discovered youth like Rajesh and Arul were active in numerous movements, while people like Bhagwan Nile have become good Marathi writer.

Although I might have been intellectually and ideologically committed to these underprivileged people, physically I was not. Brought up in clinically clean surroundings, my system rebelled against the unhygienic conditions in the slum and the poor quality of food. I would eat amongst these humble people who so generously shared the little they had with me, knowing that to refuse would hurt their feelings, and would have been misunderstood; my refusal would have been interpreted as either snobbery or, worse still, caste bias. Unbeknownst to them, I was not even aware that they were Mahars, so-called Untouchables. The acute amoebic dysentery contracted time and again then, still haunts me today as IBS (Irritable Bowel Syndrome), even half a century later.

Around that time, I saw posters of an 'Alternative University' being held in the summer holidays of 1972 at a classroom at the Ruia College. I began to attend the sessions and this was where I came in touch with the PROYOM (Progressive Youth Movement) group which was linked to the Janashakti faction of the Naxalites. It was run by two professors, Dev Nathan and Vasanti, and also one Sunil Dighe. There were a number of college youth attending the class, including Anuradha, then a student leader at Elphinstone College. The Alternative University sought to give a Marxist approach to the subjects being taught in the college curriculum. It was a good idea and attracted quite a few college students. I found the concept of an alternative understanding of education being taught in college very interesting. Besides, the teachers themselves were professors so they were well versed in the subjects from both angles, official and the alternative.

Senior journalist Jyoti Punwani, a contemporary of Anuradha at Elphinstone College, and one of the founding members of the Committee for the Protection of Democratic Rights (CPDR) and the then editor of its magazine, wrote about those times in the *Hindustan Times* immediately after my arrest on 22 September 2009:

I was fresh out of Elphinstone College, where in just one talk on the '72–'73 Maharashtra famine, the intense Dr. Dev Nathan and the flamboyant

31

Navroze Mody had turned us into romantic Leftists. Compared to them, Kobad was prosaic. Not much of an orator, despite his loud voice, and down-to-earth and friendly demeanour, you immediately felt at ease with him.

His atrocious Parsi-Hindi, his habit of bursting into the "Nadiya se dariya" hit from *Namak Haraam* (one of the few Hindi movies Kobad saw, only because it was about the working class), and his unobtrusive advice on our love lives while keeping his own totally secret – all this made Kobad more a trusted mentor than the formidable ideologue he was even then. His simplicity endeared him to our families; seeing him wash and sweep while his wife taught at college, Doon School seemed aeons away.

Quite independently, by about November 1972, the incipient Dalit Panther movement gathered momentum and came into its own. Inspired by the Black Panthers movement in the US for civil rights and the fight against racism, writer-poets J.V. Pawar and Namdeo Dhasal decided to form the Dalit Panthers, and immediately called for a boycott of the 25th Independence Day revelry, calling it a 'Black Independence Day'. Simultaneously, with the *Little Magazine* movement, Dalit literature began to blossom, speaking a new, angry language. Dr. M.N. Wankhede published *Asmita* from Aurangabad, Baburao Bagul started *Amhi* (We) in Mumbai. These magazines threw up a galaxy of Dalit literary stars including Daya Pawar, Namdeo Dhasal, Arjun Dangle, Avinash Mahatekar and Raja Dhale. Dhasal's *Golpitha* was published in 1971, its crude language causing havoc in prudish Marathi literary circles. On 10 January 1974, as a protest rally wound its way out of Bhoiwada, a large grinding stone was hurled from a building near Parel Railway workshop, and Bhagwat Jadhav died, the first Dalit Panther martyr. Violence broke out after an event where Dhasal and Dhale were speakers. Those gathered faced police repression, even policemen's kids donned khaki uniforms and reportedly joined Shiv Sainiks in assaulting Dalits. Dhale was severely injured. It was this that led to the Worli riots allegedly between the Shiv Sena and the Dalit Panthers.

The Dalit Panther movement was basically a cultural revolt against that aspect of the Hindu religion which treated Dalits as outcastes/untouchables. The Dalit Panthers propagated ideas and activities, like beef-eating, removal of photos of Hindu gods from ones houses and replaced them with photos of Buddha and Ambedkar. These activities were taboo to upper-caste Hindus. Inevitably, these notions attracted the wrath of the Shiv Sena, formed in June 1966. They utilized the 'sons-of-the-soil' theory to attack the South Indians (pejoratively known as Madrasis), who dominated the trade union leadership, led chiefly by communists, such as the Girni Kamgar Union in the textile mills.

Since nearly all of Mayanagar comprised Mahars (a major and vocal Dalit caste in Maharashtra), the Dalit movement attracted their attention. While we were fighting for basic facilities in Mayanagar, the Dalit issue, which was new to me, immediately struck a chord. I recognized the similarities between racism and casteism (though the latter, I later discovered, was much more oppressive and deeply entrenched), my personal experience and also the general experience of Indians in the UK reinforced in me the idea of what it meant to be cast as the 'other' in an unequal society.

I read all I could on the issue, particularly the collected works of B.R. Ambedkar, published by the Maharashtra government. While the Siddharth College hostel at Dadar was at the heart of the movement – and housed all its leaders, like Raja Dhale, Namdeo Dhasal and Bhai Sangare – Worli became the epicentre of pitched battles between the Shiv Sena and the Dalit youth from their respective BDD chawls in early 1974.

The BDD chawls were built by the British in 1920 as a prison, and also housed the arrested freedom fighters. They were later turned into residential quarters for workers. The largest of the BDD chawls is the one at Worli. They are three or four stories high, each family lives in a room of merely 160 sq. ft. with common toilets and bathing spaces, and hardly any ventilation. I remember going there and found the place even filthier than the Mayanagar slums and full of huge cockroaches. Worli has 121 of these chawls spread across 60 acres.

I would visit the leaders in their college hostel as well as participate in the Dalits' defence against attacks. In one chawl lived the Dalit contingent, while in the neighbouring chawl were Marathas. The chawls were now primarily occupied by textile workers, but some of the better ones were for the lower rungs of the police. The Maratha chawl that led the attacks on the Dalits was a police chawl where, people said, the sons of policemen were at the forefront of the attacks. These violent clashes – involving swords, tube-lights, soda bottles, stones and also a few Molotov cocktails – went on for nearly six months; with Mayanagar acting as the main refuge for the Dalit youth. Mayanagar, with its self-aware youth, was strategically located, just about a kilometre from the BDD chawls. Its only approach was through a narrow road, less than half a kilometre long, with the high wall of the Coca Cola factory to one side and a row of housing societies on the other. At the back there was a hill from where entry was precarious. Thus, it became the ideal location for the Dalit youth of the area to retreat and gather strength and to retaliate against further attacks. The the attackers found it difficult to traverse the half kilometre narrow road into this slum, and would invariably be forced to beat a hasty retreat.

While earlier I would take classes for the slum youth on their basic rights and the elementary tenets of Marxism, with the outbreak of the Panther movement, I began teaching classes on the Dalit and caste question amongst the youth at Mayanagar. By now I had educated myself about casteism, Dalit oppression and read the collected works of Ambedkar. I also brought to them the history of the Black Panthers movement from which the Dalit Panthers derived its name. The classes would be held on the streets adjoining the slum on a *chattai* (mat) spread under the street lights. They were attended by about a dozen young men from the slum, some of whom went on to become active members of the cultural troupe, *Aavhan*.

I had strongly argued for taking up the Dalit question amongst the Janashakti circles, one of the many factions of the then Maoists, with which I was associated. At that time the caste question was considered by all varieties of Marxists as anathema, a diversion from the class question, which was the bedrock of Marxist belief. The Janashakti leaders condescendingly termed the Dalit Panthers as Dalit lumpens claiming they were a mirror image of the Maratha lumpens of the Shiv Sena. The resistance to taking up the issue and supporting the Dalit Panthers was so great that finally to make a more convincing point I wrote an article stating how taking up the caste question in the Indian context did not go against the tenets of Marxism; to no avail. This original article, for inner circulation amongst the group, found no takers, and only the counter view-point put up by the leadership was discussed. The article too seemed to disappear, and not having a copy, there the issue ended.

In fact, in my impression, it was the Dalit Panther movement, a section of which had connections with the left, which, albeit faded out soon, and its leaders co-opted, changed the face of the Dalit movement in India, putting the Dalit/caste question firmly on the political/social agenda, which no one could then ignore, including the communists/Naxalites.

During this time I also came in contact with a circle of trade union workers who became top leaders of the unions of their respective factories, including the German pharmaceutical company, Hoechst and the multinational tech company, Siemens. They were led by a brilliant comrade, Ravi, who had been part of the historic Srikakulam struggle, the equivalent of the Naxalbari uprising that took place in Andhra Pradesh around the same time. He had been a commander in the armed units led by the legendary Satyam. The movement was soon crushed (much like Naxalbari) and the bulk of its leadership killed, including top leaders like Satyam, Chaganti Bhaskar Rao and others, but Ravi managed to escape to Mumbai, living incognito in a slum and earning a living by painting emptied egg shells (a novel idea in itself). He was equally well versed in Telugu and English, having read many of the Marxist classics.

Max was the union leader at Hoechst, while Freddie and Darius were leaders at Siemens. This trio apparently had already been inspired by Che Guevara and had revolutionary dreams even before they met Ravi. In the early 1970s when we first formed this group with the five of us, we would all be working in our own separate fields – unions, slums and students/youth, and Telegu workers in the Worli textile mills and Bhiwandi power looms. There was another excellent and simple comrade and friend, Amit Burman, an electrician working first at Bombay Hospital and then in Boisar on the outskirts of Mumbai. He died of cancer, well before my release.

This group of friends, about whom more later, formed the core of our activities for nearly two decades. They were not merely comrades but became very close friends of mine. They were at the centre of most political and ideological discussions and developments in my life, often with clear points of difference. They also became very close to my parents whom they met often when we went to their house in Mahabaleshwar for study classes. This group is important as it was the centre where most political and ideological discussions and developments took place, often with clear points of difference. Ravi, Max and Freddie married some of the gems amongst the student circles, like Suchita (married Ravi) and Meenakshi (married Max), which included Anu and her childhood friend, Neelam, as also many other PROYOM members.

This introduction to radical politics in Mumbai – relating to students, the youth, workers and Dalits – all happened within about the first three years after my return from London and before the decleration of the Emergency. A lot of the time would also be spent in study circles teaching and learning the basics of Marxism. As I already had a grounding in the subjects from my London sojourn, I took most of these classes amongst the youth, introducing the students to the economics, politics and philosophy of Marxism. Normally, the subject would be fixed in advance and all would read up and come. Sometimes we would read the texts jointly and I would explain their relevance and relation to the Indian context and contemporary events. The study circle of the leading group with the union leaders was taken by both Ravi and me with lively discussions on issues.

Jyoti Punwani wrote in the *New Indian Express*, soon after my arrest in 2009:

In the study circles he conducted, Kobad would speak repeatedly of the need to "serve the people". For him, that was no empty phrase. That was the reason he inspired so many. Some of those who attended the study circles often felt lost, unable to understand the economics that lay at the heart of Marxist theory. But they didn't give up for a variety of reasons, all of which had to do with the kind of person Kobad is. At the end of the session, you could shake your head in defeat, and he would neither pass judgment, nor force you to persist. But persist you did, because you knew if you wanted to change things, in whatever little way, these were the people you could do it with. Many of them were very well-off, but neither ashamed of their wealth, nor revelling in it. Most of their time was spent doing what they believed in – changing the lives of those at the very bottom.

While our activities were just beginning to pick up steam, the Emergency was declared bringing most activities to a standstill.

Emergency

Little did I realize that in the years after I returned from London, India was seething with discontent, which burst forth in 1973–74, which may have been an important reason for our success and growth in most fields of work in Mumbai.

Besides the Dalit Panther revolt, there was the mutiny of the 20,000 PAC (Provincial Armed Constabulary) in Lucknow, that took place in May 1973. Their miserable service conditions led them to join hands with the student protestors whom they were called to suppress. The revolt was later crushed, leading to the arrest of 600 PAC constables and the death of 13 soldiers and 25 policemen in armed clashes.

The year 1973–74 also witnessed a series of high-profile industrial actions – a 33-day strike in the jute industry, a 42-day strike of Mumbai's textile workers, a 3-month strike by junior doctors, and 3-week lockouts by workers of LIC and Indian Airlines Corporation, amongst others. In addition to all these were the two huge movements taking place in Gujarat and Bihar. In January 1974 the Nav Nirman movement was sparked by protests against the 20 per cent increase in canteen charges at the L.D. College of Engineering, Ahmedabad. It led to an indefinite strike being called of all education institutions in Gujarat and an attack on ration shops by students and working-class protestors. A few days later the call for a state-wide bandh paralysed 33 towns and resulted in a number of clashes. By early February over a hundred people had been killed, around 3,000 injured and 8,000 arrested. The chief minister of Gujarat was forced to resign.

And then there was the gigantic railway strike, which lasted from 8 May to 27 May 1974. The 20-day strike by 1.7 million (17 lakh) workers is the largest recorded industrial action in the world. It was brutally suppressed, with thousands being arrested and dismissed from their jobs by the Indira Gandhi government.

But arguably the biggest movement of all was taking place in Bihar; it began with the Bihar Students' Struggle Committee (BSSC) protesting the high fees and high cost of books and black-marketeering of commodities. In March 1974, during a demonstration against inflation and unemployment the police killed three people. Two days later groups of students assembled near the state parliament in order to prevent a meeting. The police attacked and killed five protesters. People responded with riots. Government buildings were set on fire, so was the residence of former education minister Ramanand Singh; posh hotels and warehouses were looted, railway wagons with food were opened, two media buildings were torched.

The next day, riots took place in Ranchi, Dhanbad, Chhapra, Saharsa and half a dozen other bigger towns. Railway stations, post offices, courts, state dispensaries and other government buildings were the main targets of attack. Ten people were killed by the police. Jayaprakash (JP) Narayan – a well-known freedom fighter and socialist who was involved in the formation of human rights organizations in 1974 and 1976 – accepted a request of the BSSC to 'take over the leadership of the movement', which he did on grounds that it be non-violent. A curfew was imposed on 11 towns the next day. About 22 persons died in police firings, and several hundred were arrested. Student organizations called for a state-wide strike. JP issued a public letter asking the Bihar government, led by Abdul Ghafoor, to resign.

Two weeks later, JP's first major action was to lead a 'Silent March' through Patna, with participants wearing material over their mouths, saffron-coloured scarves and with their hands tied behind their backs, to demonstrate their non-violence. At a rally following the march, JP announced the commencement of a five-week 'people's struggle campaign' aimed at bringing down the state government. Under the leadership of JP, the movement mobilized millions in Bihar. In March 1975, JP said that soldiers and police would be warranted in disobeying unjust and undemocratic orders from corrupt governments and called for 'Total Revolution'.

Against this backdrop of nationwide foment, at midnight on 25 June 1975, Prime Minister Indira Gandhi declared

Emergency, suspending civil liberties and arresting the entire opposition (barring the CPI). In a pre-calculated move, over one lakh people were thrown behind bars overnight.

Besides these movements, an added reason for the Emergency was said to be the increasing superpower conflict in the region. Since Independence, Indian leaders, instead of seeking self-reliance like China, had been closer to the USSR. With the US's rising clout and the beginning of the USSR's relative decline, the former sought to assert itself more aggressively worldwide. Besides with the economic crisis it faced back home (the oil shock and 1973 crisis that forced a shift from the gold standard) the US sought greater inroads into the economies of third world countries to increase the siphoning off of their wealth in order to ease their own economic problems. India was an important destination for the US as, until then, it had mostly been under the sway of the United States of Soviet Republic (USSR). With China a closed country, it was also a big market. This also, to some extent played out during the Emergency, where the US sought to use the forment in the country to its advantage. As a result parties more aligned to the USSR wanted to prevent this and saw the Emergency as a useful tool. That is why it was only the CPI, the party that was closest to the USSR, that did not face arrest and in fact supported the Emergency, for which they later apologized and even recanted in 1978.

During the Emergency there was terror everywhere and most activities were at a low key. Most notorious of all was Sanjay Gandhi's forced sterilization campaign in Delhi's slums. At that time, we were small fry and too insignificant for them to bother about us, but some of the leaders of the group were picked up. Except for some of us PROYOM members secretly putting up handwritten posters, most of this period was spent in study classes and writing.

41

After the lifting of the Emergency and the release of most political prisoners Anu and I, together with some others, were primarily responsible for the initiation of CPDR and the coordination with other civil liberties organizations all over the country. I would come in close touch with Justice Tarkunde whose nephew was a leading businessman in Nagpur and a good friend, as also other leading civil liberties leaders like advocate M.A. Rane of Mumbai, advocate Kannabiran of Hyderabad, advocate Gobind Mukhoty of Delhi; even Arun Shourie and George Fernandes of the then ruling Janata Party. Through these I also came into contact with the APCLC (Andhra Pradesh Civil Liberties Committee), PUDR of Delhi and some West Bengal and Tamil civil liberties groups.

Due to the pressure of the civil liberties organizations most Naxalites were also released and many of these groups began legal functioning. One of the most prominent was the PWG (People's War Group) led by Kondapalli Seetharamaiah (KS) and Satyamurthy (the famous revolutionary poet). Their opposition to some of Charu Majumdar's (original architect of the Naxalite movement) extreme views and need for mass organizations also appealed to revolutionaries like me. Ravi, who was jointly involved with me in building up the group in Maharashtra, would have long discussions with KS in Telugu. While KS had brilliant organizational sense, Ravi had deep insights into philosophy and ideology. Later, a series of splits took place in the late 1980s within the PWG in Andhra Pradesh resulting in its fragmentation. In the course of this turmoil KS apparently lost his support in the Andhra Pradesh party, and after the early 1990s the revolutionary movement advanced under the leadership of Ganapathi, a school teacher from a rural school in Karimnagar district. The rest, of course, is history with many groups uniting and forming the CPI (Maoist), of which I had been accused of being a top leader.

With a number of cases still pending against me and the matter being sub-judice I will not go into the merits of these charges; suffice it to say that the courts, not just in one case alone, but in all cases so far decided in four different states of the country, have acquitted me of all Maoist related charges.

Suppressed by the Emergency, massive workers' struggles once again burst forth post-Emergency culminating in the year-long textile strike in 1982 of the 2,50,000 Mumbai mill workers resulting in the closure of 80 mills, dismissal of 1,50,000 workers and a change in the entire character of Mumbai from an industrial hub to a trade/financial centre.

Before moving on, I would now like to present one of the most important aspects of my life – my relationship with Anuradha, her qualities and her commitment to the oppressed, as well as the love that blossomed between us.

The Importance of Being Anuradha

When I met Anu she was a student leader at Elphinstone College, and active in the Alternative University. The first time I saw her in class I saw an extremely bubbly and articulate student, raising questions, making points and being exceedingly communicative. I was very attracted to her naturalness, her spontaneity and liveliness. She was an outgoing person and did not have any of the inhibitions that stem from societal constructs. At the time we met, Anu was in a relationship with a fellow student, a sportsperson who was not politically inclined and the relation ended sometime after her activities grew.

Injustice would trigger anger in her, she could get very annoyed, but it would not linger and she would move on. She never stood on ego or prestige nor did she hold grudges. And this was not an effort, it came naturally to her. My temperament and qualities were almost totally antithetical to hers. Soon after we met, she began working with me in Mayanagar and elsewhere in the city. In the early days, most of our time together meant meetings, lengthy study classes, or sitting at my Worli Sea Face flat making posters, with little time off. We would go out late at night to put up posters, and together with others sit at the Worli home to make the handwritten posters. At most, we'd see some plays together, many by her brother and Satyadev Dubey, mostly at the Chabbildas and Prithvi theatres. It was during the Emergency, when most activity came to a halt, that our love really blossomed and we got to meet more often and spend some time together. Sometimes, after a long night of pasting posters in the textile mill areas of Lower Parel she would spend the night at my Worli flat nearby.

Jyoti Punwani, who knew Anu well before I did, had this to say about that time:

When I first met her in 1970, Anuradha Shanbag was the belle of the ball in Mumbai's Elphinstone College. A petite bundle of energy, bright eyes sparkling behind square glasses, her ready laughter, near-backless cholis and coquettish ways had everyone eating out of her hands, professors included. Elphinstone then was an intellectual hub. The Bangladesh war was just over, drought and famine stalked Maharashtra. Naxalism had come to Mumbai, at that time the industrial capital of the country. Anu, majoring in Sociology, was everywhere, inviting Mumbai's leading radicals to talk about the reasons for the drought, putting up posters that proclaimed "Beyond Pity" and urging students to get involved with the crisis in the countryside, defending this stand against those who felt a student's role must be limited to academics and at the most, "social work".

During the 1971 Bangladesh war, Anu had visited refugee camps in Madhya Pradesh with a group from college; the horrifying conditions she encountered there had an indelible impact on her, radically changing her thinking and turning

45

her towards revolutionary politics. While Anu and I worked together for all these years there was much I could have learnt from her but didn't. First, she was extremely democratic and had the knack of discussion and interaction with even those who held opposite and different views. I still recollect the numerous animated discussions she would have with Maharashtra's top theatre personalities like Satyadev Dubey, Mahesh Elkunchwar, Vijay Tendulkar and also with Sahitya Akademi Award winner Marathi writer and translator, Milind Champanerkar, originally from Amravati – people with differing views (Dubey had exactly opposite views) – without any sort of animosity. In fact, they all seemed to be very fond of her. So also it must have been in her university with her professors and students, where she had an excellent reputation. Not only was I far more rigid, I was also less knowledgeable than her in all these varied fields, with mine being restricted to Marxism, caste issues and at best economics. Her interests were widespread. Also, in the organisation, while I attracted much animosity from those with whom I differed, not Anu, though she may have had the same feelings as me. She accepted people as they were, I didn't. She was an extrovert, lively and friendly and therefore very open; I tended to be reserved and reticent.

I wrote an article about Anu on what would have been her sixty-third birthday, some of which I am excerpting here. In it, I tried to bring out her qualities and values that made her a model for not only any activist, but even for common people living their lives. Some of these were her straightforwardness, sense of responsibility, her love for fellow human beings, her passion in anything she took up, her abhorrence of any form of patriarchy or caste, and most of all standing up for justice even in minor issues. Anu was, in fact, the epitome of truth. Pretences, hypocrisy, deceit, cunning, manipulativeness were totally inconceivable to her. She would frankly speak what she

46

thought, believed, felt. There was no question of putting on an act, playing games etc. That was why she was normally at ease and put others at ease. She was an extremely principled person. It is in an unjust system or environment that Truth and Principles are the first to be sacrificed at the altar of power.

Anu, with her straightforwardness and frankness, was an example how one can move towards freedom. Most of us bind ourselves in thousands of complexities, always playing to the gallery, never being ourselves, covering up our flaws, etc. – in short, we live life deeply alienated from ourselves. Rather than being free we become prisoners of our situation. Such a person will only fuel an atmosphere of lack of freedom in any organization or surrounding. Anu, on the other hand, had the least complexities, and her innate naturalness resulted in a relaxed atmosphere for those around her (people need not be on guard), where everyone could be themselves. Anu generally brought a fresh breeze of freedom wherever she went.

Anu's warmth and depth of feeling was combined with a sharp intellect, giving an excellent balance between heart and mind. If we turn to the second aspect of love – sex-love, Anu was a truly liberated person unconstrained by the thousands of invisible threads of patriarchy/feudalism which tend to bind even progressive people in India with archaic social mores. On this issue we tend to have two extremes here – at one end women's liberation is promoted as the vulgarity associated with Western culture; at the other end its opponents (both Hindutvavadis and Islamists) promote the 'Mother image' or 'Sati-Savitri' culture. In fact, both are two sides of the same coin of commodifying women – the former as sex-objects, the latter as children-producing machines. Anu strongly felt that women had their own feelings, emotions, desires which need to be respected, and patriarchal relations, however subtle, tend to suppress these.

Anu never lost her child-like simplicity through all the vicissitudes of the movement and her academic life. This was no easy task, specifically for a woman in India's feudal-dominated culture. How then was Anu able to sustain her naturalness, innocence and simplicity in an increasingly alien environment? Besides her innate goodness and the support, she received from many an honest and sincere cadre, as also from the masses, the reasons were mainly two – first, she never aspired for post and pelf, whether in the organisational sphere or in her academic life; so, there was no need to resort to tricks to climb any ladder. Second, her commitment and high sense of responsibility and discipline resulted in her ability to excel with ease. Those with superficiality, inefficiency, irresponsibility etc. and yet aspiring for posts, favours, importance are the ones who tend to resort to all forms of chicanery, flattery, manipulativeness, one-upmanship, vindictiveness, duplicity etc. in order to push others down and push themselves up the ladder. The latter's commitment to the masses and country is generally partial as it comes with a caveat – self-promotion.

Anu's naturalness remained with her till the very end. Her every emotion, feeling, desire was reflected like a mirror. When hurt she would easily cry, when angry her face would get flushed, and, of course, when cheerful and happy her eyes would dance around like a bird. No doubt the appreciation she got from many a genuine activist, helped her sustain the beauty of her innocence. More on her activities later. Now let us turn to our families; the type of atmosphere we were brought up in from where we turned to become revolutionaries.

Family Matters

To get some insight into our lives before we became communists it may help to look at our families: all of whom lent full support to both of us through thick and thin.

Anu's parents – both communists from the old time CPI – were very supportive of all our activities. In fact, their house at Santacruz (West) was quite a centre; where activists of various hues would drop in, and receive a warm welcome from her mother and father even if Anu was not present.

Anu's mother, Kumud, was employed with the Cama Hospital till her retirement, after which she worked with an NGO till a late age; her father, Ganesh, was a public prosecutor at the Bombay High Court. Ganesh was originally from Coorg and spoke fluent Tulu. He was a simple and straightforward person. Anu imbibed some of her qualities from him. He had no airs and was down to earth, generally a misfit in our *matlabi* society. Towards the end of his life, around 1995–96, he wrote his autobiography, *From Cauvery to Dwarka*. In this interesting booklet he talks about his attraction to communism in his college days in Mangalore, when he came into contact with the communist leader Com. S.V. Ghate, who had been externed from Mumbai. This was during the Second World War. He then became active in the student union and also helped organize the peasants and bidi workers in neighbouring Kasargod. Due to all these activities, he failed his exams and returned to his parental coffee estate in Siddapur, Coorg. He later joined the army in 1941 but was eventually dismissed, as he was involved in distributing communist party pamphlets within the ranks. He then worked in the railways for six months in Mumbai, but as accommodation was difficult, he returned to Coorg, where he taught English and Science in a school run by his brother. It was then that he considered doing law and joined the law college in Kolhapur. Here too, he was not allowed to sit for his exams due to his communist activity and so he shifted to Poona Law College. By the time he completed his law exam, India had attained Independence, and he shifted to Mumbai in 1948. He stayed at the Dadar Hindu Colony, and regularly attended the Girni Kamgar Union office. It was there that he met Kumud, who was a student activist at Wilson College.

In 1950, the Telangana struggle peaked against the Nizam when twelve peasant leaders were sentenced to death. It was then that he and barrister Danial Latifi volunteered to go to Hyderabad as part of the defence team. Kumud was originally from Aurangabad, and when she had gone there he used to visit her. Meanwhile, at the very last moment the famous lawyer D.N. Pritt managed a stay order on the death sentence of the peasants from the Supreme Court. In September 1950 Ganesh married Kumud under the Special Marriage Act. They lived in Hyderabad initially and after a year Kumud shifted to Mumbai to complete BSc from the National College, staying in a hostel. Later, he too came to Mumbai and became a public prosecutor in the High Court, working thus until his retirement.

Anu's mother came from a communist family from Aurangabad where her brother, Chandragupta Chaudhary, was a two-time CPI MLA and three of her six sisters were CPI members. Like Kumud they all married communist leaders from various parts of the country.

Jyoti Punwani in the *Hindu* captured her past well in an article soon after her demise:

She came into her own late in life. A science graduate, she did her M.A. and M.Phil in sociology when she was over 45, encouraged by her daughter, and won the Vice-Chancellor's gold medal for topping her M.Phil batch. She then joined renowned feminist Neera Desai at SNDT Women's University, and would travel with her in overcrowded shuttle trains and buses to villages in Gujarat, where SNDT had decided to set up a rural development centre.

When she was around 65, Kumudben, as she was called, joined Vacha, the centre for adolescent girls from deprived backgrounds headed by feminist Sonal Shukla, becoming the oldest member there. Vacha co-director Nischint Hora recalls her contributing not just her administrative and fund-raising skills, designing unusual logos and health quizzes for adolescent girls, but also the generosity with which she would ply Vacha members with seasonal delicacies, from Gujarati pickles to Coorgi bamboo-shoot sambar.

Kumudben worked at Vacha for 15 years, till arthritis stopped her. Her home became an extension of Vacha, where visitors could leave their luggage and even spend the night. More important, though, was what she came to mean to the adolescents from nearby slums who came to Vacha. One 11-year-old especially, recalls Hora, showed no interest in any other Vacha activity; he would go straight to Kumudben. Years later, after she'd retired, he returned looking for her. Despite Vacha not revealing her address, the determined boy traced her out. To mark their silver jubilee, Vacha instituted the Kumud Shanbag Scholarship to enable girls who performed well in their board exams to continue with their education.

Kumud's personal involvement in such projects and her commitment to the work and the poor children was immense. She continued this work till a late age and even when she could not go there she would guide from her home. She continued this work right till she was forced to stop due to a fall that damaged her spine.

Though she recovered later, she was largely immobile yet mentally alert, reading profusely books and newspapers. But gradually her health deteriorated and on 12 December 2020 at 4 a.m. she passed away peacefully in her sleep. She had been uneasy for a number of days but suffered no pain. The immediate family was there with her in her last hours, and though in a state of unconsciousness the very touch of holding her hand and caressing her feet and forehead would have given a soothing effect in these final moments. She was at home and had been looked after with affection for years by the immediate family with the help of two nurses. She was cremated at the nearby electric crematorium by 11 a.m. with only her immediate family present.

When I was in jail I had a strong desire to meet her when I learnt that her health had seriously declined and her letters stopped coming. I felt that it may never happen, but I was so happy to find she had somewhat recovered meanwhile, which I observed once released. After ten years of incarceration, I reached Mumbai finally on 17 October 2019 at 4 am. By 9 am I was by her bedside. She was shocked and ecstatic at seeing me. Sunil and Reetha had kept it as a surprise. And I felt that my strong desire to meet her before she died was fulfilled at last. Surprisingly, when I finally met her, her health was relatively okay though she would only be in bed. But she was watching TV and reading – even doing Marathi crosswords – and mentally active. But the decline has been continuous right until COVID-19 times when I had to put an end to my weekly visits.

Anyhow, she lived a full life and was active till a late age. I remember Kumud as a warm person who was always affectionate to Anu's comrades and friends who would drop in. She was well read, knowledgeable, socially aware, and open-minded in her thinking; reflecting her communist youth. I felt very close to her, and throughout our life, Anu and I would long to see her, though our work kept us away for long periods. I felt the best reward was that even two days before her death when I went to meet her, even in her semi-conscious state she not only recognized me but gave a warm smile on seeing me. She even stretched out her twisted hand to mine. She could not talk but just holding her hand had a warmth that she too must have felt.

Anu's younger brother, Sunil Shanbag, has dedicated his life to theatre, doing progressive plays throughout the country and also abroad. He worked under the legendry theatre personality Satyadev Dubey from 1974 on about 25 productions. In 1985 he formed his own theatre group, Aparna and has lately formed yet another theatre group called Tamasha. Some of the plays directed by Sunil include Vijay Tendulkar's *Cyclewallah*, Mahesh Elkunchwar's *Pratibimb*, and Ramu Ramanathan's *Cotton 56, Polyester 84*; one of his most famous and progressive productions. Over the years, he has trained actors across the country and conducted several workshops on theatre techniques. Besides his major interest in theatre, Sunil has worked extensively for TV since 1985 developing programme concepts, researching, writing fiction and non-fiction material and producing programmes, films, and series. Some of his notable television works are *Yatra*, directed and produced by Shyam Benegal; *Surabhi*, produced by Cinema Vision of India; and *Bharat Ek Khoj*, directed by Shyam Benegal. His documentary, *Maihar Raag* on the legacy of Baba Allaudin Khan, won the National Award for the best non-fiction film. He also set up Chrysalis Films, an independent film company. In addition, he has worked closely with Astad Deboo (who too, passed away just two days before Anu's mother) a contemporary Indian dancer. He has also made documentaries on some of India's top scientists who have not got the recognition they deserve as also on IITs.

His recent theatre production of Shakespeare's *Alls Well that Ends Well* in Gujarati and adapted to local situations did a rave tour of the UK. With the new Covid situation he has innovated a new concept of online theatre and has three types of shows a month. He launched his Theatrenama with the on-line presentation of his well-known play *Sex, Morality and Censorship*, together with a session of discussions with the actors, producer and director. His next production on Theatrenama was an enacted presentation of Maharashtra's theatre history from 1776 to 1896. Extremely creative and with a passionate commitment to progressive theatre and writing, he has made a big name for himself and was given the Sangeet Natak Akademi Award in 2019. Having said that, in India, such talent and commitment are rarely rewarded monetarily.

Sunil's wife Reetha Balsavar was also a consistent support during the entire period of my incarceration; it was she who, together with my sister, coordinated all my legal paperwork throughout the country. Sunil and Reetha's family were virtually neighbours in Santacruz and she too went to the

54

same Bai Avabai Framji Petit Girl's High School as Anu, who was about four years her senior. Reetha passed out in 1974 and later went to London where she did a computer course in programming in 1976, and later worked in the UK from 1977 to 1981. She was a veritable pioneer in this line, as personal computers were a rarity in those days and what existed were the huge main-frame computers (occupying a full room) and using punch cards to write code. She passed her course in COBOL, PASCAL and Fortran which were the main programming tools in those days. On her return to India she briefly joined IDM – a company set up by ex-employees of IBM and then worked for two years, from 1982 to 1984. Around that time, she along with her friend Neela, set up 'Softcel Consultants', probably one of the early IT companies doing programming, systems analysis, etc with seventeen employees. It was probably a trend-setter for the future IT software industry, which today is a key aspect of Indian industry with BPOs flourishing in the 1990s and giants like TCS, Infosys and Wipro dominating this space. Yet, Softcel carved a space for itself for fifteen years and had many top corporate clients, including the Taj group of hotels. Finally, it was closed down in 1999. She then joined another software firm, RAFT, run by a cousin, Asim, till 2006. With the IT industry being taken over by the big players she started an organic shop Navdanya, which was forced to close down due to the Covid lockdown. Meanwhile she has also helped out in theatre in Arpana and Junoon. A multifaceted person, she has created a niche for herself in the IT sector which after some time grew to be one of India's major industries, but with giants dominating, pioneers like Reetha now have little chance to flower in this field.

The entire family are lovely people and each very capable in their own spheres. Their only child Kannagi is a dog lover and has a dog park mid-way between Mumbai and Pune.

Though poles apart, both sets of parents shared their acceptance of our activities and were fond of each other too. While Anu's parents had a communist background, mine were from the typical Parsi/corporate background. They could not have been more poles apart. But with time my parents veered around to our type of thinking and so we were basically all on the same plane and very close.

My parents, Adi and Nergis, were from a traditional Parsi family, though not overtly religious. My father, Adi, who was from Pune, became a chartered accountant and worked, as I've mentioned, in the pharmaceutical company GlaxoSmithKline his entire life, finally making his way up to becoming finance director. Surprisingly, my father who, while sending me to the UK had put much hope in me becoming a CA and getting a top corporate job, was not really disappointed with my decision to throw up my career in order to serve the oppressed of the country. In fact, he seemed somewhat proud of my decision. Later, he began reading books on Marxism and the Chinese revolution and he even turned strongly sympathetic to the cause.

My father had a reputation of honesty, I still remember him refusing gifts that were sent by agents to our Worli flat. He passed out of Fergusson College in Pune where he was a well-known sportsman. Throughout our childhood we used to regularly go to our paternal grandmother's house in Pune, an old rented bungalow opposite the military hospital with a huge garden and with aggressive geese, fierce dogs and lots of flowers. I still remember my cousin, Diana, who lived nearby, coming regularly to read to her in her old age. Diana now runs the organization Beauty Without Cruelty (BWC) from this same childhood place in Pune. She too was a regular support during my incarceration and would regularly send her beautiful calendars that adorned the wall of my cell right through the incaceration.

My mother, Nergis, came from an elite Parsi family that owned the Murree Brewery in present-day Pakistan. The brewery still exists in Pakistan though most of the relatives from that branch of the family have settled down in the US. Her mother's name (my maternal grandmother) was Banu Jalphiroze, she migrated to Amritsar at the time of Independence. The famous author Bapsi Sidhwa (of *Fire* and *Earth* fame) is a cousin long since settled in the US. One of her brothers, Minu Bhandara, was running the brewery until he passed away some years ago. Some relative apparently continues to run it but much of the family have made an independent life in the US with no connection with the brewery people.

My mother was a society lady but she too did not object to the path I chose. In fact, later when my grand aunt (my grandmother's sister) Shirinbai Katrak (who also donated money to build the agiary at the Delhi Parsi Anjuman, which is named after her) wanted to leave her sprawling Babulnath flat to me when she took ill, and I told my parents upfront I would use the money for the organization and for the poor, as both Anu and I had decided not to have children, neither objected. Both my parents were understanding in that they recognized our need to move away from the beaten path and venture into the unknown. The only wish my mother had was that we have at least one child and that she would gladly look after her grandchild in our absence. In fact, so was the case with Anus's mother. Of course, we did not accept the idea and used the money from the sale of the flat for the poor and our organizational work.

In those early days, organizations for the oppressed functioned fully on the basis of such donations from sympathisers and supporters. That is, it had to take care of the needs of full-timers, pay office and travelling expenses as also costs of organizational work. Unlike political parties that are funded by big business houses, and NGOs by sponsors in India and abroad, those working directly with the oppressed live a hand-to-mouth existence. Anyhow, the organization could not find many donors here in Maharashtra. Though most members live a very frugal life, the expenses mount up, and it is such donations that helps sustain our lives and the activities in urban areas. Many activists also have jobs, at least part-time, to help sustain them like Anuradha and most from the working classes.

My elder brother (by two years), Farrokh was a liberal, and while he did not fully support what he considered my extreme and eccentric views, he did not oppose them either and was, in fact, quite tolerant. He put his hands at many small businesses, even going all the way to Bangalore and setting up Indiana Fast Foods, to finally settle down in Mahabaleshwar to run the hotel when my father shifted to Panchgani in 1981. Unfortunately, he died young in April 1986. He had a heart defect, a floppy mitral valve, which required surgery which he neglected. He is survived by his wife Sheila and two enterprising daughters, Sanaya and Ayesha. A third, eldest daughter died in a car accident about ten years back. They live in Pune and Mahableshwar.

My sister, Mahrouk, two years younger to me, had just married about the time I returned from London and had shifted to Calcutta where her husband, Feroze, worked in ITC. Feroze spent most of his working life in ITC and grew to be the deputy chairman of the company before he retired. For her time, Mahrouk was quite radical in her thinking, right from her school and college days she was reading Carl Jung and other thinkers and philosophers.

Through the years we would meet off and on in Mahabaleshwar or Panchgani and once or twice in Delhi. But this was not often. She is always seeking and now is closely linked to Meenal Madhukar's energy meditation projects, which help people understand their fears, guilt and other insecurities and devise a means of removing these and taking a person towards a happy life away from the depressions and agonies that people face in their lives. She has attracted a large following and is totally committed to the cause. Having given up a well-paying investment banking job, Meenal did extensive work amongst the poor during the lockdown, distributing lakhs.

It is Mahrouk who, though she may not agree with my views, has unhesitatingly supported me throughout my incarceration, and even now, after release, continues to do so by keeping me at her Bandra home. Without her unstinting support the jail journey would have been all the more difficult. Meenal also assisted me by coming twice to Hazaribagh jail and showing me her meditation methods, which helped me enormously in my final period of incarceration and also to settle in after release.

By the time I returned from London, my father had just retired from Glaxo and my parents settled in the hill station of Mahabaleshwar. Both my parents were avid golfers, winning many trophies at the Willingdon Club, particularly my mother; both of them continued playing at the Mahabaleshwar golf course as well.

Meanwhile during the 1970s and part of the 1980s the workers' group of the five of us – Ravi, Max, Freddie and Darius – would regularly go to my parent's house in Mahabaleshwar and stay for about a week to ten days in meetings and study. The entire neighbouring area was forested and the quiet gave us time for serious discussions. Often, we would go up for our food with my parents and Ravi would have animated discussions with them. They became extremely fond of the group, especially him. What was perhaps most surprising was that my mother, who was such an 'aristocrat', got on so well with Ravi. He was a garrulous speaker and could converse on all issues under the sun. He was an extremely intense person and would get deeply involved in anything he took up or said. Though he lived very simply in a type of slum, he was extremely well versed in many spheres of knowledge and was a prolific reader.

My impression was that Ravi had a great impact on my parents, particularly my father, drawing them deeper to Marxism; and at the personal level he became, I think, closer to them than I could, as my nature was more reserved. My father was already sympathetic to the cause. With my parents, my group of friends would discuss the Chinese revolution, the ongoing Indian revolution, philosophical questions like human nature, and many more topics. In fact, when I met Max after my release, after decades, he recollected my mother saying that human nature does not change, so it is difficult to get people and society to change.

Amidst all this, my mother died of a heart attack in 1984 at a relatively young age. I was not there at the time, as we had by then settled in Nagpur and only came to know later. Though Anu and I were regularly in touch with them, those were not the days of cell phones and we had no phone in our frugal rented accommodation. The only other contact was through letters.

Thereafter my father was on his own, now removed to the hill station of Panchgani, about 20 kilometre from Mahabaleshwar, and a centre of many boarding schools. The reason for the shift was that Mahabaleshwar is second only to Cherrapunji in the amount of rainfall it receives. During the monsoon my parents would shift to a Parsi dharamshala in Panchgani for 3–4 months and then spend a month on repairs and maintenance on the house. That virtually meant six months wasted, which was becoming more and more difficult with age. Besides, they were able to buy a beautiful plot in Panchgani on which they built a bungalow.

In the mid-1990s my father passed away peacefully in his sleep. Again, I was not present and we were shocked to hear the news as he was very fit, though 81 years of age. He was extremely close to Anu and me and we would regularly go to meet him in Panchgani until his last days, as would some of our comrades. Interestingly, after my release Anit Burman's wife, Anita, a village girl from Palghar, reminded me that they had gone to his place in Panchgani on their honeymoon. His passing away left a big vacuum in our lives, as he was a solid support we could always count on.

Comrades in Life

In November 1977, after the Emergency was lifted, Anu and I married at a small celebration at my parents' home in Mahabaleshwar with only both our parents and some relatives present. By then Anu was a lecturer, having finished her MA and MPhil in Sociology from Bombay University. The magistrate had to be brought from Satara (I recall a bottle of whiskey being a necessary inducement), the district headquarters, 35 kilometre away at the bottom of the ghats, to sign our official marriage certificate.

With the Emergency lifted, Anu and I became active in the civil liberties movement throughout the country, which followed in the wake of the lifting of the Emergency. The Janata Party's defeat in the 1980 elections and Indira Gandhi's return to power made these all the more relevant. This was also the time we were both instrumental in the formation of CPDR (Committee for the Protection of Democratic Rights) in Maharashtra.

I take recourse in Jyoti Punwani's accounts of the time, not just because they provide perspective to the past but also because years of incarceration have played cruel tricks on my mind and memory. She wrote:

Those were the days of "parallel" cinema. Marathi amateur theatre was blossoming at Dadar's Chhabildas Hall. The Dalit Panthers had exploded onto the Marathi literary scene. Adil Jussawala's New Writing in India was still making waves. Forum Against Rape, Mumbai's first feminist group, had just been founded. Anu, by then a lecturer at Wilson College, was immersed in all this. With her wide range of interests, she succeeded in linking the human rights organization she and few others founded after the Emergency with the city's intellectual ferment. Among other things, the Committee for the Protection of Democratic Rights (CPDR), demanded that the State stop acting lawlessly with Naxalites even though they rejected its laws.

Thanks to Anu's ability to talk as intelligently with George Fernandes as with Satyadev Dubey, her brother Sunil Shanbag's mentor, the cream of Mumbai's intellectuals supported this demand. Playwright Vijay Tendulkar and reformist Asghar Ali Engineer were CPDR's president and vice-president.

After marriage, we began living at Worli. Anu's earnings from her lectureship took care of most of our simple and basic needs. She first taught Sociology at Wilson College, and then at Jhunjhunwalla college in Ghatkopar. During this period, I would sometimes help my brother Farrokh in his Friendly Ice Cream (later Kentucky Ice Cream) business, as I needed a source of income. My needs were limited and the major expense was travelling around Mumbai, which I did mostly by bus (there being no railway station near Worli).

The ice cream was made at home in the traditional sancha, with cream added. Despite, or because of, its excellent quality and the laborious method by which it was made, the ice cream business made little profit; moreover, it was unable to compete with the big chains and folded after a few years. The exquisite quality is still remembered by our friends Roshan, Govind and Jyoti. In fact, later in an article immediately after my arrest, journalist Jyoti Punwani wrote:

> Kobad Ghandy was among the three who signed as witnesses at my marriage. IIis family's ice cream was served there, much to the distaste of older guests who frowned at the strawberry chunks in a dessert supposed to be smooth and synthetic. Fresh strawberry was the flavour that rewarded us at the end of our study circle afternoons in the vast, empty expanse of Kobad's sea-facing flat.

Later, when the Worli rented property was sold by the landlords, we made a tidy sum from my share of the proceeds (due to the then prevailing tenancy laws) which we used partly for living, but mostly for organizational work.

From Worli, we shifted to 1st, Pasta Lane, Colaba where our neighbours were Govind and Roshan Shahani – both lecturers of English Literature at Jai-Hind College – who became good friends. Govind was also a leader of the teacher's union (BUTU), of which Anu too was now a member. It may seem a digression, but I particularly remember Govind's mother, who was exceptional for her age and had extremely liberal and progressive ideas. Perhaps that was to be expected: she had been a freedom fighter and continued to live by her Gandhian principles of simplicity. Soon after release when I went to visit Govind and Roshan, the place looked exactly the same, except that the famous eating joint at the beginning of the lane, Kailash Parbat, had expanded substantially. But otherwise, all the old buildings in the vicinity were just as they were forty years back; it's probably skyscrapers are not allowed in the area due to the naval dockyard nearby. Or else they would have been swallowed up by the real estate sharks as most of Mumbai elsewhere. Of course the old lady was no more and the two little kids that we knew were now also English lecturers in the US.

Both of us continued in CPDR for a couple of years, but felt we needed to do more grassroots work. It was then that we began to toy with the idea of moving to a more backward area of Maharashtra.

Jyoti writes:

They weren't social workers who visited slums while servants looked after their homes. From sweeping to washing up, these wealthy 20-somethings did it all themselves. Not everyone of course, could – or even wanted to – live like this. "Toughening up" for the revolution (that it would come about seemed a certainty) took up a lot of time then – the long hikes up the hills outside Mumbai; the study camps in spartan surroundings, where we had to sleep on a mat, and wash up after eating. But Kobad knew few of us would take the plunge that he and his wife Anuradha Shanbag had already decided on. Yet, they created the space for us to do what we enjoyed the most, be it in PROYOM or CPDR. For them, revolution wasn't only class war, in which few wanted to participate, sacrificing our comfortable lives, facing police bullets. If you wanted to change the unequal system, you could make your two-bit contribution wherever you worked, and Kobad would make it seem important.

Those formative years left most of us with some basic premises that have stayed with us: the state was exploitative; the police oppressive; elections rarely changed the lives of the majority of people for whom democracy meant little – these, have been substantiated again and again.

While working in Mumbai, Anu and I thought it was time to do more grassroots work and live more deeply amongst the masses with whom we were working. As an important area of work was with Dalits we finally decided to move to Nagpur, though we knew not a soul there.

Grassroots

In 1982 we finally decided to shift to Nagpur which was then the heart of the Dalit movement. The entire Vidarbha region was also where extensive mining, particularly coal, was taking place.

Jyoti continues:

It was time for Anu to grow into a successful academic, the type who writes books and attends international seminars. Instead, in 1982, she left the life she loved to work in Nagpur. The wretched conditions of contract workers in the new industrial areas near Nagpur and of Adivasis in the forests of Chandrapur had to be challenged. Committed cadres were needed. In her subsequent trips to Mumbai, Anu never complained about the drastic change in her life: cycling to work under the relentless Nagpur sun; living in the city's Dalit area, the mention of which drew shudders from Nagpur's elite; then moving to backward Chandrapur. In Marxist study circles, "declassing oneself" is quite a buzzword. From Mumbai's Leftists, only Anu and her husband Kobad, both lovers of the good life, actually did so.

In truth, we never considered it a sacrifice, just a part of life as a true revolutionary. It is true the places we took on rent were simple and so was the food.[3]

We knew no one in Nagpur when we moved there. Anu got a job as a postgraduate lecturer in Nagpur University and I a temporary writing job in the Sunday edition of *Hitvada*, a reputed English daily, which had supported the freedom struggle in the pre-Independence days. With the help of a socialist, Nagesh Chaudhary, we were able to find a reasonably priced accommodation to rent in Laxmi Nagar. The place had a leaky roof and whenever it would rain, we would spend the night removing buckets of water.

As the main field of activities was amongst the Dalits, within a few years we shifted to Maharashtra's biggest Dalit basti, Indora.

In a 2009 article for *Open* magazine, Rahul Pandita wrote about those times, saying:

[They] rented two small rooms at the house of a postal department employee, Khushaal Chinchikhede. "There was absolutely nothing in their house except two trunksful of books and a mud pitcher," he says. Anuradha also worked as part-time lecturer in Nagpur University. Later, Kobad would also come to live there. Both would be out till midnight. Anuradha used a rundown cycle to commute, and it was later at the insistence of other activists that Kobad bought a TVS Champ moped... Indora was notorious for its rowdies. "No taxi or autorickshaw driver would dare venture inside Indora," says Anil Borkar, who grew up in Indora. But Anuradha was unfazed. "She would pass though the basti at midnight, all alone on a cycle," remembers Borkar.

Indora was such a dreaded place that middle-class people were scared to go to that area after dark due to the impression that it was a nest of crime and were shocked to find we were living there. Such impressions are easily created in impoverished Dalit and Muslim localities because of inbuilt biases and a certain amount of petty theft due to extreme poverty that gets magnified.

A typical day in Nagpur would start with Anu cycling/ busing to university, over 15 kilometre away, leaving early in the morning after having breakfast. I would do some of the cleaning up of the rooms and then meet the Dalit members of the community in our basti.

Working amongst Dalits we hoped to arouse them not to accept their existing status that their religion sanctified. We encouraged them to stand up for their rights and study both Ambedkar and Marx. Ambedkar would give deeper insight into the caste issue, while Marxism would keep them away from identity politics and help them unite with other oppressed, even from other castes. The two ideologies would show them the path as to whom to target and whom to ally with – i.e. target Brahminism (the ideology) and those who propounded it and not all upper castes; on the contrary one needed to educate those from the other castes (like the OBCs and even upper castes) to drop their casteist feelings. We would encourage inter-caste love marriages to help facilitate this unity. The point was not to consolidate caste, even Scheduled Caste sentiments, but destroy the caste system from its roots. One had to counter identity politics amongst Dalits which the Dalit political leaders promoted for their vote-banks.

Many of the youth of Indora were attracted to our views and joined our organizations of student/youth, especially the cultural organization, Aavhan. Jyoti, the daughter of Khushal Chinchkhede (the postal employee whose first floor we rented), and her friend who stayed across the road, Jyotsna, were active in our organization.

In Nagpur, we used to travel all over the city on cycles in the notorious Vidarbha heat. Earlier our residence was reasonably near the university where Anu taught. Indora was virtually at the other end of the town. Her schedule was so hectic that only strict discipline, her high level of commitment to any task she took up, and her inexhaustible stamina enabled her to do justice to both her students and to her social activities.

Because of Anuradha, Devanand Pantavne, a black belt in karate turned into a poet and the lead singer of a radical cultural troupe. Pantavne remembers her as a stickler for deadlines. 'She would get very angry if we took up a job and then didn't deliver on time,' he says. Another young man, Surendra Gadling was motivated by Anuradha to take up law. Today, he fights cases for various activists and alleged Naxals. 'She is my guiding light,' he says. He is at present in jail as one of the accused in the so-called Koregaon Bhim case, though he lived and practised in far off Nagpur. It is not without reason. Anuradha led by example, living the life she wanted the *basti* boys to lead.

Jyoti continues:

Anu's lawyer-father may have left his family estate in Coorg to defend communists in court in the 1950s, but she had never seen deprivation. Despite her own rough life, neither did Anu make us feel guilty for our bourgeois luxuries nor did she patronise us. On the few occasions she would suddenly land up over these 25 years, it was as if she had never left. She had the same capacity to laugh, even at herself, the same ability to connect, even with management types, the same readiness to indulge in women's talk. But with those closest to her, she seemed unnaturally detached.

69

Her parents doted on her, yet she didn't take every opportunity she could to meet them. I realize why now... When her father died, she couldn't go home. That was also the reason for her harsh decision never to have children, though her parents would have willingly brought them up. That was one bond she knew would draw her away from the life she had chosen.

In those days in Andhra Pradesh it was a norm if a young couple got married and both were active revolutionaries the male member would have a vasectomy in order to avoid children which would require additional attention and distract from one's activities. Anu and I, having decided to dedicate all our time to the poor, followed this norm after marriage.

In the morning Anu would attend her lectures. Then, in the afternoon, she and I would meet up and we would jointly go and meet people in the city like Prof. Sudhakar Joshi, Nagesh Chaudhary and numerous other social activists. In the evening there would be some public function or meeting. Often we would also go to the MIDC (Maharashtra Industrial Development Corporation) area, Khaparkheda and Kamptee to organize the workers into trade unions. In trade union work Anu began organizing the molkarins (household labour) of Nagpur and then in various other sections. She was actively involved in organizing the 5,000 strong construction workers of the Khaparkheda Thermal Power Plant near Nagpur and led many a militant struggle, notably a three-month strike which faced huge repression. She also organized the powerloom workers of Kamptee (some 15 kilometre from Nagpur), all of whom were Muslims and lived in horrid conditions. Anu went to jail numerous times in the course of these struggles. In 1993 she helped organize coal mine and construction workers in Chandrapur.

In 1994, a Dalit woman, Manorma Kamble, working as a maid in an influential lawyer's house, was found dead with the lawyer's family claiming that she had accidentally electrocuted herself to death. But the activists feared she had been raped and killed by the lawyer. Anuradha led an agitation, and it was due to her efforts that the case created ripples in the state assembly and in Parliament. In India, one of Anuradha's trusted lieutenants was Biwaji Badke, a four-foot tall Dalit activist. Every morning Badke would come to her house and share all news with Anuradha over tea, recall friends. Later, when he was diagnosed with throat cancer, Anuradha brought him to her house and nursed him for months. Others recall, her house in Indora was open to everyone.

In the urban areas the nature of work entailed making people aware of their rights and organizing them to fight for it. In the trade unions that is easy to conceive as it is against the factory owner for better wages and working conditions. For Dalits and for women, it takes on a different character and is mostly against the system of caste and patriarchal oppression. An important weapon of building awareness and organization was through songs. Maharashtra has had a long tradition of *Lok Geet* (peoples' songs) from the time of the legendary Amar Sheikh and Anna Bhau Sathe of the CPI, who travelled around the countryside writing and singing songs on the life of the people and the need to struggle, since the 1940s. Their troupe would only have a 'dafli' and 'dholak' as musical instruments. We had our own *Aavhan Natya Manch* with present-day Amar Sheikhs in Vilas Ghogre and Sambhaji Bhagat. They wrote and sang songs that became popular, particularly those on Dalit and women's issues. They were mostly in Marathi, but also in Hindi.

The Dalit youth of Indora whom we organized were primarily attracted by these songs, and they themselves being

71

talented, soon started staging programmes all over Vidarbha attracting more and more Dalits. So was it with the women's organization, but here we would also take up specific issues of torment, like that of Manorma Kamble putting cases against the perpetrators or taking direct action like a morcha (procession) against the individual or family to educate them to change. Also, Dalits and women in our circles were encouraged to stand up for their rights in their private lives as well, and not tolerate any humiliation or oppression wherever it may come from. Anu was the mass leader in all these struggles, both amongst Dalits and workers. She would regularly be called to speak at public meetings organized all over Vidarbha. She was a good public speaker and spoke as fluently in Hindi as in Marathi and was able to keep the audience spellbound.

Most activists tend to have the approach of neglecting their professional duties. Not Anu. She made time for her lectures, grading her students' assignments, as well as the activist work we were both immersed in. Sometimes, she had an article to write, and often worked late into the night. Her lectures were very popular and she was loved by her students and the academic staff alike. Over and above this, she would share in the housework which we both did. I, though, was never good at cooking, while Anu made excellent rotis. Besides, for long periods I was away and Anu would have to do all the housework herself.

~

As I mentioned, the region near Nagpur was the site of various mining operations. Anu and I, together and independently, often travelled to Chandrapur where coal mine workers and others were being organized into the Akhil Maharashtra Kamgar Union.

I would also go to some rural areas in Bhandara district – about 50 kilometre from Nagpur – which had large numbers of bidi workers, all Dalits. Nearly every hut would have the entire family, including children, rolling bidis. Contractors would supply the leaves and the tobacco, which these families would role into bidis. The bidi king of the area was Praful Patel, a top leader of the Nationalist Congress Party (NCP). The money these families made was a pittance for their effort. They were paid per bundle, and each bundle comprised a hundred bidis. Most of them, though based in villages, owned no land and were entirely dependent on the bidi industry for their survival. Organizing them was difficult, as there was no factory floor where the workers would gather and all were dispersed in their own houses. Besides, it would be difficult to survive if they went on strike for their wages. In fact, when we sat and talked, they would continue the rolling of bidis, their hands working mechanically like machines. I was not particularly successful in getting them much relief, though the money they earned was raised marginally.

We would also travel to Amravati and Wardha districts where students were being organized. Sometimes our travel took us to the northern regions of Amravati, bordering Madhya Pradesh, where the bulk of the famous 'Nagpur oranges' grow. Even the students' body there called themselves the California Students' Organization. We would often eat luscious oranges direct from the trees. In fact, there was a sympathetic orange farmer in the Nagpur region in whose fields we held study classes for 5-6 days, right under the fragrant, orange-laden trees.

We would also often visit Ramtek, about 40 kilometre away, and climb up to the famous Ramtek temple. I knew some locals who had land in the village and we tried doing work there amongst the peasantry, but did not get too far. I remember the Ramtek temple more for the aggressive monkeys that would attack us on the long climb to the top. Especially if we had any food on us there was little chance of saving it from the monkeys.

In Wardha we also went to the Gandhi Ashram several times. I remember a particular experiment they had conducted there which inspired me. They showed that on a half-acre plot of land an entire family of five could survive for the whole year. It made me wonder why then this could not be implemented for the vast number of marginal farmers throughout the country. Of course, that would entail a regular supply of water and terminating the exploitative debt, reducing the price of inputs and switching to organic farming, as also getting a reasonable price for the produce they sold. In fact, it was here, the heart of Vidarbha, that was to soon become the suicide capital of farmers of the country.

I remember often meeting the top leader of the Shetkari Sanghatana of Vidarbha, Vijay Jawandhia, who himself was a cotton farmer with 40 acres of land. He would explain at length the economics of cotton growing that was pushing the farmer to penury. This was the mid/late 1990s when suicides had not begun as Bt cotton had not been introduced yet. With the introduction of Bt cotton in 2002, the number of suicides began to reach epidemic proportions, as the seeds were very expensive and the yield was not much due to lack of irrigation facilities. Besides, Bt was only effective against the Bollworm insect, not others, so limited spraying was also necessary. Besides, cotton prices have always been depressed so that the textile mill magnates could extract maximum profit. Jawandhia was very clear in all these calculations and would, with facts and figures, show how exploitative the system was for the farmer and how only the input companies, moneylenders, wholesalers and textile magnates gained from the vast lands of the once famous black cotton soil of this region.

~

We spent about twenty years in Nagpur, involving ourselves, as I have recounted, in Dalit activism, trade union movements, women's movements, as also amongst bidi workers of villages in neighbouring Bhandara district. This covered much of Vidarbha region, particularly the districts of Nagpur, Chandrapur and Amravati. But it was the various Dalit struggles that shook Maharashtra in these three decades, after the initial Dalit Panther movement that specifically attracted our attention.

The Dalit Struggles

Through the two decades of our stay in Nagpur, Maharashtra was shaken into awareness by four major Dalit movements (after the Dalit Panthers of 1973–74); Indora, where we began living, was a major centre of these movements. There was first the movement, in the mid-1970s before we went to Nagpur, for the removal of the ban by the then Maharashtra government on Ambedkar's book, *Riddles in Hinduism*, which I had categorized then as India's Voltaire-type analysis of Hindu religion. As a result of this movement the ban was finally lifted.

Then there was the massive movement for the re-naming of Marathwada University as Ambedkar University, to pay homage to work done by Dr. Babasaheb Ambedkar for the educational development of the Marathwada region. In these movements the youth of Indora would traverse the length and breadth of Vidarbha arousing the Dalit youth through the songs composed by the famous Lok Shahir, Vilas Ghogre (who, sadly, later committed suicide) and Sambhaji Bhagat. The Namantar song by Bhagat virtually became the anthem of the Dalit/Namantar movement of Maharashtra. The demand was first made in 1974 and the movement grew in leaps and bounds for sixteen years starting in 1978; it was only in July

1994 that the university was renamed the Dr. Babasaheb Ambedkar Marathwada University.

The other movement to shake Maharashtra was the Ramabai Nagar killings. On 11 July 1997, a statue of Ambedkar in front of Ramabai Ambedkar Nagar – a predominantly Dalit urban colony in the city of Mumbai – was found to have had a garland of sandals placed around its neck, in an act widely seen as a desecration. The outraged residents of the colony complained at the nearest police station, Local Beat No. 5 Pantnagar police, which happened to be located a few metres from the statue. The complainants were instead directed to the Pantnagar police station. A crowd of protesters began to form, and by 7 a.m. had blocked the highway that ran in front of the colony.[4]

A team of State Reserve Police Force (SRPF) members arrived a few minutes later, and opened fire on the crowd with live ammunition. The firing continued for 10–15 minutes, and killed 10 people, including a bystander who had not been involved in the protests. The protests then grew more violent. At approximately 11.30 a.m., a luxury bus was set ablaze. In response, about 25 police officers entered Ramabai Colony, deployed tear gas and began a lathi charge. By the end of the day, 26 people had been seriously injured, and Local Beat No. 5 had been destroyed by the protesters. The protest spread throughout Maharashtra, paralysing the state for four days. No action was taken against those who desecrated the statue or the police who were complicit.

Finally, there was the horrifying incident of Khairlanji village in Bhandara district where an entire Dalit family was brutally lynched by upper castes. In this incident, 50-60 upper-caste villagers massacred the Bhotmange family – Surekha the mother (45), and her children, Sudhir (21), Roshan (19) and Priyanka (17). Surekha's husband was the only survivor, and died of a heart attack in 2017. The brutality with which it was done was unbelievable. The mother and daughter were paraded naked in the village and gang-raped to death, the genitals of the boys were crushed with stones and the corpses callously thrown into a canal. For a month the incident was ignored by the mainstream media and it was only on 1 November 2006, when a fact-finding mission set up by progressives and Dalit organizations published the gory details that the truth emerged. Soon, protests engulfed all of Maharashtra, but the cruelty with which these were suppressed was unimaginable. A fact-finding report of the CPDR stated that police attacked Dalit bastis, thrashing young and old, men and women, abusing them in the filthiest terms. School and college-going boys were tortured in custody.

Angered by these killings as also the desecration of Ambedkar's statue in Kanpur, Dalits in several parts of Maharashtra went on a rampage, setting three trains on fire, damaging over a hundred buses and clashing with police in violent protests that left four persons dead and over 60 injured.

As the state witnessed protests for the second day, authorities imposed curfew in Nanded town of Marathwada region, Pimpri in Pune district and Nandurbar town in north Maharashtra following incidents of violence there.

Two persons died in police firing at Osmanabad in Marathwada, while one each died in Nanded and Nashik during protests. Five compartments of the Mumbai-Pune Deccan Queen train were torched by a mob of over 6,000 people at Ulhasnagar in Thane district, 56 kilometre from Mumbai.

The reason for the Khairlanji massacre: the Bhotmanges had attained a certain amount of economic independence coupled with cultural awakening – the mother was assertive in confronting upper-caste harassment and the children were more educated than others in the village. Forty-six people were charged but the case was weakened by the police, doctors, and officials (mostly all Dalits themselves); finally only 11 people were sentenced, many of whom gained relief from the high court. In fact, it is said that the main masterminds were not even in the case and only the small fry were convicted. The case and its aftermath shook the conscience of all progressives in Maharashtra. Surprisingly, though the Naxals have a wide presence in the neighbouring district of Gondia, this seemed to have had little impact there.

These four major upsurges, and many smaller ones, in which we played a role, helped widen the awakening amongst Dalits of Maharashtra indicating that they were no longer going to take their oppression lying down. And this awakening of Dalits/Mahars of Maharashtra has, to some extent, grown as a vast awakening of Dalits throughout the country, including the relatively socially backward states of Uttar Pradesh and Gujarat.

Right from the earliest days the communist organizations hesitated to take up the Dalit issue. Together with Anuradha, I went on to write numerous articles supporting the Dalit question from a Marxist view-point, the arguments being specifically published in long and detailed articles in the English weekly *Frontier* from Calcutta, and the Marathi monthly *Satyashodak Marxswad* brought out from Dhule by Sharad Patil, as far back as the late 1970s. In fact, Anu and I went on to devote much of our life to organizing Dalits in Maharashtra, living for over 15 years in Maharashtra's biggest Dalit basti, Indora, in Nagpur.

It was Anu who wrote a number of articles throughout her political life which has been the most comprehensive Marxist approach to the caste question in India. Her first essay was 'The Caste Question Returns', published by *Frontier* responding to an article by Gopal Guru's 'Understanding Ambedkar – A caste and class Paradigm'. Next was an essay 'Movement against

79

caste in Maharashtra' presented at the AILRC seminar tracing the history from the Bhakti movement. The last article she wrote was on the Khairlanji killings in the January 2007 issue of *People's March*, entitled 'Gruesome Massacre of Dalits: Dalit fury scorches Maharashtra'. But these were mere the building blocks to her magnus opus – the most comprehensive piece on the caste question (from a Marxist/revolutionary view-point) was written by her and posthumously published in *Scripting the Change*. I am of the opinion that this nearly 100-page article is so analytical it needs to be introduced in the texts at the university-level (if necessary, with amendments) as well as in all Marxist and other progressive circles. Yet it seems to be ignored by both. Though it would be too long to reproduce it here I bring out the main points she presented:

1. A detailed historical account of the evolution of caste and classes in India right from the Vedic period (1,500 BC) to the present;

2. Traces the consolidation of untouchability to the feudal period beginning from about the second AD when the Manusmriti is said to have been written;

3. It traces the history of the strong anti-caste movements, particularly the Bhakti movements in India and those of Phule, Ambedkar and Periyar;

4. It seeks to counter the earlier communist's notions that caste exists only in the superstructure and will automatically fade away with the change of the economic base; and

5. It outlines 29 major points for the annihilation of castes to be undertaken by revolutionaries and social activists.

Summing up, she says: 'Even during the revolution, while destroying it at its roots in the base itself, we shall have to struggle against caste discrimination and prejudices wherever it occurs.' She concludes that even after the revolution 'at the ideological and cultural plane, the fight against Brahminical practices, pujapath, superstition, rituals, and any and every symbol of hierarchical superiority, etc., shall continue, while upholding one's right to practice one's faith... we shall have to emulate and learn lessons continuously to create the new person, the socialist person. In the Indian context it means, specifically, eradicating all caste sentiments and ingrained thoughts of superiority through a continuous process of cultural revolutions.'

Today, after the Dalit awakening it is difficult for communists to oppose the issue like they did earlier, but they appeared to reduce its importance in the social and revolutionary project by not bringing it to the front of the agenda, partly to pander to the subtle caste sentiments amongst other Hindu-background cadres and even the public in general, many from the upper and other forward castes as also OBCs who have anti-Dalit sentiments. But, in the long run, such appeasement only helps perpetuate the caste system; a major factor in India's backwardness and divisiveness.

It continues to confound me as to why Indian communists are unable to recognize the importance of caste abolition to the democratization of Indian society, particularly as many of their earlier leaders were from Maharashtra, which has a strong social reform tradition. After all, the caste system permeates every aspect of the peoples' lives; besides which, it is highly oppressive against untouchables; let alone racism, it is probably worse than slavery.

Its negative features are many besides being oppressive: First, it is very patriarchal in its attitude to women, as witnessed by the large number of rapes of Dalit women, mostly unrecorded; second, it is particularly claustrophobic and negates, in practice, the concept of uniting for the nation, as caste sentiment does not extend to the entire country crossing caste barriers, so the country is perpetually divided, making it easy prey for foreign conquerors who play one caste against the other; thirdly, it gives importance to the advance of merely one's own caste and not of the country as a whole; and last, but not the least, it goes to the extent of even dissuading one to love whom one likes, eat what one likes, and numerous other onerous and exclusive cultural practices.

Yet the communists have negated this key issue. The reasons could be many: from a mechanical interpretation of Marxism to the Indian condition, as also of the base-superstructure theory, to the remnants of traditional thinking among upper-caste Marxists leaders. After all, ideas, including caste sentiments, inculcated from our childhood days are deep-rooted in our subconscious, and these do not get automatically eradicated with the adoption of some ideology without a conscious effort.

Today, after an elementary study of psychology I can understand how deep-rooted these caste sentiments must have been that even a Marxist and those with a scientific understanding of society were unable to break through the imprints of childhood amongst much of the upper-caste leaders. Studies have shown that the major part of our sub-conscious is formed (programmed) till the age of seven (that is, before reasoning ability develops), mainly through perceptions formed from our environment. These programmes get reflected in the bulk of our emotions at a later age and reflected in our habits, tastes, likes, which tend to act independently of our conscious mind which is, of course, more powerful. So many of our values, like, say, caste feelings, patriarchal ideas, ingrained likes and dislikes, fears, guilt, mistrust, are formed in our childhood and acquired

82

from our environment at that time and cannot change simply by induction of ideology. It will require independent efforts to fight some of these values, which are deeply embedded in our subconscious since childhood, and keep coming to the fore again and again, however much we try and suppress them.

Whatever the reason, the Dalit issue and caste eradication in a country like India is an important, if not key aspect for the democratization of society – at both macro and micro levels.

Bastar: Walking the Forests

We returned to Mumbai just before the turn of the century, in 1999. Anu had been asked to leave by the Nagpur University authorities because of her activities – her work amongst Dalits and the fact that she'd become a popular mass leader regularly addressing public meetings, and her work with trade unions and women was increasingly coming under the scanner of the cops.

Soon after leaving her university job, Anu went to Bastar and spent two years gaining much experience of life there and women's issues amongst tribals. Bastar is in south Chattisgarh bordering the three states of Andhra Pradesh, Odisha and Maharashtra.

Whereas I had gone there earlier on rare occasions to study the movement and the developmental work, she had first-hand experience, staying there continuously for over two years. She was known there as Janaki (another name for Sita) and after she died in 2008 a memorial in her honour was built at Abujmarh in Chattisgarh according to the book on the Lalgarh movement by Snigdhendu Bhattacharya (2016). Abujmarh is known as the 'Naxal headquarters' in the mainstream media.

Together with the other mahila (female) comrades, Anu helped to develop the women's organization KAMS (Krantikari Adivasi Mahila Samgathan) in the area. KAMS is said to be the biggest women's organization in the country with about 90,000 members and is, what Arundhati Roy calls, 'probably one of India's best kept secrets'. Anu would recount that in Bastar the organization was very particular about supporting women's rights and any complaint by the women cadre was taken very seriously by the organization, just as Anu would herself do while in the urban areas. Due to a support system, she said, that helped women develop their individual abilities and grow as equal partners to their male counterparts in all spheres, they developed a self-confidence unthinkable amongst backward tribal women. Not surprisingly, the media has time and again reported that the top leadership positions at various levels were held by women, including in the armed formations. As a rule, members were allowed to marry only two years after joining the squad/platoon. At the time in question, the organization had not quite addressed the issue of couples wanting children. Typically, the husband (never the wife) would have a vasectomy operation so that both could contribute equally to the movement.

The initiative of the local women and their awakening to consciousness was to be particularly seen in the songs they themselves began writing. Some of these were reproduced in *Scripting the Change*, and provide a glimpse into the life of women in Bastar.

In one particularly popular song, Kamala laments about the marriage forced upon her by her elders and goes on to vividly describe the slave-like labour she performs at the house of her in-laws:

I labour all day, but then my in-laws
Call me a lazy daughter-in-law!
To collect the leaves, to bring the firewood it is the
daughter-in-law,
...
I cannot go anywhere, Sangam Pandu,
He takes the cows and bulls and sells them off
He drinks and spends the money, my man.
He never brings anything, not even clothes,
As if he doesn't know he has a wife and children.

This was a particularly popular song amongst the women. Then there was the song written by the squad women in North Bastar:

The red flower, sister, is flowering
Let us follow the path of the red flower
In the village, the elders, sister
The elders threaten and suppress us, sister
In the house it is mother and father
They marry us off, sister...

The feelings of a young girl forced into marriage have been poetically expressed in another song, which goes like this:

In the darkness of no moon
In the light of full moon
In the deep forest I am alone,
I put my foot forward, I take a step backward
Wherever I step it is dark, brother.
Their only daughter, this bright beauty,
This beautiful face, they have ruined, brother
They have forcibly married me off, brother.

Then the song ends with hope:

Yes, brother yes, I have heard your view
I will no longer stay in the darkness
I will go forward towards the red dawn.

Anu told me there was such close interconnection between the organization members and the villagers, that they virtually treated all the children of the village as their own (an aspect brought out sharply in the film *Chakravyuh* by Prakash Jha). In big things and small, according to Anu, the organization would give opportunities for women to develop their individual personalities. For instance, she would recount how women could be seen writing songs and poems for the Gondi cultural magazine brought out locally; women trained as medical practitioners and as 'barefoot doctors', and in all organizational structures. Women were also playing lead roles in the developmental work at the village level – building cooperative irrigation projects, afforestation, promoting fish breeding, developing agriculture and animal husbandry were some of these significant activities. Anu helped develop these together with other women leaders, many of whom were originally from Andhra Pradesh, who played a stellar role in all these activities.

In 1997, I had visited Bastar for about a month when the movement was not yet banned, and wrote a booklet on the development work being done in the area. From what I gathered, it was in 1981 that some twenty students/youth from neighbouring Telangana first entered Bastar (and Gadchiroli) with the intention of working amongst the local tribals. These activists would inform me that when they first arrived on the scene in 1981, the people barely wore any clothes (women a towel around their waist and men a

86

loincloth), they were totally uneducated, let alone modern medicine, they did not even know the basics of agriculture and animal husbandry. They spent much of their time hunting and living a hand-to-mouth existence, constantly exploited by tendu-patta contractors, bamboo contractors (for the paper mill) and also the Baila Dila mining contractors. The tribals were paid next to nothing for their labour. A full half century of independence had passed them by with no difference to their quality of life from the British period.

When I visited, it had been fifteen years since the Telangana youth activists came in contact with the locals in Bastar and in spite of being continuously harassed by police, the people, through *shramdaan* (voluntary community labour) had built over a hundred water bodies for irrigation in the area. The Andhra Pradesh activists had taught the local people agriculture, fruit growing, animal husbandry and fish-breeding, trained hundreds of barefoot doctors, and started primary education amongst the locals in their own language, Gondi. In addition, these activists organized the masses to campaign against the contractors to increase their wages. For the first time in their lives the tribals began earning a living wage. Most importantly, through education – they had by then developed textbooks for up to class five in Gondi – and increasing their class consciousness, treating them as equals with respect and raising their economic status, the self-confidence and self-respect of the tribals grew. The leaders helped adapt political songs from Andhra Pradesh to local folk tunes in Gondi, which were exceedingly popular and educative. At the drop of a hat the tribals would burst into song and dance, which they love.

It was into this atmosphere that Anu entered Bastar towards the end of the century. Anu used to say those two years were the richest in her life. Tribal women are, like her, very simple, straightforward and natural. Being good at languages she was able to pick up Gondi. As she had an incisive mind, I remember her saying that Gondi was more akin to Tamil, rather than any of its neighbouring languages (Telugu, Hindi, Marathi, Odiya) and would try and trace the reasons behind it through anthropological studies. That was Anu researching life and society anywhere and everywhere. It was a tough two years, as life there is not easy, particularly for a 46-year-old with arthritis and yet to be diagnosed, systemic sclerosis.

She went out of her way to gather as many PhD studies on Gond tribals to provide source material to cadres. During the peak of the famine in 1977 she saw hundreds of people perish of starvation in other tribal areas. But here, she observed the revolutionaries resorted to seizing grain from the hoarders and distributing them amongst the starving masses, thus preventing a major calamity. During this period, intermittent attacks of malaria, the terrible dry heat of summer, coupled with famine conditions took a toll on her health, and she lost 10 kg by the time she came back. She never made a show of her own suffering, always bearing pain with dignity, without complaining or letting others know.

Besides these two years when we were apart, even in those fifteen odd years we spent in Nagpur, Anu was by herself much of the time while I would be away. In fact, in much of our lives together, we spent paradoxically more time apart, as we both had independent and different fields of work. This, to some extent, affected our relationship, but Anu could fulfil much of her emotional needs, being a friendly, unassuming person who was greatly loved by all.

Though Anu's health deteriorated significantly on her return from Bastar, she did not let this tell on the level of her activities and was the same bubbly self.

The Worst Night of My life

By about 2000, Anu had developed severe arthritis and was also diagnosed with the auto-immune disease, systemic sclerosis. This was taking a serious toll on her health, but she didn't reduce the level of her activities. Moreover, staying in rented places with poor facilities, upon our return to Mumbai from Nagpur after 2000, had made life more difficult. I too was not giving her sufficient attention, but she never demanded it, and made light of her illness. I now feel I did not give the auto-immune disease the seriousness it deserved; not that much could be done about it, as it has no cure. Yet, building immunity would have helped fight the disease, which I could have helped in.

In 2008, in spite of her poor health she accepted an invitation by the Jharkhand Maoists to take a class on women's oppression with the leading mahila tribal activists of the area. Walking through forests with her bad knees and poor health was real trauma. Apparently, her class was a hit with the tribal girls, it was recorded and the audio shared on cell phones, some in Jharkhand jail had also heard it and informed me. I was later told by some who attended the classes, that the girls accompanied her as far as they could and, with tears in their eyes, bade her farewell as she disappeared over the horizon, tripping and falling over the rough terrain.

By then she had been hit by the deadly falciparum malaria which neither she nor the women activists were aware of. I was not around when she returned to Mumbai, and the malaria was not diagnosed in time. When I returned, I took her to a well-equipped hospital where she was already being treated for systemic sclerosis. We went to the hospital in a bus, merely to get some test results, but soon after reaching, the falciparum hit her so suddenly that she went into coma. While travelling she never once gave any indication that her condition was so serious. She was on ventilator in the ICU the entire day and finally passed away that night (early next morning) on 12 April 2008. I had spent the entire day and night by her side, hoping for her recovery but by early morning doctors came with the terrible news. The shock of her death shook her mother particularly as she was very fond of her, the father having passed away earlier in 2001 after suffering for years with Alzheimer's disease.

It was the worst night of my life. The death was least expected. The suddenness of Anu's passing shocked me to such an extent that I could not recover for years, even after my arrest. The very thought of her, or mention of her, would bring tears to my eyes. Nor had I the luxury of grief, as within a year and a half of her death I was arrested. During interrogation, the Andhra Pradesh IB were sensitive enough to stop raising the issue of Anu when they noticed my reaction.

Ironically, the day before I had left Delhi for Bombay in order to meet her, I had vowed to myself, I would now cut down my activities and spend more time looking after Anu. Obviously, this decision came too late, and I regret my insensitivity for not having taken it earlier. Somehow in my mind Anu was invulnerable, as I was the one who often fell sick. Imagine, in the two years she was deep in the malaria-ridden Bastar heartland, she did not get malaria (vivax) that often, whereas when I went for a month, even after taking a prophylactic dose of lariago, I was sure to get it.

On 20 April 2008, soon after Anu's death, Jyoti Punwani wrote the following article in the *Times of India*:

Cerebral malaria can be fatal, but people have been known to recover from it. Anuradha Ghandy, however,

90

didn't stand a chance. Already weakened by the sclerosis when she walked into the hospital, it was too late. Within 24 hours, she was gone. By the time her vast circle of friends was informed on the evening of April 12, the 54-year-old had already been cremated.

That Anu managed to evade arrest for so long, was an indicator of the ruthlessness with which she effaced her identity. This, of course, meant isolating herself from all those who would have given up everything to nurse her... Anu could have followed medical advice and given herself the break her body so badly needed... that wasn't her style.

Just climbing stairs had become an ordeal five years ago. Yet, days before her death, she was in some jungle where malaria was probably an inevitability.

At the time of her death Anu was studying the problems facing women comrades in the revolutionary movement. She was deeply involved in the enquiry of the varied forms of patriarchy that women had to face every day, so as to enable them to grow to greater leadership responsibilities.

Anu was the epitome of what a good social activist should be. No doubt there has been recognition of her role in serving the nation and its people through the annual Anuradha Ghandy Memorial (AGM) lectures in Mumbai, as well as her posthumous book, *Scripting the Change*, edited and published by Shoma Sen and Anand Teltumbde (both of whom, ironically, are in jail today on allegations of being so-called Urban Naxals), with an excellent foreword by Arundhati Roy and released at a function by former chief justice of the Delhi High Court, Justice A.P. Shah. The AGM was formed by friends of Anuradha, like Gurbir Singh, Susan Abraham, Bernard D'mello and others who knew her and/or had worked with her as activists at some point in their lives. In the formation of the AGM it was advocate P.A. Sabastian of the CPDR who played a pioneering role and organized the first memorial lecture by Samir Amin, the well-known Marxist economist, which drew a huge audience. I am told that the AGM lectures have drawn packed halls and have had other outstanding speakers as Jan Myrdal, Baburam Bhattarai (a one-time top Maoist leader from Nepal, the party, from which he split is today de-facto leading the government), Arundhati Roy, Dalit poet/activist Meena Kandasamy and Angela Davis, founder member of the Black Panther Party and pioneer of the Black Lives Matter movement in the US.

To these tributes, I want to add an additional and important facet of her which I presented elsewhere too: it was the values she held which to me were unforgettable. Wherever she worked and whomever she met, Anu reached out and touched the lives and hearts of all. More than being respected as a leader she was loved as a person by one and all.

In this context, I was inspired to write this ode having read a poem by Rumi in memory of his soulmate and idol, Sham Tabriz; a fate similar to what I had faced. It was published on the occasion of her sixth death anniversary in *Mainstream*:

Your Face
You may be planning departure, as a human soul leaves the world taking almost all the sweetness with it.

You may be going. Remember you have friends here as faithful as grass and sky

. . . .

I have broken through to longing now,
Filled with grief I have felt before,
But never like this.
My work is to carry this love,

Soul opens the creation core,
Hold on to your particular pain,
That too can take you to God.
My work is to carry this love,
As comfort for those who love you,
To go everywhere you walked
And gaze at the pressed– down dirt.

Jalaluddin Rumi translated by Reynold A. Nicholson

I do not know about the soul.
But her inner radiance lives on,
As a message of human values
Coming from a deep compassion for the underprivileged.
Grief, there is no doubt,
But time heals the wounds of the heart,
And now acts as fuel to the fire,
that brings light amidst the darkness,
through the message of her life.
Anuradha lives on, like a dew drop
on the petals of humanity.

Kobad
Tihar Jail 1
High Risk Ward

With a Little Help

What I realized after my release (and to some extent within jail)
was that, not only my immediate family but also many relatives
and friends have supported me (and so Anu) throughout the
period of my incarceration and now even after. None of these

background and live comfortable lives they, being generally good-hearted, have a yearning for a better society. In earlier times when we were confined to our left circles we would not reach out to such people and tended to brand them in a single brush as 'bourgeois'. Unfortunately, we communists use ideology as a dividing line between good and bad, not the nature of the person. So, the vilest elements in the left could be supported, but gems in ordinary civil society ignored.

I have described in this section the nature of my activities over a period of four decades in service of the oppressed of our country. None of it was illegal, but as the government could not put these points in my charge sheet they brought in the Maoist link, and through fake confessions before the police put cases all over the country on me, linking me to violent incidences, most of which I had not even heard of, let alone participated in. No wonder I was acquitted in all those cases. During my long incarceration, besides human-rights organizations, no doubt many of whom subscribe to the Maoist ideology, there were also numerous independent individuals who lent support, directly or indirectly. Most had no ideology just a concern for justice. There was my sister, Mahrouk, who was there from the very first day of my arrest, as also my sister-in-law, Reetha. Both played a key role in the support system from the outside. Then there was my classmate from Doon school, Gautam Vohra, who campaigned extensively for my release and also raised funds for my medical treatment. There were senior journalists like Jehangir Patel, the editor of *Parsiana*, who even visited me in Tihar, though he is elder to me and blind in one eye. Also, journalists Sunetra Choudhury, Uma Vishnu, Sumit Chakravati (editor of *Mainstream*), Diana Bhatnagar who brings out the magazine *Beauty Without Cruelty*, and numerous journalists like Jyoti Punwani, Sudheendra Kulkarni and others, all of whom assisted

Choudhury, Uma Vishnu, Sumit Chakravati (editor of *Mainstream*), Diana Bhatnagar who brings out the magazine *Beauty Without Cruelty*, and numerous journalists like Jyoti Punwani, Sudheendra Kulkarni and others, all of whom assisted by bringing out the truth in the media in varied ways. None subscribe to radical thinking but supported me just from the view-point of justice. In addition there were the top leaders of the Communist Party of India, like the late A.B. Bardhan, the then Rajya Sabha member D. Raja, and the Viaskhapatnam secretary of the local CPI unit who assisted me. Besides there were many others, some of whom are mentioned later as well. After being released I found there was support coming from sources whom I never knew like a vast section of the Parsi community, many Doon School students, and quite a section of the middle classes. Most of these were not even leftists let alone radical, just simple justice-loving people.

Why then the ten years in jail people ask? That question needs to be addressed to the rulers and their legal system which can virtually be twisted at will by the police and government to let off big criminals involving crores and imprison sincere activists working for the poor. This is not surprising, as the entire legal infrastructure is still the old colonial one created by the British. We see this happening more and more nowadays, as both state and central governments are increasingly using the system to crush any form of dissent.

This is seen as anti-national by India's ruling elite just as it was by the British. Have we then come full circle? Are we back to the type of colonial rule, only with whites being replaced by browns? That I leave to you to consider, for the moment let's traverse the over decade long journey through Indian prisons that was imposed on me, that too as a senior citizen without a single conviction except for a minor 420 related charge of supposed impersonation in the Delhi case.

Notes

1. As far as power corrupting, the attempt of the Cultural Revolution in China was to precisely try and control that, for which their most popular slogan was 'Bombard the Headquarters'; i.e. criticize the top leadership. That it failed is a matter of further analysis, of what went wrong.

2. In fact, through the decades, communist revolutions/ movements helped resist violence/reaction at major points in world history, not only in Russia and China, but also Indo-China, the Koreas, Indonesia, Chile, and numerous other places. They suffered inhumanely for this. Cuba was a particularly successful exception, that too, right on the outskirts of the US.

   The first communist revolution was the Paris Commune which lasted barely two months, from 18 March 1871 to 28 May 1871, when there was a brutal massacre of the Communards by the earlier rulers. The Paris Commune occurred in the wake of the Franco-Prussian War and the collapse of the Second French Empire under Emperor Napoleon III in 1870. It was the unstable Third Republic and the over four-month siege of Paris that facilitated the Paris Commune. Communards was the name given to the activists of that movement. Marx and the Communards did not expect such brutality as they had set up one of the most democratic, non-violent systems ever.

   Later, the first successful communist/socialist revolution happened in Russia during the First World War in 1917 under the leadership of Lenin. For the first time in the history of society did the oppressed become the rulers led by the Communist/ Bolshevik party. The first experience of building a more egalitarian society that had been ravaged by war – a socialist economy – was under Stalin, after Lenin's death on 21 January 1924. But the young fragile economy had little time to consolidate as the Great Depression enveloped the West from 1929. This was followed by the Second World War where Russia faced the brunt of Hitler's forces and lost two million of its countrymen.

The next major communist revolution was in China under the leadership of Mao. Once again, it was during a war – the Second World War – that the major struggles took place and they achieved victory in 1949, fighting the inhuman brutalities of the Japanese fascist aggressors and their collaborators at home. In fact, the major communist revolutions in the world took place during major wars when central governments and the state were relatively weak. With victory of the Chinese communists, they too tried to set up a more egalitarian society learning from some of the errors of socialist construction in the USSR – particularly the point of an over-centralized state and party. These experiments at decentralization both in the sphere of the economy – walking on two legs – as also in the sphere of the state apparatus and party, did not sustain after the 1970s.

It was against this backdrop that in India the Communist party was formed in 1924 and played a major role in the freedom struggle against the British. Unfortunately, the Indian communists were unable to sustain their goodwill by effectively applying the general ideological tenets of Marxism to the concrete reality prevailing here. The problem appeared to be that they treated Marxism more as a dogma than a guide to action replicating policies from either the USSR or China. As a result, they never grew into a significant force and also split a number of times. A major division took place in 1967 which resulted in the formation of the Maoist party, inspired by the Naxalbari peasant uprising.

The 'Naxals' sought a new path from the earlier two parliamentary parties (the CPI & CPM). The CPI was the united party formed in 1924 and the CPM was formed in 1964, having split from the parental party. In early 1967 peasant cells were formed in Siliguri district by local leaders of

97

the CPM (Communist Party of India-Marxist). These were led by Charu Majumdar (CM) and peasant leaders Kanu Sanyal, Jangal Santhal, many of whom were later killed. From March the peasants started seizing land from the local big landlords. Peasant committees were set up within four months. Clashes began to take place between peasants and landlords. The government brought in the police and an inspector was killed. On 25 May the police killed nine peasant women and a child in firing. By June, peasant committees gained control of landlord land and power in the entire region and were supported by strikes of the Darjeeling tea garden workers. But in July the government crushed the incipient revolt by sending in the para-military forces. Though crushed locally the uprising inspired the youth and students, throughout the country, but particularly in Calcutta. As the leadership of the CPM did not support the peasant struggles of their local cadres, CM have a call to come out of that party and launched the new party, CPI(M-L). This was decimated by 1972 when their founder and leader, Charu Majumdar, died in jail and the thousands of student activists were brutally killed by the then Congress government.

The term Naxalite/Naxal is the popular name for the various trends of those groups that are Marxists and also accept the Maoist ideology – like Janashakti, CPI(Maoist), CPI(M-L) Liberation (which won a large number of seats over 30 other such groups; while the generic term 'Left' refers to the general spectrum of all Marxists, communists and even socialist parties, groups and individuals in the country. Today the term Naxalite is used by the media for the party, CPI(Maoist), which is the largest of the Naxalite groups and is the only one to be banned; none of the other 30-odd Naxalite/Maoist groups have been outlawed. The ban is because they state in their programme that the seizure of power is only possible through armed struggle. Most of the 'left' work amongst the poor, though they have

98

their different methods and strategies, but their goal is generally a peoples' democratic transformation, where the majority can enjoy a decent living, in a truly democratic framework. Of course, many of these have been absorbed into the trappings of corruption and power-politics, propping up the existing status quo, and are only in name socialists/communists.

Later socialism collapsed in the Soviet Union and in China too the system veered towards capitalism after Mao's death, though the communist party has continued to exist as the ruling party. In Vietnam too, after inspiring the entire world with their struggle against the US and their victory, the system soon reversed to capitalism. In spite of these reversals the socialist system has been seen to pull the most backward countries of the world out of poverty and today China's economy has begun to challenge that of the US, by far the largest economy in the world. Also, earlier, post-Second World War, the USSR was the only country to be able to challenge the US's might and worldwide domination. Both Russia and China were one of the poorest countries in the world, somewhat like India, before the revolutions, and additionally, both were ravaged by world wars and civil strife. Yet, they could recover and even become major powers through socialist development unlike the countries of Asia, Africa and Latin America. Whatever may have been the other weaknesses, which resulted in their reversals, this reality cannot be denied.

3. Both Anu and I had a sweet tooth but we rarely indulged ourselves, except when we went to our parents' homes, when they would go out of their way to make something special that we liked. I, of course, missed Parsi food, a lot of which has gur (jaggery) in nearly all meals. Anu loved any non-veg food and we both enjoyed anything sweet, whether dessert, ice-creams, anything.

4. https://en.wikipedia.org/wiki/1997_Ramabai_killings#cite_note-Narula(Organization)1999-1

SECTION II
A DECADE-LONG JOURNEY THROUGH INDIAN JAILS

This section deals with my life in the numerous jails I was sent to. There are various facets of jail life which I shall try and capture here. First I recount my entry into Tihar, my very first experience of an Indian jail; next I narrate the conditions in the various jails, but mostly in Tihar where I spent the longest time; then I tell the story of the interesting people I met in this jail journey which helped throw some light on scamsters, terrorists, Kashmiris and lastly, revolutionaries and social activists; next I recount the fascinating stories of some of the top Dons I met in jail; and finally I trace my tiresome judicial procedures until my final release.

Life in Indian Prisons

Most Indian jails I suspect, certainly the ones I went to, are constructed in exactly the same way. They all seem to follow the colonial-era British Jail Manual, rewritten over the years with minor changes made by respective states.

There is only one entry to the main jail through two sets of formidably huge gates, no matter how big the jail is inside. The rest of the jail has a huge wall surrounding it. For example, both Patiala (in Punjab) and Hazaribagh (in Jharkhand) jails had about 30-40 acres of land within the jail for agriculture (in Hazaribagh this land also had a big pond with fish), yet the entry is only at one place and also those farms are encompassed within the same high walls. The first gate has armed police outside and prison guards within, who open the gate only if the person is authentic – checked through a small window in the solid iron gate. Once one enters the area between the identical second gate, some 30 metres away, the jail guards check everyone and everything, including the staff who come in. In some jails, like Tihar, metal detectors are also used as scanning equipment, in addition to the physical search. For inmates the latter can be humiliating, for staff it is more perfunctory. If all is well and there is permission to enter the main jail, another set of guards open the second gate, and one enters the main jail. Never are the two gates allowed to be open at the same time.

All the main offices of the jail lie between these two gates at the point of entry itself – on either side and also upstairs; there can be 2-3 floors. Long corridors stretch on either side with the offices attached and stairs going upstairs. Where the walls of the office structure ends the high walls of the prison start. The offices of the superintendent, deputy superintendent (DS)/jailor, the convicts record office, the undertrial record office, as well as other official offices all lie here. That is why, the way the jail is designed, inmates do not have access to these offices/officers as one needs a written permission/ pass to enter the gate from the jail side which also has a small window through which one can request or show the pass.

Thus, to check our own records or meet any official is next to impossible and can be terribly humiliating. For the smallest request, written consent is necessary from the superintendent or the deputy superintendent, this very process is made cumbersome by the mere construction of the jail as prisoners are not allowed into this area. For example, in Tihar even to take a pen and paper to court we needed the superintendent's written permission. In jails in South India the superintendent would do weekly rounds and so was accessible, but in other jails there was no such procedure. In Hazaribagh jail, the superintendent during my time would each day meet the newcomers, and at that time one could get access to meet him after an application had been passed.

Once inside the jail, the residents would be divided into separate wards, each enclosed within high walls. In Tihar the High-Risk Ward (HRW), with its independent security and two additional sets of gates, was a veritable jail within a jail.

Tihar Entry

When I entered Tihar, I was shocked at the level of humiliation one is subjected to. I was stripped and searched; personal details were taken for the umpteenth time, there was an insistence on recording one's 'caste'; the removal of footwear before entering an officer's room (like in a mandir); and all other colonial and feudal norms one imagines died with the British Raj are followed here.

After passing through the two huge and intimidating gates of Jail 3, I was led to the HRW, which houses the phansi kothi, meant for prisoners sentenced to death. This HRW was the one with the maximum security of all the HRWs of Tihar's ten jails.

Tihar is a massive complex of ten jails, nine of which adjoin each other with their entire independent structures and managements. In all there are about 15,000 prisoners; and I believe, today, six more jails have been added in Delhi, the construction of which was going on while I was still there. Its official capacity is 6,500 prisoners but in 2012 alone the occupancy was double that.

The staff of the prison, like the police, are mostly locals – Jats from Haryana – while the entire security operation has been handed over to a battalion of the TSP (Tamil Nadu Special Police). This has been the case since 1984. It is said the reason for bringing in the TSP is because the higher authorities themselves could not trust locals for security purposes. The officials felt that as many of them came from the same villages as the inmates, they could be related, and there was a higher possibility of corruption amongst them. Though, such a situation of utilizing another state's forces does not exist in other states.

The young Tamil security force were more decent and understanding, once they understood the system and the type of inmates. Many of the Tamil staff, who had become quite friendly with me, would often chat about their lives, and it was they who gave me many details of their working conditions. The other staff were mostly cruel and vindictive, though they behaved in a very servile manner with those who had money.

As I did not have many belongings when I entered jail there was nothing much to search except a sling bag (still have it) with mere toiletry items given by my sister-in-law, Reetha Balsavar, who landed up at my very first court hearing. Yet, after a thorough search I was led to the HRW, where the entire search procedure was repeated. Each time, we were made to walk through metal detectors, and also physically thoroughly searched with a hand-held metal detector. One wonders at the impact of these high levels of radiation over the years.

When I entered the ward for the first time, it was past 7 p.m., so all the inmates were already locked up in their respective cells. As I was being taken to Block A, I was greeted by a warm smile from none other than Afzal Guru who, standing at the gate of his cell, said he was expecting I would be brought to this ward in Tihar after reading about my case splashed all over the newspapers.

He immediately offered any help as I was taken away by the guards to Cell No. 4, which already housed three inmates, including Delhi's top don, the dreaded Kishan Pehalwan. They offered bedding and shared their dinner which they had not yet consumed. Of course, I was so shaken by the events that hunger and sleep both seemed distant. My first night in jail, with four of us cramped in a cell, was difficult to pass. The others in the cell were mostly criminals and we had nothing much to communicate with each other.

Although each cell is meant to hold a single inmate, due to overcrowding, three inmates are often housed in a cell together – either one or three are allowed, never two. Once locked away you have no interaction with others in the ward. Only when the cell gates open can one interact with others in the ward. Besides Afzal, there were many interesting persons like the Khalistanis, another don, and some Islamists. Between 6 a.m. and 12 noon, when we were again locked in our cells for three hours, we were free to mix with the others in that block of the ward, including Afzal. There were no further restrictions on any inmate, at least then. Although Afzal did say that in his first few years of incarceration he was never allowed out of the cell.

Next morning, I was shifted to the last cell in the block of eight cells where my two fellow inmates were two Khalistanis (actually one was a smuggler of guns and drugs from across the border with Khalistani leanings). Even before being shifted to this cell, as soon as the gates opened, Afzal was there inviting me for tea in his cell; a routine that continued for over three years, till his hanging in February 2013. He had a knack of converting basically hot water into an excellent cup of tea. He had a half-litre white thermos flask (which I asked for as a memento after his hanging, but nothing was given) in which he filled the hot 'tea' that came from the jail kitchen, to which he added milk powder and a few tea bags purchased from the canteen. We would have it with the two slices of bread (made in the jail bakery) provided by the jail.

It was over these cups of tea and evening walks in the ground adjoining the phansi kothi that he introduced me to the Kashmir situation, Islam and its progressive aspects (directly opposed to what the fundamentalists propounded), and, most importantly, Sufi thinking, in which he strongly believed. As this was my first experience in an Indian jail, he was reassuring, helpful and mildly sympathetic to the cause of the oppressed people in India, unlike the Islamists, who saw no difference between the communist or other parties. For them, as long as a person was not a Sunni Muslim, he was either a potential convert or an enemy.

'A' Bloc (B Bloc was behind) where we were kept was adjoining a big ground (separated by barbed wire of course) which had a lot of trees like jamun, ber, pipal, and at the corner of which was the locked phansi kothi. Only the three of us (including Devinder Pal Singh Bhullar, the Khalistani leader facing a death sentence) had permission to these grounds. In the initial phase of my incarceration the superintendent was helpful and allowed me to plant tulsi, guava, dhaniya patta, and provided me with a water hose for watering the plants. This ground was the only peaceful place in the jail. Often, I would sit alone in these grounds, watching the little squirrels prancing around and reflecting on life in jail and the world outside. Many a time I would purchase a packet of peanuts from the canteen, which they loved and scrambled for. When they felt any danger, like a cat in the vicinity, they would make a 'tic-tic' sound, alerting all the other squirrels who would scamper up the trees. It was also here that much of the ideas for the six articles I wrote on 'Freedom and Peoples' Emancipation' (published in 2012 in *Mainstream Weekly*) crystallized. Such serenity one never found again, as the grounds were permanently shut after the hanging of Afzal Guru in 2013. Later, a 20-foot double wall came up completely shutting off this ground and phansi kothi from the ward. Why double, no one could fathom, whom were they trying to protect – the squirrels or the lifeless bodies after hanging.

Here I was, an undertrial, no sentence had been handed down to me, but I faced daily humiliation, worse than that of convicts, who were at least given responsibilities and could move around the jail relatively freely. Here, one did not have any rights and we were all at the mercy of the staff, who could act as per their whims and fancy.

Sleep had to take place with the bright lights on and the switches outside the cell. If by any chance we tried to cover the bulb, the warder, while on their night rounds, would yell at us and we would meekly have to obey, otherwise punishment would follow. As far as I can remember, according to the UN, this is a form of torture (to prevent sleep); as darkness induces the hormone melatonin which induces sleep, while light triggers the hormone cortisol, which keeps you awake. Throughout my stay in Tihar, I was in a cell with a CCTV camera, being watched day and night. In the HRWs every second cell has one. It is perched just above the toilet so that except in the bath/toilet you are under 24-hour surveillance – while resting, while eating, while sleeping, while exercising, while reading – all the time Big Brother is watching you. As if that weren't enough, the guard outside, constantly peeping through the bars, made one feel like an animal at a zoo being stared at by tourists. I felt much the same as those poor animals locked up.

Every day one had to swallow some form of indignity or the other. Any person wielding authority in the jail can order inmates around; and one has to obey or get punishment. In the HRS, if one falls ill, no medicines are available unless the DS gives written permission for the inmate to go to the hospital. Even to move from one place to the other in the ward was dangerous as one could be attacked any time by bladebaaz, a group of blade-wielding inmates, who were purposely put in the ward to terrorize us. Soon, I mused, that my sensitivities would likely get numbed, having to quietly follow orders over the pettiest of things. Then we had the dalals, our fellow prisoners, who were more vicious than the staff. Often, the staff would act through these dalals to teach a lesson to some recalcitrant inmate. It could be a slash on the face by a blade or worse.

Such was life in this new abode.

Prison Life

Living conditions differed drastically from jail to jail; those of the South, where I spent about two years appeared more humane. Nothing of course could be as bad as Tihar, where, unfortunately, I spent my maximum time – nearly seven of the ten years. Tihar was not so bad when I first entered, but over time I found that one right after the other was snatched away from us continuously. Life had been reduced to a living hell by the time my Delhi case ended in June 2016 and I was transferred to Hyderabad jail.

Of course, in jails, we are de facto stripped of our citizen's rights, as even undertrials have no right to vote. One is denied the right to participate in any election without even having been proved guilty. It is another point that even if proven guilty, no one has the right to strip us of this right. Of course, the big mafia can get elected from within the jail, but the ordinary citizen – undertrial and convict – is disenfranchised. This issue is never raised by any of the parties and it is not written in any jail manual, as far as I know. In addition, conjugal rights are also not allowed for undertrials; a basic instinctive need is denied, adding to the many frustrations and humiliations in jails.

Rather than merely recount my jail stay chronologically, I will deal with the various facets of prison life separately in the following sections. These include the living conditions, mulaqaat system (which helps us keep in touch with the outside world), medical facilities and police and escort systems.

Living Conditions

Of the ten years of my incarceration, I spent 6¾ years in Tihar, nearly a year in Hyderabad jail, a month in Patiala jail, and six months in Vishakapatnam jail. After release and re-arrest I spent 1¾ years in Jharkhand jails and finally two months in Surat jail and custody. There are some things common to all jails like the food timings: lunch at 10.30 am and dinner at 4.30 p.m. When I came out others were wondering why I so much relished hot meals as one rarely had a warm meal throughout the ten years of my incarceration. In a Tihar kind of jail where we were locked up in the cell at 12 noon and then again at about 7 p.m., one would try and utilize the period that we were in the open doing exercises, interacting with others, where games were possible playing them or merely interacting with others. The locked away period was used for eating, reading, washing and cleaning and, of course, sleeping. To change the timings to those when meals are served was not feasible, as it would detract from our ability to interact/exercise while in the open ward. It was also the only time we could get sun.

Tihar jail
In Tihar, unless one is totally insensitive or has thick skin, the jail is structured to crush you. Inmates have zero right as persons and the smallest activity is treated as a 'concession' by the jail administration. For example, in the HRW in Tihar, you are not allowed to step out into the main jail unless you apply and get written permission from the DS. The same rule applies to medical treatment of any kind. It can take days to arrive by which time you could be dead; or it could be immediate if you have the right connections with the staff.

Justice V.R. Krishna Iyer, a pioneer in judicial activism and criminal justice reform in India, outlined numerous rights of prisoners, hardly any of these are followed. Although as undertrials, we are supposed to be strictly under the jurisdiction of the judge and not of the jail, even a minor application to the court has to proceed through the jail authorities; and any complaint has itself to be vetted by the superintendent. It was

Krishna Iyer who also firmly believed that undertrials should not be made to languish in jail and it was he who is known for his stand which was a taboo till then in the Indian judiciary: 'Bail is the rule, and jail, the exception'. But in many states in India, including Delhi, the courts act in an exactly contrary way. I was told that in some states, like Uttar Pradesh, West Bengal and some states in southern India, bail is far more routine.

To give an example of the meaningless and insensitive rules that governed us, we were not even allowed to donate our bodies to medical science in case of death. A fellow inmate once acquired a form, which we duly filled and had counter-signed by a close relative; it was rejected by the superintendent and the forms were torn up.

Inmates generally prefer to stay with others as they have nothing to do if alone. With others they can chat, pass time in varied ways (like playing cards made from the boxes of purchased items), smoke joints together, plan their nefarious activities, etc. Also, many were actually afraid of ghosts and djinns and did not wish to sleep alone at night.

After the first three months I was fortunate to be given a cell to myself, which was convenient for my study and writing. The magistrate had ordered I be given a table and chair due to my slip disc and spondilitus problems which very much facilitated my study. I was probably the only inmate in Tihar to have a table. Though there is a well-stocked library in the jail I was denied access to it. Tihar also has a wide spectrum of Indira Gandhi National Open University (IGNOU) courses, over and above the school certificates (standard 10 and 12) and graduation courses, it offers. But as a 'Naxalite' prisoner, I was denied permission by the superintendent to do any of the courses I had applied for, including a six-month course in Human Rights. In fact, it was in Jail 3 itself that there was a very good IGNOU Centre.

As far as maintaining my mental sanity, by being focussed on study and writing, I was able to maintain a purpose in life and an outlet for my thoughts and feelings. As Voltaire once said: 'Shun idleness. It is a rust that attaches itself to the most brilliant metals.' In jail most people really have nothing to do, because the jail organizes neither sport nor study. These, at best, have to be devised by the inmates themselves, crossing numerous hurdles. If there is TV they watch that; otherwise they gamble; in Jharkhand many inmates (including me) played ludo.

I would try and push to the back of my mind the daily humiliations I faced in jail and the frustrations from delays in court hearings and try to focus on my study and writing. Mercifully, there was no restriction on writing and one could even purchase pen and paper from the canteen. The problem was in sending these articles out, as strictly one is not allowed to print articles from the jail. I would find the means to get the articles posted, mainly due to the high levels of corruption in the jail. Almost anything was available at a price. As for reading, newspapers were freely available in the jail, and magazines I got from my sister regularly through the post. Earlier, books too were briefly allowed to be given at the mulaqaat.

Although, as I mentioned, I had no access to the library, there was a good Samaritan, a fellow inmate, working in the library who would, in the first three years, provide me books, particularly the excellent IGNOU notes on the history of philosophy. I made extensive notes from these – as also the newspapers and magazines I had access to – of any item that I thought was of interest to my writing.

Thus, by keeping mentally active I was able, to some extent, ward off the depression and lethargy that comes easily to inmates; mostly from having nothing to do and the tensions of the jail system and judiciary but also from neglect from the family who, after some time, begin to consider the inmate as an additional financial burden. An idle mind, as they say, is a devil's workshop. In jail it can be both 'devil' as well as breeding ground for all sorts of worms, reptiles, insect, et al, that eat away the brain cells and push a person to depression and also suicidal tendencies. It is ironic that while, on the one hand, every means possible is used to mentally torment the inmate, on the other, all forms of string/rope, blades, phenyl are strictly banned to prevent a person from taking his own life. As a result, often in jail we are unable to hang our clothes, we cannot shave nor properly clean the room/ward or the toilets, as all these items are treated as contraband. This made life even more difficult and cumbersome.

Whatever little rights I had enjoyed at the start of my confinement in Tihar were, over the six years and nine months, systematically eroded. By the time I left for Hyderabad jail, the inmates at Tihar had practically no rights. All this was done in the name of security – to supposedly stop contraband from coming in or being used – when in fact, the bribing and procuring continued unabated as the main carriers were said to be the staff. In fact, they began to command a higher price as a result of scarcity from the ban. The heightened restrictions were not merely due to a change in management, though that may well have been a factor. There was never an occasion when the reverse happened: no relaxing of the rules. Because the mindset of the authorities is such that they do not want to see anyone happy inside jail. The more people are tormented the more they appear to get a nefarious thrill. Not to mention, the more the restrictions, the more the illicit earnings of the staff to get around them.

I was earlier allowed a transistor which was later stopped. Wrist watches too were later forbidden and the one I used for years was taken. TVs were never allowed in the HRWs.

Legal visits (which take place independently of mulaqaat in the DS' room), which were once allowed daily, got restricted to once a week. Because I had cases slapped against me all over the country, I was faced with increasing problems; if, say, a lawyer came from Maharashtra, Andhra Pradesh or Punjab, and meanwhile a Delhi lawyer had already come that week, the former would not be allowed to meet me and would have to return. As I wrote to my classmate Gautam Vohra on 12 September 2013:

> Earlier any number of lawyers could visit an inmate on a week day. Now it has been restricted to one. Also, the inmate is allowed one visit by a lawyer each week. And this too for a mere half hour. Which essentially means that the prisoner is denied his rights to legal advice. He is not allowed to telephone his lawyer. In fact, here everything tends to get more difficult. I believe we will be enclosed behind more and more walls, that are coming up all over. Am still trying to obtain the status of senior citizen so that I am put in the ward with them that adjoins the hospital. Now once again have been given the phone facility to ring two relatives, so can be in touch with my sister. Do not know how long this will last. On the previous occasion, I enjoyed the phone facility for three-four months before the jail authorities changed their mind.

In Tihar there was a ridiculous system – de facto punishment for all the inmates for a single person's fault. If anyone made a mistake, whether that person was punished or not, an entire system would change. Just one example: it was alleged that the political leader Om Prakash Chautala, serving a ten-year term for corruption, would call his lawyer every day so that he could continue his political activities from within the jail. Due to his misuse of this facility, the legal mulaqaat was restricted to one lawyer's visit per week and only one lawyer could come at a time. Chautala, of course, faced no punishment but the entire jail did. This is but one example; many more could be cited for all the new restrictions that kept being conjured up by the authorities to torment us and restrict our rights.

Earlier, we were allowed to take all papers to the court. Later, depending on the whims of the superintendent or the police escort, not a piece of paper nor a pen was allowed. We were thoroughly searched while entering the lock-up at the court, though we had come from jail after being searched and brought under heavy police escort. Obviously, the purpose was not security but to humiliate and demean the person.

As for the food in Tihar, it was generally diluted and watery; though I was told that on paper the amount allocated for each prisoner daily was quite substantial. Earlier, a canteen facility was provided from where food could be ordered, but for that one needed lots of money; this was closed down in the final years. A dry canteen was there for one's daily needs, which also sold fruit, vegetables and milk. In the HRWs we received water twice a day so there was no shortage, as in Jharkhand and some other jails. Yet, on the whole Tihar was a nightmare and unfortunately because of the slow process of my case it was there that I spent the maximum time.

Actually, the worst harassment in my entire ten years in jail, was the new rule in 2012 to shift en bloc all HRW inmates every three months from one HRW to another. Earlier, only those who were caught doing wrong (say, with contraband) were punished with such a transfer from one jail to another. In other words, such transfers amounted to continuous punishment for every HRW prisoner; as a result, those who did wrong were no longer afraid, as anyhow the transfer would happen for all HRW inmates. In effect, this system therefore encouraged wrong-doing.

The transfer was a humiliating process: we would be informed only an hour in advance giving us no time to pack our belongings properly; we had to carry all our belongings ourselves and get everything through three lots of searches (one while leaving the jail and two while entering the new jail). Even for a young person this was difficult but, at my age, with all the orthopaedic problems, it was debilitating.

In the 'new' jail, one had to re-apply for all the permissions (like medical diet, subscription to newspapers), which could be granted or denied. By the time these permissions came through, if at all, one was again transferred. Not only that, in the new jail there would be a scramble for the better cells which obviously the younger people and regulars managed to get more easily.

As I wrote in a letter to Gautam Vohra as far back as 10 December 2012, when the transfer system had just started:

> [T]he new DG [director general] has begun wholesale transfers of High-Risk Ward people from one jail to another. Today is the second such move in four months. Fortunately, they have not transferred me, probably as the hospital is in this jail. For me it would be impossible at this age and in this health. Here they don't bother. The last time they transferred a person whose BP was around 250 saying "You can take treatment there". These transfers take place with just one- or two-hours' notice. In that time, you have to pack all your belongings and go.

After Afzal's hanging in February 2013, the ward was closed for repairs and we were all shifted to Jail 1, which had just been renovated. As, at the time, UP's top don, Brajesh Singh, had been just shifted to our HRW, we considered moving to the same block together in Jail 1. In Jail 1 we spent over a year together with just five of us in the three cells in Block D – Brajesh Singh, Tribhuvan Singh and their assistant, Farooq in one cell; I and a Phoolan Devi (one-time dacoit turned SP MLA) undertrial, one of the seven persons implicated in her killing, alone in the other two cells. It was because of Brajesh Singh's presence (until around 2014, when he was acquitted in the Delhi case and sent to Varanasi jail) that the transfer was not that traumatic, as he was able to get people to assist and no one dared cross him on which block to choose.

Unfortunately, after his departure a vindictive superintendent sought to forcibly transfer me, as I had organized the ward inmates to petition against a few notorious staff members. The following letter to Gautam Vohra, dated 7 December 2014, details what happened:

On 16th morning I refused to go stating that unless the superintendent signed a statement to the effect that I would be given all the facilities that a senior citizen is entitled to, I would not budge. At 1.30 the AS (assistant superintendent) in charge – a notorious fellow – came with 10 hoodlums and forcibly began removing my samaan, saying orders were orders and that his job was to get me out. After they packed my belongings – threw everything in boxes – they would have lifted me physically if others had not intervened and taken me on a stretcher. My samaan was parked outside the gate of Jail Number 2. But I insisted on meeting the superintendent. I had prepared a petition for going on a hunger strike along the lines of the press note earlier given to my lawyer.

After an hour's wait hanging around the gate, they took me to the superintendent's office. He said that orders were from the DG and he was powerless. Then he went on to question me as to why I was incessantly petitioning. Some of the staff here, since the last three-four months had been particularly unsavoury – harassing continuously to extract money and or goods – a despicable lot. I had been writing directly to the DG regarding this with the signatures of the entire ward. It was this that the jail authorities vehemently objected to. Let alone protest, mere peaceful petitioning is treated as a crime and seen as insubordination. We must silently tolerate the harassment and corruption.

When I explained the contents of my press release, the superintendent asked me to return to the gate, saying that they would think over the matter and, if necessary, talk to the DG. From 1.30 to 6.30 p.m. I had been sitting at the gate in the burning heat, when they informed me to return to the ward. Fortunately, I am back in Jail 1. Jail 1 is the only decent HRW with some open space, which we are allowed to use for two hours in a day. All others are like cages. Actually, we need to campaign either for the Senior Citizens ward or to stay put in Jail 1.

Though this punishment was reversed I was put on the three-monthly transfer list (which had now become bi-monthly) for the first time. The next two years were a traumatizing period when little study and writing could be done. First, from Jail 1, we were transferred to Jail 2 (where Chotta Rajan is now kept, with the whole HRW to himself, with VIP facilities), then back to Jail 3 again, and within a few months to Jail 8 – the worst HRW amongst all the jails. These transfers were taking a heavy toll on my health, and so it was then that I decided to go on a fast-unto-death against my transfers. Chotta Rajan was put in this ward of Jail 2 and for his protection no one was allowed to meet him even within that jail. He was, in addition, given extra security, and we would get news about him from his TSP securities when they were rotated. He was petrified that Dawood's people would get at him, so extreme precautions were taken for him, making him a veritable state guest.

In 2015, before going from Jail 3 I requested the superintendent to stop my transfer. He refused. It was the same superintendent who, when I entered jail had been relatively supportive, but had now turned extremely nasty, probably at the behest of some political/police higher ups. First, the punishment for supposedly going late to the court and now transfer to a jail where the cells were so small they had no space for a table and chair. A few months earlier at the peak of summer he got warders to threaten to beat me, supposedly because I was late in going for the court date. When I explained my health condition and that many others had not yet gone they began physically roughing me up. When I later complained to the superintendent he supported them and, on the contrary gave me a punishment by stopping my mulaqaat for three months.

Anyhow, as soon as he refused to cancel the transfer, I gave him a copy of the notice for hunger strike which I had prepared in advance, and then proceeded to Jail 8, though my BP was already high. On reaching Jail 8 I gave a copy of the hunger strike notice to the superintendent there too. Here the AS and other staff were quite obliging but as the hunger strike lasted for seven days, and my health started to deteriorate, I was put on intravenous saline.

As my hunger strike gained media publicity and was also raised in the court, the then DG of prisons (later CBI chief), Alok Verma, personally intervened. He ordered that I immediately be transferred back to Jail 3 (which has the main hospital) and not be shifted again. He showed considerable concern later as well; when my health worsened, he ordered the RMO (head medical officer of entire Tihar over the senior medical officers or SMOs in each jail) for my detailed health report, and for his personal intervention. The RMO showed a lot of concern as well in his personal capacity.

Yet, in 2015 as well, there was no peace as the new superintendent of Jail 3 began 'repair' work in our ward, starting from my cell, which was the first. It was another matter that repair work had just taken place a year back with the entire ward being vacated for over six months. As a result, I was forced to move to a cell with three other inmates, including one of the Nirbhaya rapists, Vinay Sharma, a vile sort. This disturbance went on for 3 to 4 months with little repair work getting done, except breaking up my cell so it was rendered unusable. Considering my arthritis and need for a western toilet life once again became intolerable, made worse by living in close proximity with rapists and their ilk.

Yet, in the midst of these horrors and constant humiliations, the lives and works of men who had made history would bring me comfort and solace. In my nearly seven years at Tihar, I repeatedly drew comfort and strength from the prison writings of Kenyan writer Ngugi wa Thiong'o prison writings:

Maximum Security: the idea used to fill me with terror whenever I met it in fiction... A year in Kamiti [Kenya's top prison] has taught me what should have been obvious: that the prison system is a repressive weapon in the hands of a ruling minority... The rituals, seemingly petty and childish but rigorously followed to the letter by decorated guards, serve to make political prisoners feel that they have been completely cut off from people and hence from group solidarity... which alone keeps men and women going, even when menaced by truncheons, nailed boots, tear gas, and death whistling bullets. They must be made, not just to know, but to actually feel that, with the links cut, they are now adrift in an ocean of endless fear and humiliation. They are not introduced into the ocean gradually. They are thrown into it to swim and stay afloat anyway they know... or plunge into the depths and drown.

What I witnessed in Tihar was similar to what Ngugi mentions here. It was not just that mere individuals with authority were criminal minded, but the very system was constructed to break the individual; mind, body and soul; though as yet political detainees were few. And it is only within this system if one encountered a decent person would there be mild relief.

Another person whose writings inspired me with hope and with the feeling that all was not lost was Subhas Chandra Bose, one of the tallest leaders of the country, whose role has been hugely downplayed by our rulers as well as the communists. Some of Bose's quotes, at random, which kept my spirit alive:

'One individual may die for an idea, but that idea will, after his death, incarnate itself in a thousand lives.'

'Life loses half its interest if there is no struggle – if there are no risks to be taken.'

'No real change in history has been achieved by discussion.'

Bose, who died under mysterious circumstances, was surprisingly highly revered by most of the inmates, including

LIFE IN INDIAN PRISON

the Tamilian TSP police. I was under the impression, till then, that it was only the Bengalis who looked up to him; but a Tamil policeman from the Madurai area told me that in their villages no wedding takes place without a photo of Bose, even today. He explained that a large number of Tamilians from his area had been a part of Bose's INA (Indian National Army), who were recruited in Malaysia and other such places, where there was a large Tamilian population. As he himself said, Bose lives on in the hearts of the people of our country, though the rulers have sought to erase his memory.

Hyderabad, Patiala and Visakhapatnam Jails

Finally, it was in June 2016 that I secured relief from the horrors of Tihar with my acquittal in the main UAPA case, while I was found guilty in the minor 420-related charges (of allegedly using fake identities).

Meanwhile, Cherlapally jail, Hyderabad, readied itself for my arrival with Ganesh, a Naxalite who had already served 20 years in jail, getting a cell ready for my arrival and chicken biryani from the canteen; a non-vegetarian meal after nearly seven years, as Tihar was strictly vegetarian. Ganesh was to go on parole the day before my arrival, but postponed his departure to settle me in. As there were no other Naxals, the ward was filled with young NDPS (Narcotic Drugs and Psychotropic Substances Act, 1985) undertrials. These youth had been arrested on drug charges (they were running a chemical company that allegedly began making chemical-based drugs) and were all very well educated, extremely warm and cooperative. It was they who took care of me after Ganesh left.

Due to major prison struggles in the 1990s, in Andhra Pradesh at the time Naxalite prisoners were given the status of political prisoners. Excellent wards were constructed specifically for Naxalite prisoners in this jail. Each cell had a TV, running water and a wash basin, 2-3 cells would also have a Western-style toilet, and each had a block on which to sleep. The food was good and the tea was like at home. Mulaqaat, with both visitors and lawyers, was allowed inside the DS's room sitting on chairs.

After Tihar, it would appear that I had ascended from hell to heaven! The ward had been planted with all sorts of fruit trees – coconut, guava, mango, papaya – drumsticks, lots of curry patta plants and heaps of roses and mogra, all by Ganesh. There was a badminton court on one side but due to my arthritis I could not play. The food, as I mentioned, was excellent compared to Tihar and the inmates and staff decent people. I would do yoga on a platform under a neem tree and in the evenings another young NDPS undertrial and I would take long walks outside the ward, with me teaching him spoken English (he was fluent at reading English).

After about six months at Hyderabad jail I was taken to Patiala by train to appear there for a different case. I had expected to be presented and immediately return, but the judge insisted I remain there until the case was being heard; so I was sent to Patiala prison for the twenty days that the case lasted. As it happened it turned out for the best.

The Patiala jail covered a huge area as it was from the Maharaja's times. The bulk of the inmates in the jail were there on drug-related cases which is a serious problem in Punjab. I was put in the hospital which housed a number of 'VIPs' and other well-connected inmates. The biggest was a co-accused of one Bhola, ex-IGP and reportedly a major player in the drug mafia of Punjab. Bhola's associate (cannot remember his name) took me under his wing and every evening when I returned from court gave me an excellent home-cooked meal. As I've mentioned, in most jails people with money have access to all benefits. In all the jails I noticed the big-time underworld generally had a liking for Naxalites as they too had a Robin-Hood type image. Also on the very first day some Sikh leaders (I think they were Nirankaris) learning of my arrival came up to me and said they had a system of phoning and I could use it anytime I wanted. When I did, I found it a sort of social service for poor inmates to which the authorities also seemed to turn a blind eye. In addition, a friend of my erstwhile co-accused (whose charges had been dropped) – a Dalit Sikh – met all my expenses in jail and was very keen to know more on the philosophy of the movement. The entire day I would spend at the court each day and return only in the evenings. Overall, the stay in Patiala was relaxed and the court procedures fast and efficient. One observation was that the entire Sikh community with whom I came into contact – inmates, lawyers, judge and even the entire police escort – seemed to have immense respect for Naxalites. I thought it maybe due to their religion which has much humanity in it.

Once my cases were over in Telangana, I was taken from Hyderabad to Visakhapatnam in a police van in a torturous 16-hour journey. I am still unaware why they chose that mode of transport instead of a train. In Visakhapatnam jail, while most of the trees (except papaya) had been cut down, much of the ground was covered with gongura plants, the edible sour leaves which are much relished in Andhra Pradesh. The ward was an exact replica of the Hyderabad one. Every Sunday, chicken dish was provided by the jail and this would be quietly further cooked in the ward with gongura and spices, making for a good meal. The food here was even better than at Hyderabad, as we would also get an excellent breakfast – upma, haldi rice and vada every alternate day, while on Sundays we got puri and sabji.

One alleged Naxalite leader, Chadda Bhushanam, who was an educated tribal from the area, but had spent many years working in Odisha, took complete care of me, getting new clothes made by the jail tailors and ordering ayurvedic supplements. He had earlier spent many years in Odisha jails before being acquitted.

Besides him, there were two others in this special ward; one was in for life for his involvement in the infamous Paritala Ravi killing at the behest of the Reddy landlords; and the other person, who was from Tirupati, where his family ran the main restaurant at the bus stand there, was serving a ten-year sentence in a rape case. I came to know much about the politics of Rayalaseema (the region in Andhra Pradesh where most CMs come from) by talking to the former, and about many aspects of the Tirupati mandir and the famous tasty ladoos from the latter.

The superintendent of this jail had a reputation of being extremely honest and was a very decent person, though feared by the staff. It was not surprising that his promotion to IGP was delayed, but that meant he was with us for an extra four months. That was in fact fortunate for us.

During my last days at this jail, on 31 August 2017 a letter came from the Ministry of Home Affairs in Delhi asking for a detailed report of my health condition. I only learnt later that it was at the behest of CPI leader and then Rajya Sabha member D. Raja who not only requested his colleague, Visakhapatnam CPI secretary to visit me, but also met the then Home Minister Rajnath Singh who sent this letter seeking my full health report. The local CPI unit has been very supportive even now when I went for my court hearing in March 2020.

After release from Visakhapatnam jail on 12 December 2017 and re-arrest four days later by the Jharkhand police, I had to spend the next 1¾ years in Jharkhand jails.

Jharkhand Jails

Never have I seen any other jails – and I have been to five others in four states – that are so completely dependent on the convicts to run the place than what I saw in Jharkhand. In a state with maximum unemployment, the jails employed the minimum possible staff. The few official staff comprised mainly retired army personnel, who were available cheap, getting paid a flat ₹20,000 per month, with much unpaid overtime and little leave; they had, in addition, their monthly pension of ₹30,000. That is why, though new jails are being commissioned, ever since the formation of Jharkhand in 2000, there have been just 250 new recruits to the jail staff in the entire state in these twenty-odd years.

While in Jharkhand, I was first put in Tenughat sub-jail where my case was registered. But after three months I was shifted to Hazaribagh Central Jail as the facilities, particularly medical, were not good and it was affecting my health.

Tenughat sub-jail is a small jail with just about 350 inmates. I was put in the hospital which was the best possible place, but of the twenty-odd patients there, four were serious TB patients coughing blood and sputum. There were very few facilities in this jail but the police officer in-charge of the area, Jaat saheb, instructed the jailor to provide all my needs, which they did to the best of their abilities.

The jail having few facilities, for the first time ever I had nothing to read and with only inane TV on it was particularly boring. The most popular channels were the Bhojpuri ones, full of vulgar songs and cheap comedy. They were difficult to watch. Fortunately, I suddenly remembered the book by Supreme Court Judge Rohinton Nariman on the Zoroastrian religion advocate Dashrath had given me just prior to my arrest by the Jharkhand police in Hyderabad. Dashrath had been given the book a year earlier by senior advocate Fali Nariman who was arguing my case in the Supreme Court. When I began reading the book, I was so impressed by the content (before that I knew little of the religion into which I was born, just some customs) that I finally wrote an elaborate review and sent it to the fortnightly Parsi magazine *Parsiana*, which featured it in the 21 March 2018 issue.

In this jail only the unconnected and poorest ate from the jail kitchen (called bansa), all the others were organized into 'chulla' groups who would take their share of the rations, add their own (purchased) masala, and make decent meals. The biggest such group was that of the Maoists – about 30 in number – and it was with them that I ate.

In trying to find out something of Jharkhand life and the movement I found none of these alleged Maoists was in any way knowledgeable; except for one, Sitaram Manjhi, who was a mass leader allegedly linked to the movement. Sitaram was a Santhali tribal and belonged to a big village along the Hazaribagh–Giridih border, with a population of about 4,000. Others in the organization were least interested, particularly those in the military formations, who could not tell me the minimum details of village life (though they were locals) as they seemed to have little contact with the locals once they joined the military formations. Their only attraction later seemed to be the adventure of that life, the power they wielded and the relatively better living conditions.

I reached Hazaribagh Central Jail, which was to be my new abode for the next one and a half years, on 23 March 2018 at about 8 p.m. The jail was closed. After the routine search (the searches in all other jails were no comparison to those in Tihar) I was led to the Ahmed Ward, where all new inmates are housed for a day before being sent to their respective wards by the superintendent. There were 90 people in that ward with just two toilets, but instructions had been given to make it as comfortable as possible. Needless to say, one could hardly sleep. Fortunately, that first night there was a BSF inspector, serving a three-year term for insubordination (he hit his officer or some such thing), who spent much of the night explaining how horrible the conditions were for the ranks in the Central Forces. After that I never saw him again.

Later in the morning I met the superintendent, Hamid Akhtar, who was an extremely decent person, but disliked in the jail as he was seen to be a strict disciplinarian. He assigned me a separate room within the hospital premises, with a toilet and verandah and asked the excellent doctor, Dangi, to give me the medical diet I requested. Though the best possible facilities were given, at the ground level there was no water which had to be brought from far, and the medical diet had to be organized from the kitchen. Fortunately, the superintendent agreed that I may keep a help for all this, and Bajiram was more than willing. Bajiram Mahtao was the ex-Naxal who first met me and introduced me to some of the other Naxals. In this jail there was relative freedom to move around. Of course, they too had the equivalent of a HRW, but only a few Naxals were in them. Most were in the wards outside.

As these jails were primarily run by convicts, everything was arbitrary at the ground level and the handful of officials who came on transferable jobs were dependent on the jail mafia. There were no real rules in place; and even if they did exist, they were flouted and only money counted, even for one's legitimate needs. There was no proper system for receiving money where a percentage would be cut. All other jails had coupon systems, but Jharkhand jails only operated on cash. The large number of 'Maoists' in the jail, instead of countering this mafia control, were often a part of it, sometimes leading it. Ironically this very book itself has been felicitated in some way by the Jharkhand jail superintendent who kindly allowed me the facility to practice computer typing in the jail computer class, which I did for a full nine months for one hour every day. If it had not been for this my typing speed would have been half of what it has been.

I could write a whole treatise on Jharkhand from what I discovered from the lengthy interviews I had with people; I'll keep that for another day. However, it was a bizarre experience, but its very strangeness made it unique. After witnessing the law-based structures of jails in Andhra Pradesh/Telangana, Jharkhand seemed to resemble a Congo-type country, where no rules applied. Even though there were helpful and supportive individuals around – the Jail Superintendent, the SP of Police (Bokaro) and other police officers, judges, lawyers, etc. – they were helpless in the face of anarchic structures that governed all. Besides in the economy, these anarchic and arbitrary systems could be also seen in the jail, police and judiciary. In the jails it has already been mentioned that nearly every aspect of the jail system was being run by the criminals themselves. If we turn to the police escort system, they ignored any orders to be taken to the hospital or even the courts. The judges too, would not act against them if an inmate was not produced as instructed. It was probably the only state where the inmate was not produced in the court even during the trial nor when a production warrant was issued – everything was done through video conference. The sessions court would not give bail in even the flimsiest of cases so everything had to go to the high court, putting an immense burden on the latter. If we turn to economic activity, all work was done through contracts and sub-contracts with no law of the land applying – whether for labour, the environment or forests and agricultural lands.

In Jharkhand jails, many people commented that unlike the other Naxal 'leaders' I was portrayed as much in the media who had come to the jail I was the first who lived simply. Others had pots of money and people would flock around them for that reason, including the lower-ranking Naxals. The main reason for gaining the respect, not only of the ordinary inmates (though not the Naxals) but also of most authorities, was the fact that they saw me living simply, eating jail food and taking no favours that money could buy.

Finally, after getting bail in August 2019, I was transferred to Surat jail, which was to my last prison abode.

Surat Jail

The DSP (deputy superintendent), Jadeja saheb, who had done my formal arrest in Surat, was a batchmate of the jailor at Lajpore Central Jail in Surat and had requested the latter to make reasonable arrangements for me when I reached. Ten days prior I had been in police custody under the excellent care of the DSP and his juniors.

An entire ward was emptied out and I was put in it alone. The next day, when the superintendent (in charge of all Gujarat jails) came from Ahmedabad, he ordered four people to stay with me to keep the huge ward clean. In front of the ward there was a lawn, convenient for yoga, walking and contemplation of the future. Also, the don Fazlu Rehman, whom I had met in Tihar, contacted me from Ahmedabad jail and told his Surat lawyer to make arrangements for some good food and any other needs. The lawyer, Sheikh, came twice and brought some excellent Mughlai food.

Yet, this jail had such strict rules that it would have been very difficult to live there for long. Inmates were allowed just one 50-paisa postcard per month to write letters home; the phone facility was restricted for most, and only allowed for those involved in minor crimes; the hospital facilities were difficult to access; all writing paper was confiscated upon entry, as also many other things normally allowed in other jails, and one was not allowed out of the ward. Fortunately, my bail was passed within a month and a half due to the efforts of advocate Panwalla and his office, who did the entire case pro bono.

In Surat, many of the young jail staff (recent recruits) were intrigued to see a revolutionary (Gujarat has no such history) and were very interested in learning more about both the Dalit and tribal issues, which I was reasonably well versed with. These youth were themselves quite knowledgeable and interested in knowing more. I never met jail staff elsewhere with such a keen interest in social issues, not even the young new recruits in Jharkhand. They too would explain to me at length the conditions in their villages, the different regions of Gujarat and their varied cultures, the topography of the state – all very interesting as I knew nothing about the place. In turn, I introduced them to the Dalit movement in Maharashtra, the history of tribal revolts against the British and general issues which they were interested in.

It was during this time at Surat jail, sitting on the lawn, that I began to think of a jail diary and started making jottings of things that I could remember. Earlier, I had never considered writing one.

Finally, on 16 October my sister came all the way from Mumbai, furnished the surety and managed to reach the jail just in time for my release. She was helped in this by a young drama enthusiast, Vaibhav. This was possible primarily due to the cooperation of the Kathor court magistrate, the local lawyer, Atodariya, and the police. With the superintendent and jailor also being very cooperative I was out by about 7 p.m., and after some formalities we drove straight to Mumbai through the night in a cab she had already arranged. At 4 in the morning we reached her home where Meenal, who stayed on the third floor, stayed awake the entire night, to welcome me with flowers. Meenal who runs an organization (MPFY – My Prayer For You) helping people to understand the energies around them and does healing for herself and others had made two trips to Hazaribagh together with my sister to work on my release by showing me how I could change my energies and also meeting the superintendent and SP. While I was in Jharkhand jail, she taught me the method of working on one's energies to take away the frustrations and bring positivity in one's approach. With nearly ten years in jail and no light at the end of the tunnel, I needed it. It made me more relaxed and surprisingly from then on everything worked well right till my release from jail and even after.

Contact with Relatives and Friends

In spite of a Supreme Court judgement saying contact with family and friends is a key factor in the rehabilitation of an inmate, the jail system makes any contact with one's kin as difficult as possible. In this respect, Tihar was particularly bad. There were two ways of being in touch – either the phone or meeting directly at the jail or court.

Earlier no phone contact was provided, but later due to a court judgement the jail authorities were compelled to provide it. Here too there was a world of difference between Tihar and the other places. While at all the other places, barring Gujarat where the phone was only available to those with minor cases, any phone number could be registered and dialled – relatives, lawyers, friends. Quite naturally no proof was required for anything. At Tihar only close relatives were allowed to be phoned, that too only after a post-paid bill was shown as proof and an affidavit that the person was a close relative. No lawyers, no friends, no other phone calls were allowed. Also, to change a name of the person registered for the call, while it was easy in other places, in Tihar it was a lengthy process. Often the phone facility would be stopped for HRW inmates. Besides, the number of phone booths were so few that utilizing the facility was yet another nightmare; it was restricted to five minutes per call just twice a week for the HRW prisoners at Tihar, and also at other places. Of course, at all jails the number of phones was so few that invariably it was a massive rush to get our five minutes.

Mulaqaat (meeting with visitors) was the most looked-forward to event in the jail by all the inmates, including myself. It was our only real contact with the outside world, however limited.

As with most aspects of jail, there was a world of difference between Tihar and the other places when it came to mulaqaat rules and practices. At all other places anyone could just come and meet an inmate during the stipulated time, if it fell within the once/twice a week criterion. In these jails all the visitor was required to do was produce an identification, but in Tihar it was a long procedure with numerous conditions attached. As there is nothing much to say about the other places, since the procedure was simple and straightforward, I will outline the system at Tihar which could test anyone's patience.

Mulaqaat at Tihar was consistently made more difficult and unfriendly. I am surprised (and very grateful) anyone ever came. First, the inmate had to make a 'booking' on the phone, which often took hours to connect as there was only one number for all the jails in the Tihar Complex to access – that is, one phone number for 15,000 inmates. Earlier, anyone was allowed to meet, but later the authorities imposed a restriction on HRW inmates – we were to provide a list of ten names and only those people would be allowed for mulaqaat, no one else. On my list were my sister and other relatives, some friends and the rest were human rights activists.

As PUDR (Peoples' Union of Democratic Rights) activist and regular visitor for me, Moushumi Basu, says: 'and one cannot come without the telephone appointment. At the mulaqaat there are several check-points: mulaqaat time for getting passes is at 2 p.m. and the final mulaqaat is at 4 p.m. for 20 minutes. The first check-point is where the food items (when they were allowed) and clothes are screened. Earlier we could carry food, but that was later restricted only to rotis; no rice, dal, mutter paneer; then that too was stopped; then fruits were stopped; finally, only those eats were allowed that were made and sold at the Tihar shop made by inmates.' The reasons given for these restrictions was that it was through food that contraband items were smuggled in like tobacco, charas, blades, etc. But even after these restrictions the amount of contraband in the jail never decreased as the bulk transporters were not inmates but staff.

Home food was not only a pleasure compared to the insipid jail food, it was also a sort of bonding between the family and the inmate. It was the main source of pleasure of the inmates, and they would wait expectantly for the visit and food. I too would wait expectantly for the food and was disappointed if any visitor came without it. But most relatives and friends who were local would bring food. On the HRW mulaqaat days twice a week all would wait expectantly to see if their names were in the list. You could see their faces light up when they discovered their name, while the others returned dejected. But, once the food was stopped much of the enthusiasm was reduced, though still the mulaqaat was the major event to look forward to for all.

Moushumi continued: 'If we had to bring medicines or books it was a major problem as we would have to go to the PRO and show the letter that gave the permission for these; clothes, no metal buttons, no mufflers, no pyjamas with draw strings, and one time the fellow refused me a black coloured trouser saying no black allowed. All this at the first check-point; after which you have to go through a personal frisking process where they seek to ensure that we are not taking any contraband inside – no phones, keys, bags (only cloth bags), no pens, no water bottles (imagine, in the Delhi heat). The third check-point is the window where passes are issued – your details are verified and a picture is taken of the visitor – a guy sits and consults his diary and makes notes. After the passes are issued there is one more screening of bags, shoes, etc, and then you are allowed into the prison complex. You walk down the high walls with guards staring down at you – as they know you are there to visit a high-risk prisoner (others are in the morning). From here on it is a long wait – a constable would come and collect all the passes – there would be drop-outs and late comers and he would wait for all and then take the passes inside. One more round of checking and then we could meet the inmate. The checking is done by a mix of Home Guards, Delhi Police and TSP and an intelligence person where the passes are issued. The entire process takes about 3–4 hours plus the booking and travelling time. It's very bureaucratic and frustrating and though you are a visitor to an undertrial it's like you too (i.e. family members as well) are also on trial. Of course, those with money-power can avoid all this'

All this had an enormous impact as many would then just avoid coming given the time wasted. As getting health foods required permission that itself was difficult – first the SMO would have to OK it and then the superintendent would either accept or reject. Again all this was easy for people with money but for me it was a real pain, having to face a lot of humiliating questions by both the SMO and superintendent as to why these were needed and as they were not doctor-prescribed and on what basis!!! Often they would refuse permission.

Earlier whenever a visitor came for me, they would bring home food, fruits and other eatables. All would bring it: both relatives and friends. It was a real pleasure to eat home food given the rotten stuff we were given in Tihar. Though no non-veg was allowed other meals with nice rotis/parathas and fried rice made all the difference. First food was stopped; then fruits were restricted and later stopped. Earlier books too were allowed, but later these too were stopped. Good food at least once a week and proper reading material made all the difference to the drab life within jail. As mentioned, it was the most looked forward to event by me as well as by all in the jail.

For a period in 2014, the then DG at Tihar passed a draconian rule which barred HRW prisoners from meeting any visitors. We appealed against this decision but there was no response. Through a synchronised hunger strike of HRW prisoners of the nine jails, we put pressure on the authorities. We received threats and appeals, but finally the rule was withdrawn.

When the mulaqaat or meeting with visitors finally takes place, it is through speakers fitted to glass windows on both sides and lasts about twenty minutes. Such is the arrangement in Tihar, in other jails it's through a mesh and one can hardly hear the visitor due to the noise from others.

Then there is mulaqaat during court appearances; which was such a torture in Delhi that often due to the humiliation the process entailed I felt it was better to avoid it. In Delhi we were prevented by the police (unless a decent inspector came) from talking to our lawyers, let alone any relatives or friends who came to court. Strictly, only with court permission was a mulaqaat allowed in the lock-up within the court premises where we were kept before the hearing is announced. This was difficult to obtain, as the application has to go through the superintendent first, who may or may not allow it. Besides, getting to meet him itself was a tiresome procedure. Finally, if one managed to get permission from the jail superintendent and the judge, one would get five minutes, with the cops breathing down your neck and pulling you away.

Yet, in spite of all these coercive methods at Tihar, it called itself an ashram for prisoner reformation. In actual fact there is no effort in the direction of reformation, in fact the environment is more conducive to greater criminalization where the ordinary inmate has to resort to extortion within the jail to get the money for his daily fix. Most petty criminals plan to become big-timers while they are inside, learning the tricks of the trade from the bigger criminals and developing new contacts and liaisons.

In the Hyderabad and Visakhapatnam jails, mulaqaat for Naxalite prisoners was relaxed and took place in the DS's room. Of course, for the ordinary prisoners it too was through a mesh, but there were many rooms so one did not see big crowds and shouting. In Jharkhand it was bad, speaking through the mesh, even with the lawyers or family members that came all the way from Mumbai. One had to shout to be heard. Sometimes there was a phone system where we could speak to one person at a time. Jharkhand jail had very restricted mulaqaat timings with only one visit a week allowed for undertrials and once a fortnight for convicts. In all other jails it was twice a week for both. Besides, the mulaqaat here included that of the lawyer, whereas in other jails it was never part of the mulaqaat system. Nowhere else was the procedure as long drawn-out, cumbersome and humiliating as at Tihar. Of course, in Patiala and Surat I was only there for very short time so not familiar with the mulaqaat procedures.

Medical Systems

The ten years of incarceration have taken a toll on my health, for which, of course, there is no compensation. All my pre-existing health issues like blood pressure/heart, slip disc, spondylitis, IBS (irritable bowel syndrome) and prostrate/urinary problems got aggravated over the years. In addition, new problems have also been created of arthritis, sciatica, skin, eye and memory loss. This was not surprising given the late age at which I was arrested, 62, and the harsh conditions and long term of jail life.

What put the maximum strain on my health was the Delhi and Jharkhand escort systems to courts and hospitals; the 2014–16 period of jail transfers at Tihar and the hunger strike that followed; the dislocation from the cell due to 'repairs' in Tihar in 2015; the continuous transfer to various jails in the country; attending court dates at far off places by police van and/or train, and last but not least the poor quality of food, particularly at Tihar. Not to mention the continuous necessity of picking up weights like buckets of water, luggage during transfers, and not being given a Western toilet or a block to sleep on in Tihar for many years, added to all the orthopaedic problems. Of course, things could have been much worse if it had not been for my regular yoga and exercises. Given that I had learnt yoga as far back as 1976 from an Iyenger student in Pune and later had friends who helped improve my skills further, it was easy for me to pick up where I had left off. Also, long before my arrest I had been taught physiotherapy exercises for my orthopaedic problems which were useful. Normally, as the cell gates opened early, I could go out in the ward yard and do my yoga. In the Delhi winter it was nice doing it in the sun.

As Ngugi writes in *Wrestling with the Devil: A Prison Memoir*, 'It is the paramount duty of all political prisoners to keep physically fit. Any bodily disablement can considerably weaken their will or forever damage them... At Kamiti, disease and family were the two most frequent means of tormenting political prisoners. First disease. It was the most dreaded hydra in Kamiti Prison. "Whatever you do," the other political prisoners had told me, "try not to be ill....'"

The only positive aspect in Delhi was that I was lucky to get fair and considerate judges and magistrates who ordered proper medical attention. So, by far the best medical treatment I was able to get was while I was in Tihar. The judges I had, first Judge P.K. Jain and later Judge Reetesh Singh, sensitive to my age and health problems, continuously ordered I be treated at the top government hospitals – AIIMS for most ailments (eye, skin, prostrate/urinary, etc.) and G.B. Pant for my BP and heart problem.

The medical attention one received within Tihar depended largely on the nature of the SMO. This was particularly so in Jail No. 3 where the main hospital, physiotherapy unit and dentist clinic were located. For my orthopaedic pains, while in Jail 3, I would regularly take physiotherapy treatment as the unit was manned by two excellent therapists. On occasion we would get nasty SMOs who would not allow anything unless paid handsomely, but on the whole they were decent.

Nonetheless, by early 2012 Tihar had already begun to take its toll on my health. My eye-sight began to weaken with severe pain in one eye. And with high BP, I developed a heart complication which showed up as 'ventricular ectopic' and 'triggering'. Fortunately, I managed to receive decent medical attention for these conditions, including cataract operations of both eyes by the top doctor, Tityal, at the AIIMS.

In Hyderabad jail there was an excellent lady SMO, Dr. Kapoor, who was very sensitive to the inmates' needs, and a large medical staff who were also very cooperative. For my ailments Dr. Kapoor sent me to Gandhi Hospital as well as NIMS (Nizam's Institute of Medical Sciences) where I was able to get good attention. Of course, the dentist was a bit difficult and I probably lost one tooth because of him. Yet, when one tooth weakened, he sent me to Osmania General Hospital to see if a root-canal could be performed. When the young dentist there heard I was a Naxalite prisoner, he showed a lot of concern and said though the roots were weak he would try his best. After my release I went to a top dentist in Mumbai who, after examination, said the person who had done the root-canal had done a superb job.

Visakhapatanam jail had a reasonable medical system. It was during my stay there that I was sent to the King George's Hospital for my prostrate problem, where the senior urologist said it may be difficult to diagnose the actual cause of the frequent urination from within jail as a number of tests would be necessary. It was at his suggestion that I took bail, though my case was at the last stage. But of course, I was re-arrested within three days, not given a chance for the tests.

The Tenughat sub-jail in Jharkhand had virtually no facilities for anything. No medical diet, and worse, no proper medical facility. In place of the doctor (who rarely if ever came) there was a compounder who attended to the inmates (and who was no doubt good). A senior lady doctor twice recommended me to RIMS (Rajendra Institute of Medical Sciences), Ranchi for my prostate/urinary problem, but I was never sent. Also, there was no separate ward for TB patients and I was kept along with them. When these details of my health and lack of treatment appeared on the front page of *The Telegraph* on 23 March 2018, I was immediately transferred to Hazaribagh Central Jail.

In Jharkhand, at the Hazaribagh Central Jail, unlike the rest of the other jails, the hospital had barely any staff. All other jails would have a full-time SMO and another doctor, plus a compounder to dispense medicine, plus some nurses, MOs and other support staff. Here, the jail had just one doctor who came for a couple of hours every day, and many days not at all. There was no other staff, everything from dispensing medicine, giving injections, taking BP, administering intravenous drips, taking blood samples, treating urgent cases, virtually everything was done by semi-trained convicts, taking their commissions. Ironically, the overall chief at the hospital was a Maoist. There was a lady's section within this jail but they had no separate doctor. Not surprisingly, during my stay at the hospital, there were about five deaths of the elderly. Also, the hygiene levels at Hazaribagh were atrocious. Though there was supposed to be a separate cleaning staff, little of value was done – not only by the administration, but also by the inmates. Leftover food would be thrown around and rot, there were no urinals, and as water was in short supply, many in the hospital would not take a bath for weeks. The hospital was infested with mosquitos, flies, and all sorts of insects, including bedbugs; the only jail to have them.

Getting to RIMS for treatment was next to impossible. Not only because the doctors rarely recommended it but in spite of that, the police escort system was so bad that they responded sometimes after months.

While I was there, though the Jharkhand Human Rights Commission wrote a scathing report on the medical treatment that I was getting and that I be immediately taken to RIMS, the police escort took another two months to act and the pain of the ten-hour long round road trip probably did more damage to my slip disc than the examination at RIMS (over in two minutes). Later, at the instance of Maja Daruwala, senior advisor of the Commonwealth Human Rights Initiative in Delhi, the NHRC headquarters also sent a very senior representative from Delhi to take my report firsthand. They could only further recommend being sent to RIMS, which again took one month to implement because of the atrocious police escort system in Jharkhand. None of the SMOs who later came were like Dr. Dangi, who retired a couple of months after I came to Hazaribagh jail. He was the doctor in-charge when I first entered the prison and ordered all the facilities given my age and health problems. He was from a simple family in Chatra district. He was very considerate towards all – rich or poor, not making any distinctions. Unfortunately, he had been given the dual responsibility of looking after the state malnutrition programme which occupied much of his time. Inmates in the jail said they had never seen a doctor like him. But he soon retired. Others who came were no comparison.

Police and Escorts

Again, if we turn to the police escort system that took us to the courts and hospital nothing could be as bad as in Delhi. When inmates have to be taken to the court, hospital outside or during jail transfers, there is a police escort system that has to be involved to make sure the prisoner does not escape. Depending on the level of the crime that much security would be allocated.

In what I can only put down as an attempt to intimidate, during these trips to court and hospital in Delhi I would always be accompanied by a massive posse of police – four with bulletproof jackets, fifteen-odd with AK-47s, a number of SIs and an overall inspector in-charge. Given my age and health condition this display of force for mere travelling, was entirely unwarranted and a torturous experience. Not only that, the police personnel in Delhi were generally rough, uncouth and corrupt.

I would be driven in a van which had three gates, each locked from the outside, and finally deposited in a suffocating cage just behind the driver's seat, and locked from the outside. The dons in the high-risk ward said, in summer, they never sat inside the cage, but when I requested likewise on health grounds (in peak summer I would feel faint while travelling, which was evident even to the judge, who commented on my health a number of times) they would not allow me to sit outside. These high levels of 'security' continued even after the Delhi court granted me interim bail on health grounds.

Fortunately, I was never handcuffed as that required a court order. Each trip to the court or hospital was a nightmare, and in Delhi's polluted summers it was probably a major reason for my declining health.

In none of the other states was the police and escort system even a fraction as traumatic as in Delhi. I would usually travel in a jeep or car and with limited police force; in Surat and Punjab they were particularly considerate. I estimated that if one calculated the salary of all the escorts and accompanying police vans the total cost of each trip in Delhi would exceed ₹50,000. What a waste of peoples' tax money which could have been better used for the poor.

In addition, at Tihar, I was forced to the jail gates well in advance, and we were made to hang around in the blistering sun until it was announced that my police escort has arrived. Once when I was a little late during peak summer due to dizziness and nausea, 4-5 jail staff (not TSP) came to my cell threatening to beat me if I did not hurry up. When I told them about my health, they became more aggressive mishandling me. When I complained to the superintendent not only did he support his staff, but also punished me by cancelling my mulaqaats for a month for 'insubordination' and another month for going late. It was the same superintendent who was there when I entered jail – who seemed a different person earlier – and the one also responsible for transferring me to the HRW in the worst possible jail No. 8 where I had to go on hunger strike to stop such transfers.

Even in the long-distance travel there was a world of difference between the Telangana, Punjab, Jharkhand and Surat police on the one hand, and the Delhi Police on the other. The former were sensitive, supportive and helpful given my age and health condition. If they were cautious, they were not overtly so, resulting in a relaxed atmosphere. They never demanded anything and would often offer any food they had brought from home. The Delhi Police were just the opposite in every way – aggressive, demanding, always playing on the security angle and making the trips as uncomfortable as possible.

In Telangana/Andhra Pradesh, as also Jharkhand and Punjab, the police seemed to have some respect for Naxalites and treated me like a political prisoner. Senior officers in all these places would often discuss with me the state of the economy and the future of the country. In Surat, although they were not familiar with the Naxal issue (no such history there), it was the only place where they knew who Parsis were. They too were very decent and made good arrangements while I was in their custody.

All said and done, except for Delhi, the police acted decently – it is not so much the individual but the corrupt colonial criminal-justice system that makes them oppressive; besides having to dance to the orders of politicians, which compounds the situation.

~

This then is a brief account of the conditions of life in Indian jails – over a decade basically as an undertrial – dealing with its many facets. Tihar was a nightmare as was their police escort system, but what was even worse, as we shall see later, was the agonizing uncertainty of the entire judicial process which operated on the whims of the police/politicians. For the present let's turn to a more interesting and pleasant topic – the people I met in jail.

I joined the Doon school in 1958. This group photograph of that year has me standing in the second row from the top (*third from right*). Also seen here are my friends, Ishaat Hussain (*top row, seventh from right*), Gautam Vohra (*top row, eighth from right*) and my brother Farrokh, (*second row from bottom, second from left*).

At the Mumbai airport in 1968 on my way to London to study
chartered accountancy.

Anuradha and I on the day of our wedding in Mahabaleshwar in 1977.

With Anuradha in Mumbai, a few days after our wedding.

Anuradha's commitment to the oppressed and women empowerment influenced her work as a change-maker.

Standing (*third from left*) with my parents and friends.
My parents (*first and second from left*), supported me in all my endeavours.

The building that has replaced the Mayanagar slum as part of the government's rehabilitation programme.

At a friend's house in the mid-1980s.

© PTI

Being produced in a district court in Patiala in 2016.

Covers of *Aavhan* song book and *Parsiana*, which did a cover story on me in their April 2014 issue.

Of the ten years of my incarceration, I spent more than six years in Tihar, and the rest in jails in Hyderabad, Patiala, Visakhapatanam, Surat and in the sate of Jharkhand.

With Anuradha's mother, Kumud Shanbagh. I was released from Surat jail on 16 October 2019. The very next day on reaching Mumbai, I went to meet her. During my time in prison I would correspond with her and even speak to her on the phone. She was bedridden for a while and finally passed away on 12 December 2020 at the age of 91.

Political Associations

Though Tihar was the jail with the worst conditions, it was also the jail that taught me the most about many aspects of Indian society. The few parliamentarians I met in jail were a knowledgeable lot. Tihar also gave me a detailed insight into the police-criminal nexus when local Delhi criminals would tell me of the hafta they would have to pay the police monthly to carry on with their activities. Of course, much of this is already in the public domain. I also found out a lot about the big-time dons of North India and their lives. I gained clearer insight into the politics of the Kashmiris, Islamists, Khalistanis, all of whom were lodged in the HRWs of Tihar. I acquired a picture of the life in Jharkhand and the revolutionary movement there of which I knew little till then. Last, but not least, at least in the first couple of years, I had access to the excellent IGNOU notes which gave me an insight into the history of philosophies and before the disturbance of transfers began, had time to reflect on my near half century of activities.

Parliamentarians

At the end of 2011 the 2G Scam individuals came to Tihar jail. As they were all in Ward 4, the VIP ward, I had access to them only during the legal mulaqaats. Sanjay Chandra of Unitech and the Reliance directors, Gautam Doshi, Umashankar and Hari Nair, in particular, became quite friendly. As Chandra and I had the same lawyer, Rebecca John, he would carry messages to her through his lawyers that visited him in the jail. The Reliance directors would discuss at length the injustice of their case and explain its details. There were a few other 2G people in Tihar but many of the main accused were in other jails.

A few aspects of the case struck me, but I did not ask as it may have resulted in embarrassment for them. Why was the Reliance chief, Anil Ambani, not put in, and only the directors and executives made scapegoats? Is it not the norm that money passes many hands for any contract awarded, so why the big fuss at the exchequer losing thousands of crores, when that is continuously happening both before 2G and after? Though they claimed that it was their rival Airtel that forced the action, what was the deal that was worked out that let them out so soon?

Towards the end of 2011, the BJP 'cash for vote' scam accused entered the jail. One of them, Sudheendra Kulkarni, who had been an aide to former prime minister Atal Bihari Vajpayee, and was at that time heading the Observer Research Foundation, came to Jail 3; in the same ward where the 2G scam accused were held. We became very good friends in the short time he was there. He was yet to publish his book on Gandhiji, *Music of the Spinning Wheel*, and we would discuss the draft and I gave my comments. Though we had differing views on Gandhiji, I realized that on economic theory we held similar views – of making the village the centre for all

148

development and for building upwards. The major point of difference was of course the caste issue on which I felt Ambedkar had greater clarity. Then there was Gandhiji's stand on non-violence, which seemed unclear as he fully supported recruitment of Indians into the British army for the war in which thousands were killed; his views on celibacy (brahmacharya) and raising it to a major aspect of his life was odd, as sex is a normal instinctive need; amongst others. On the question of simplicity as well, there were similarities. Why, Arundhati Roy, too, after visiting Bastar, had once referred to the Naxalites as 'Gandhians with guns'.

Sudheendra explained he was from IIT, Powai where the former Goa chief minister, Manohar Parrikar, had been his classmate. In college, Sudheendhra said he had been a left supporter but later became disillusioned with them and joined the BJP. He was now in jail in a case associated with them. Though I had not as yet written my six essays on 'Freedom' I would discuss some of my new ideas with him and he would share his understanding of Gandhiji. It was probably the only real intellectual discourse I was able to have in my entire ten years in jail. It was a very interesting period and I would try and get out of the HRW to meet him as often as I could.

Upon his release Sudheendra wrote a series of articles in the *Indian Express* entitled 'My Days in Tihar Ashram'; in one of them, entitled 'I met Gandhiji in Tihar', published on 11 December 2011, he said:

Within a couple of days of my arrival in Tihar, I met an inmate who introduced himself with rare candour. "Unlike you," he said, "I am someone who can be called a criminal. I headed a criminal gang and have committed several murders." Soon I came to know a lot from him about the general profile of the prison population. "I would like to meet some interesting inmates," I told him. His response: "Would you like to meet Gandhiji?"

I was curious to meet him because, as a left-wing student activist in Mumbai in the late 1970s and early 1980s, I had heard the name of Kobad Ghandy. He was a spirited campaigner for the protection of democratic rights in the aftermath of the Emergency. But how, I wondered, can I meet him since he is lodged in the high-risk ward, whose inmates have severe restrictions on their mobility? As luck would have it, I got to meet Kobad several times in the course of my 52-day stay in Tihar. Haven't the wise said, "Where there is a will, there is a way?" We exchanged several letters. He even took the trouble of going through the 650-page manuscript of my forthcoming book on Mahatma Gandhi, and sent detailed comments, many of them appreciative of my hero, but also some critical.

I conveyed to Kobad that I am inflexible in my condemnation of violence as a means of political activism and acquisition of state power. All violent revolutions in history have failed to achieve their stated objectives. Mankind should learn the right lessons from its own historical experience and search for a new path for social change, based on truth and nonviolence as attempted, with partial success, by Gandhiji.

It came as no surprise to me that Kobad is engaged in profound soul-searching through a rigorous study of the communist movement. He is asking himself serious questions about why communist movements have failed all over the world, including in India. Some of the conclusions that he has arrived at are

150

startling. He, of course, remains an unapologetic foe of capitalism and believes that the internal crises in capitalism could once again force it to inflict enormous violence on mankind, just as they did through the two World Wars in the last century.

Experience has led Kobad to begin a deep study of religion, philosophy and psychology especially why power corrupts and corrodes human nature. Being a Parsi, he has found new light in the teachings of Zarathushtra. The values he cherishes, he told me, "are those epitomised by my late wife – simplicity, straightforwardness, self-sacrificing, absence of ego/ arrogance and childlike. The New Man needs to be like that – heart of a child, spirit of love and affection, but with the mind of a scientist. But it is difficult to acquire these in this world. Let us hope that I can find some answers to these in the few years left of my life. I will continue the search."

Kobad, 63, is suffering from multiple ailments. However, neither his medical condition nor his incarceration has taken away the amazing glow from his face, a glow that reflects his courage of conviction and the inner peace of his being. He finds his peace watching squirrels play in his ward, tending to the tulsi, rose and guava plants that he has planted, and devoting 7-8 hours daily to reading and writing…

There is so much to write about Kobad, my friend. For now, let me say just this: This "Gandhiji" does not deserve to spend his last years in jail.

I was astounded to read the article and though I had discussed my unformed views on 'freedom and values' I was not sure I was worthy of such fulsome praise with all my flaws.

151

What also came as a surprise was the other inmates' impression of me when they introduced him to me.

Obviously, our interactions had been brief but being the only communist prisoner within the Tihar atmosphere, I suppose there was a difference from the others. As Sudheendra writes, the 'strange but deeply satisfying rapport that we built in the course of our several interactions… transcended our conflicting ideological affiliations.'

There was one more interesting encounter that took place around the same time. One evening the superintendent called me to his room. When I went in, I was astounded to find Samajwadi Party leaders Amar Singh and Jaya Prada sitting there waiting to meet me. Amar Singh was at the time said to be one of the top 'brokers' in political circles, a close friend of Amitabh Bachchan and close to Mulayam Singh (he recently passed away after a long illness). After a brief discussion on the nature of our two cases, Amar Singh went on to say how they had recently been part of a Bengali film on the Naxalite movement. At that time Naxalism seemed all the rage and carried a somewhat romantic Robin Hood image.

The positive response I obtained from most of these well-connected individuals may have been a result of the media hype around my arrest, which I had not, till then, realized. After all, one rarely sees a top Naxal (as I was portrayed in the media) who is from Doon School and London returned. Stuff ideally made for films.

No wonder then, in the two years after my arrest, three mainline films appeared which claimed to have been inspired by my life and work for the oppressed. Prakash Jha's *Chakravyuh* (in which Om Puri is said to have played me), a well-researched and mostly accurate portrayal of the movement; Mani Ratnam's *Raavan* (in which Abhishek Bachchan was advertised as playing me), which I never saw but from what I could assess had nothing to do with me or my activities; and another lesser-known film, *Red Alert*, with BJP politician and actor Vinod Khanna playing a Naxalite.

Khalistanis and Islamists

Way back in the early 1980s I remember writing an article supporting the Anandpur Sahib Resolution (1978) on centre-state relations demanding a greater federal structure for India; giving more powers to the states. I understood the Sikh movement to be an extension of this, calling first for more powers to Punjab, and when brutally crushed, for a separate country. But here, in jail, I was shocked to find that the Khalistanis had turned fundamentalists, their main goal was no longer more powers to the states, and they were busy targeting the many deras which they claimed were polluting the purity of the Sikh religion. Ironically, most of these deras are supported by Dalits who do not get the recognition within the existing present-day Sikh religious establishment, run by the Jatts who dominate the Sikh Gurdwara Prabandhak Committee (SGPC), the top Sikh religious body. In fact, I was told that in virtually every village in Punjab there are separate Jatt and Dalit gurdwaras.

This was a shocking revelation for two reasons. Firstly, I had known many kisaan leaders from Punjab and even spent a month doing a survey in the villages over the peasant suicides in the cotton belt. Yet, never once did I get any inkling whatsoever of the extent of the caste/Dalit factor there. Incidentally, most of these leaders were from Jatt or upper-caste Brahmin backgrounds. Punjab has had very strong kisaan organizations and powerful peasant movements mostly led by left parties/organizations; yet the Dalit issue never seemed to be on their agenda, though Dalits are said to comprise 32 per cent of the population – the highest percentage in any state. It showed the impact of economism in these movements where such an important aspect of Punjab life was negated and merely the economic issues, no doubt very serious; were of prominence. But, judging from the farmers movement against the three laws, things seem to have changed during my ten years of incarceration, as they seem to be successful in rallying entire Punjab society around them.

Secondly, as far as I knew the major reform that the Sikh religion brought in was against the caste system. Therefore, I would have assumed any 'orthodox' Sikh to oppose the caste system and support the integration of Dalits into their fold which the Guru Grant Sahib emphasized. Yet these Khalistanis, again mostly Jatts, who claimed orthodoxy could negate one of the most important tenets of the Sikh religion. Also, the gurdwaras are meant to be open religious centres where anyone can enter – regardless of religion, gender or caste – yet in their social life the caste factor appeared extremely rigid. By targeting the deras supported by Dalits, the Khalistanis appeared to me to be doing a disservice to their religion, rather than promoting it.

While many of the older lot were in for their involvement during the peak of the Khalistan movement, the newer generation had been arrested for targeting some of the religious gurus. My first observation was of Devinder Pal Singh Bhullar, a top Khalistani leader, accused in the 1993 Delhi Bomb Blast Case, who was involved in a whole lot of rituals, was a strict vegetarian and would not even touch an egg. Not a strand from his beard should fall or be cut, and other rigid practices. It gave me a completely different image of what the movement was all about.

Another one of their leaders, Jagtar Singh Hawara, an accused in the assassination of Chief Minister Beant Singh in 1995, was openly linked to the Sikh priesthood and was, in fact, elected to an alternate body of the SGPC, while in jail. In November 2015, the Sarbat Khalsa declared Hawara as interim Jathedar of the Akal Takht replacing Gurbachan Singh. But Hawara had a charismatic past when in 2004 he escaped from the maximum-security jail at Burail, Punjab by digging a 90-foot tunnel. He was recaptured in 2005 and had since been in Tihar. Unlike Bhullar he was not that rigid, a pleasant and jovial person, who would regularly exercise with me in the ward whenever we were together. Of course he was relatively younger and physically fit, while Bhullar later was admitted to the mental hospital.

It is a tragedy that what started as a movement for greater federalism (more power to the states) ended in this sectarian fashion. In fact, these top leaders in Tihar seemed to have no knowledge of the earlier movement and the Anandpur Sahib Resolution. Of course, the government of that time pushed them in this direction with Operation Blue Star and later the anti-Sikh pogrom. Not surprisingly, I was told that some of the Khalistani faction leaders are based in Pakistan, just like the Islamists; both being encouraged along the fundamentalist path.

Another set of extremists were the Islamists who were even more fanatical in their approach. When I entered jail, one of the first persons to meet me and talk with me was a Pakistani who was linked to the ISI. His only intention in the entire conversation was to try and utilize my disorientation by the arrest to convert me to Islam. He played on my insecurities to great effect. While Afzal introduced me to the humanitarian aspects of the religion, the bulk of the IS (Islamic State), ISI (Inter-Services Intelligence of Pakistan), IM (Indian Mujahideen) people were fanatics. On many occasions I remember arguing with them about how throwing bombs in public was counter-productive and inhuman as it kills innocents, including Muslims. But they would not accept any argument and would say such collateral damage is inevitable in any conflict. They were in total awe of Saudi Arabia – no doubt the fountainhead of their Wahhabi ideology and probably their funding – and were disinterested in any other movement. They spent the bulk of their time reading their religious texts and if they ever spoke to any of us it was only with the intention of converting us to Islam. Their fanaticism went to such extremes that they would see Shias and Iran as one of their major enemies; even the very mention of Sufism would make them angry.

I gathered that their intolerance went to such extreme levels that the IS–ISI–Saudi types would not tolerate the milder Islamists like the Muslim Brotherhood. In fact, it is alleged that the Saudis promoted a coup and massacre of them after they were elected to power in Egypt by perfectly legitimate means. The level of this fanaticism can be understood by the fact that even though a number of states, like Turkey, Qatar, and others supported the Muslim Brotherhood and their government, these Wahhabi elements masterminded their destruction with a military take-over, with the US and other big powers looking on.

From these facts it appeared that the Pak-Saudi Axis seemed to turn all organizations into fundamentalists to promote their geo-political agenda; much of it at the behest of the US. After all, the US has used aggressive Islamist ideology in the Middle East to counter first the communist influence in the 1970s and 1980s, and later the Soviet influence in the region. In fact, both the Khalistanis and the Islamists in India seem to have become the other side of the RSS coin, each fuelling the other.

On hearing these accounts, I began to wonder how legitimate movements against injustice can be turned on their head if those leading them are not grounded in the realities of the situation with a proper focus to distinguish enemies from friends. 'Divide and Rule' is a common ruling class policy, in India effectively used by the British. It may not be a coincidence that the RSS and the Tablighi outfit were both established in the 1920s. It is also known that about the same time, it was the British who installed the Wahhabi puppet in Saudi as king to counter the Caliphate movement. While Muslims are a victim of Hindutva policies in India, fundamentalism is counterproductive to fighting communalism. In fact, it further fuels support for the Hindutva agenda.

Till today both the issues of greater federalism and anti-communalism is even more relevant than in those days as, over the years there has been greater centralization of power and with the Hindutva project anti-Islam has reached peak levels. Unfortunately, these issues are being ignored by even the political opposition, or, at best, used for vote-bank politics. Neither have much impact.

Kashmiris and Afzal

I noticed that while a lot of those from Pakistan (mostly from the Punjabi areas) were influenced by the Islamic fundamentalist philosophy, those from Kashmir were purely against the Indian State's oppression in Kashmir and were against violence that entailed bombings in civilian areas and targets, which to this date seems rare in Kashmir. From what I could gather, most don't have any ideology as such but feel stifled by the presence of Indian forces in Kashmir.

It seemed many were not favourable to Kashmir joining Pakistan and wanted an independent Kashmir. In fact, Afzal told me that in the early stages of the movement, when the

Jammu & Kashmir Liberation Front (JKLF) demand for an independent Kashmir was at its peak in the 1980s, Pakistan used its network to kill many intellectuals advocating Kashmiri independence. In fact, he said, the writings of Maqbool Bhat, the first Kashmiri to be hanged in Tihar and a JKLF member, are banned not only in India but also in Pakistan. Afzal was the same – he distrusted Pakistan as much as he did India. He felt that Pakistan was using Kashmiris as cannon-fodder in their geo-political games with India. Ironically, I did not hear of any extreme fundamentalists being hanged.

Afzal, though had strong faith in Islam – he did his namaz five times a day, observed a strict Ramzan, had a strong belief in the afterlife (Jannat), opposed idol worship and dargahs, had a mistrust of Shias – was not a fundamentalist. He was a Sufi and had done a detailed study of the six volumes of Rumi in Urdu. He showed a keen interest in socialism and would often quote Iqbal who he said once wrote: communism + God = Islam.

At our daily morning chai sessions, he would give much information about life in Kashmir, Islam, Iqbal and Sufism. Afzal was well read, having studied people like Noam Chomsky and other anti-imperialists. He was the only person in jail fluent in English so we would talk in English or Hindi (he could speak but not read the latter). He would outline the background of Islam in Kashmir saying that most were recent converts and most of the leaders with names like Geelani, Sayeed, Guru, etc. were all Brahmin converts. And in their homes, many still followed some of their earlier rituals. He would picture the beauty of Kashmir and say that such a heaven had virtually been converted into a hell and an open prison with troops at every step. It was Afzal who also introduced me to the writings and history of the Muslim Brotherhood, who, it seems, always followed legal forms of struggle though many of their top intellectuals were hanged, right from the time of Nasser.

Maqbool Bhat was hanged on 11 February 1984, while Afzal was hanged hastily on 9 February 2013 – both are buried side-by-side inside Tihar, in the ground we once walked around. While Bhat's writings have been published, though banned, Afzal's extensively detailed diary has not seen the light of day; probably burnt by now. In fact, none of his belongings were given to us, though we asked for them. Besides Afzal, there was another Kashmiri inmate I was close to; Rafique, a simple intellectual from Kashmir, in no way connected with activities there or in Delhi, who was later acquitted. Rafique and I had some items that were lying in Afzal's cell (books, a thermos and some other stuff); these too were not returned to us.

It all happened very suddenly. On 7 February 2013, we were asked to shift immediately to B Block at the back, as A Block was supposedly being white-washed. Those at the back had been moved out earlier in the day. Later in the day we, with the shutting of a side gate, were cut off from the view of the phansi kothi ground. We gathered from staff that much work was going on there. This raised more doubts that it was being prepared for a hanging, as, after all, no one had been hanged there since 1989 and it would require much repair. The staff, in order to throw us off, said the area was being spruced up because they were expecting an international delegation, but people had their doubts that it could be either Bhullar or Afzal. Even amidst this tense atmosphere, Afzal would say, calmly, 'If there is to be a hanging it will be me, not Bhullar.' And so it was.

On Friday the 8th many went for the mulaqaat and in the process saw the level of work going on at the phansi kothi. The suspicions increased. That evening we were all tense and I remember telling Afzal, while we were being locked up, to have a good sleep and not worry. He only smiled but did not say anything. Worry we all did. All in the ward hoped, of course, that nothing would happen, but I remember thinking of asking Afzal for his diary, just in case. I, naturally, dropped the idea as it would make the tension much worse for him; making it seem there was a strong chance that something would happen. No one knows if Afzal really slept that night as no one in the ward ever saw him again.

The next morning was Saturday, 9 February 2013. The gates did not open at the usual 5.30 in the morning. Everyone was getting restless expecting a search party, as, only on such occasions was the opening delayed. At 6.15 they finally came. Afzal's being the first cell, it was opened with Afzal saying, 'It is already late for namaz do the searching after we finish'; and he walked out for his namaz. Within a few seconds, he saw that after letting him out, they locked his gate and did not open any others. He realized what was in store, and so did all of us in the other cells. The law officer led him to the cell in A Block where he had stayed all these years.

The staff was apparently in tears on seeing his courage while going to the gallows, and they said while he was walking towards the phansi kothi from his cell – barely a three-minute walk – he wished all the staff lined up and asked the officers to take good care of them. Except for the most corrupt, the staff quite respected him as he was not fanatical, was highly disciplined, lived simply and was of a jovial temperament.

As I wrote in my letter to Gautam Vohra on 18 February 2013:

Just as I was settling down to read again, as AIIMS said it was ok, (I had a cataract operation in one eye) our entire existence has been destabilized... Besides the trauma of this taking place virtually before ones very eyes – Afzal was the most well-read person in

160

here and had a very liberal view of Islam – the idyllic ground is now a graveyard, completely shut.

His bravery at the time of hanging probably came from his firm belief in Jannat. He once told me that when he died, he would just be waiting to meet Mohammed, Rumi, Iqbal and all the other prophets there – a better future than the hell he faced in Tihar. He had been trying desperately for many years to get transferred to a jail in Kashmir to be near his family, which was his legal right. He was very fond of his mother, wife and son, Galib. Once when he had access to someone's mobile, I remember him singing ghazals on the phone to his wife, which continued for nearly an hour. His family would regularly visit him once every 4-5 months (his wife was a school teacher and could not afford to come more often). He would particularly look forward to Raksha Bandhan, a day when they were allowed inside the jail. Unfortunately, he could not move the Supreme Court and get the transfer order for lack of assistance from his people outside the jail on the issue. Though they would regularly visit him he would be quite frustrated with the lack of any progress on what to him was most important and a simple court procedure. Though advocate Pancholi of PUCL, would offer help and was very cooperative, his assistance was not taken by those outside. Now of course one understands why this transfer petition was resisted: if he happened to be in a Kashmir jail this surreptitious and out-of-turn hanging would have been difficult.

Unfortunately, Afzal Guru has been demonised and now it comes out that even his Delhi trip at the time of the parliamentary attack had been planned by an intelligence police officer who was recently caught with terrorists. Apparently, although Afzal mentioned this fact in his statement, it was ignored by the courts. In fact, if one reads about his whole court proceedings there appears to be a serious travesty of justice.

While talking to these Kashmiris and comparing them with the fundamentalists, I conjectured that the government needs to think more seriously about dealing with the more rational elements, rather than the fundamentalists to try and solve the Kashmir issue. After all, many similar issues have been settled all over the world, like the Irish question, Kosovo, Sudan and elsewhere; then why not Kashmir which would release thousands of crores in military expenditure each year for India's development. The issue is between the Indian government and the Kashmiri people, quite rightly Pakistan should be kept out as they muddy the waters with their own agenda. Why even today, the states in the US, as also the Scottish, Welsh and Irish in the UK, have more independence from their central government than Indian states ever enjoyed. That is, in fact the essence of a federal structure; which India needs to consider seriously, given that in Indian states even the languages are different, unlike the US or UK. At one stroke not only the Kashmir, but also the Northeast, Punjab/Khalistan, Tamil and other related issues could be solved. What massive saving to the exchequer that would result in. As the Indian rulers tend to mimic the West in everything, then why not learn from the federal structures of those countries instead of further centralizing everything?

Revolutionaries and Social Activists

Towards the end of the 1990s Andhra Pradesh was facing a state terror of unprecedented proportions where any and every youth suspected of sympathy was allegedly being killed in fake encounters by the Chandrababu Naidu government.

162

The Congress, led by Rajashekar Reddy, won the 2004 elections purely on the plank that they would have peace talks with the Naxals. The peace talks lasted a month when top leaders were accommodated in the state guest house and took representations from all sections of society regarding their problems, apparently including the police union. When talks broke down, the main Naxal leaders were allowed to return to the Nallamalla forests where they resided. But apparently, we are told, that during this legal period the police watched all who came forward and when the talks broke all hell was let loose. It is said they never recovered from this onslaught.

I noticed when I was in Hyderabad jail the younger generation knew little of the revolutionary movement and it was not even in their consciousness. This surprised me as this revolutionary tradition has existed since the days of the separate Telangana movement of 1948. I was given to understand that Ganesh was one of the last of the Naxal arrests; not surprisingly he was the only Naxal in the entire ward.

When I reached Hyderabad jail, and entered the separate 'Naxalite ward' I was greeted by Ganesh, extremely soft spoken and gentle, who had spent twenty years in jail and was respected by one and all there. He was arrested in 1997 after a shootout and injury in Guntur district. He said he was one of the last of the Naxal arrests in erstwhile Andhra Pradesh, as after him they stopped with the formality of arresting and began killing all in fake encounters. By that time, the Radical Students' Union (RSU) had veritably swept all the schools and college elections of Andhra Pradesh. The RSU was said to be the front of the PWG – the Maoists in the state. By the mid-1990s the RSU had won practically all the student union elections throughout the schools and colleges of then Andhra Pradesh (i.e. today's Telangana and Andhra Pradesh). The entire student and youth of the state were drawn towards revolution. Yet, when I reached the jail the younger generation just a decade later seemed not to know a thing. However, the staff, who were between 40 and 50, were mostly sympathetic having been associated in some way with the RSU in their youth.

Unfortunately, Ganesh's case was taken by the CBI and he was given a life term. In Andhra Pradesh at the time, life convicts were often released after 8-10 years on the basis of good conduct. Nowadays, throughout the country the state governments set up a board headed by the chief minister, which is supposed to meet every three months and take a decision on life-term convicts to be released. It is no longer automatic after 14 years as it was earlier. But in cases decided by central agencies, like the CBI, the decision has to be taken by the centre.

In Ganesh's case the entire Telangana parliament and police had long back agreed that he should be released. In fact, so sure was he and human rights groups of his release that he actually got married to a revolutionary's widow during one of his parole trips. Unfortunately, being a CBI case, the central government had to pass the order and they consistently refused to release him though the local police and government passed resolutions in his favour. So he continues to languish in jail, while his wife pines for his release.

Later, another alleged Naxal leader, Varanasi Subrahmanyam, came to this jail and Ganesh too returned from parole after four months. From then on, chess became an important part of the day as all three of us were avid chess players. They would invariably beat me.

~

In Visakhapatanam jail, as I mentioned earlier, I befriended the educated tribal Naxal leader (said to be a state committee member) Chadda Bhushanam (CB). He was from the forest areas of Visakhapatanam district and joined the movement when he was very young in the early 1990s. While in the 5th class he took the ITDA test and gained admission into the Gurukul School. He first worked in the student organization, RSU, and later in the Gurukul area in Koyyur, which was famous for the huge tribal revolts in the 1920s. He said that by 1990 the RSU had swept all the schools and hostels including the women's hostels and CB became a mass student leader. He led many militant struggles against liquor barons, strikes on student demands and organized many 'Go to the Village' campaigns. Here, groups of students go to the villages for 15-30 days, stay in the huts of the poorest and eat whatever food they are given, and educate them on their rights, while themselves learning about the condition of the people.

When state pressure increased, his parents opposed his activities and he joined a squad. By the early 2000s he was said to have been promoted to leadership and transferred to the Orissa (present-day Odisha) area of AOB (Andhra–Orissa Border) region. This was the huge bauxite belt with the (in) famous Niyamgiri hills. Bhushanam recounted: This bauxite belt comprises the two Orissa districts of Narayanpatna and Koraput and the Vizianagaram district of Andhra Pradesh Vedanta, Nalco and Indalco operated on the Orissa side and Jindal, Nalco and a Dubai-based company on the Andhra Pradesh side. At that time another Naxal group, Janashakti, had organized the masses into a huge mass organization in this entire region – the Chasimulya Sangathan (CS). Since the earlier 30-40 years the entire tribal land had been seized by non-tribals (Sundi community). The CS primarily organized the tribals for their lands against the non-tribals, and also against the liquor barons.

Bhushanam further said: After the Maoist entry in 2007, initially the relations with the Janashakti were good, but later the CS split and the Orissa section went with the Maoists. The worst tragedy then unfolded – for up to six months in 2009 there were major clashes between the two factions of the CS. Thousands would take part on either side – all tribals. The mining/bauxite barons took advantage of these clashes and funded and organized the terror outfit 'Shanti Sena' amongst the non-tribals. Together with the weakening through the division, the CS, according to Bhushanam, had a tribal consciousness and not a class consciousness and so would also target poor non-tribals. This facilitated the spread of the Shanti Sena. Later, in 2010 the leader of the Shanti Sena (a Congress lawyer) was killed and the Sena collapsed.

The government acted fast to fill the vacuum, and moved in a battalion of the CRPF and unleashed terror on the mass organization. Initially there was resistance to this move and a two-week bandh was organized with a total blockade. He said that it was so effective that the CRPF had to bring their rations by helicopter. Until then the unchallenged leader of the CS was a person called Linga. As his stature grew, apparently he became very autocratic, and with the repression he and his small inner circle capitulated, resulting in mass arrests, particularly of the 80-odd village leaders. By 2012–13, the CS, now participating in elections, had won all panchayat/block elections and had access to crores of funds. The leaders now allied themselves to the ruling Biju Janata Dal (BJD). With the mass organization, particularly its leaders, now hostile to the Maoists, the squads/party lost their base in the villages and found it difficult to survive. Though mass sympathy remained in the face of opposition from ground-level leaders, it amounted to little. Apparently, it was at such a time that their top leaders were also arrested. This weakened the movement even further.

This example seems to be a common pattern in most Naxal areas. With the collapse of the mass movement due to repression, either the entire work collapses or the squads/ party end up alienated from the masses or turn into roving rebels collecting money from contractors for their food and existence. With this the movements collapse or go round in circles. From what I gathered, through reports in Jharkhand and in Telangana jails, a similar pattern resulted in the collapse of the movements there as well, with, no doubt, local differences.

This then was the picture one acquired from a top local leader of the Niyamgiri mass movement. Bhushanam said that with the collapse of the movement a massive network of roads could be seen snaking over all the hills of the area – to facilitate bauxite transport and police movement. A similar situation was reported to exist in Jharkhand according to activists in jail there.

∼

While in Jharkhand's Tenughat jail I came to know something about tribal culture when I took an active part in the Sarhul Pooja (a major tribal festival in February). The 'temple' was in the courtyard just in front of the hospital and comprised only a stump of the Sukhwa tree, which is what they worship. The tribals worship nature and the whole process, though now a little bit Hinduized, did not involve any gods or goddesses. A chicken was sacrificed, and the drops of blood from it sprinkled over the Sukhwa stump and the area around it. We all had the Sukhwa white flowers in our ears. We then, one by one, led by the jailor, broke coconuts next to the stump. Afterwards, rice wine was distributed (in jail only 5 kg of rice was allowed to be made into wine by the authorities, basically fermented) to a few (I too had a taste). Later, prasad was distributed – khichdi made with the sacrificed chicken in it. Finally, of course, there was a lot of merriment with Nagpuri music playing and everyone dancing. Surprisingly, it is not their Santhali music that is popular but Nagpuri songs.

The bulk of this forest belt of Jharkhand is called Chota Nagpur and the general language is Nagpuri, though they have their own tribal languages as well. The other big forest belts are called Santhal Parganas (SP) and Saranda. It is basically these three regions that comprise most of Jharkhand. The state has a number of other tribal communities as well, primarily Mundaris, Ho, Ganjus, Oraon, and a few others. Santhalis are primarily in the Chota Nagpur and SP areas and have their own language as well as a distinct script. The others are mainly in the Saranda belt. All speak their separate dialects although, much like the Sarhul Pooja, strangely, it is Nagpuri songs that are most popular on the TV and radio.

When I was shifted to the Hazaribagh Central jail I discovered that much of the mafia there were the Naxal prisoners themselves. Yes, as I said, they did make a beeline when I came, but for one purpose – money. The jail scenario was such that all movement leaders (even lower-ranking ones) had a reputation of having pots of money. When they found I had none and in fact needed their help (not knowing a soul in Jharkhand) they disappeared, rarely to be seen again in the entire one and a half years of my stay there. I asked them to find a decent sevadar to help bring the water and other items as I had orthopaedic problems and could not lift weights, but no help was forthcoming. These Maoists appeared completely different from what I had earlier observed (and read about) in Bastar.

These Jharkhand Maoists seem not to have taken much from the great Jharkhand revolutionary tradition. As little is known about this history and it was something I had no knowledge of prior to jail, I will, in brief, recount what I learnt. All these heroic freedom struggles where thousands of

Adivasis gave up their lives, have been consciously kept out of our history. There is no official historical record and what can be gathered is through the oral history of the tribal people and some informal research by enterprising individuals like Gladson Dungdung.

Freedom Struggles in Jharkhand

An entire book could be written on what ails Jharkhand's economy and the dominating impact of the contract system. Yet, what astounded me while talking to others, was that it was the people of Jharkhand, particularly the tribals, who made the greatest sacrifices fighting the British; in fact, long before the Congress was established and the official freedom struggle launched.

Jharkhand has seen a series of revolts against the British and zamindars dating back to the 1770s, mostly by its Adivasis. That is over a century before the very formation of the Congress Party. Unfortunately, the fruits of these struggles have not accrued to them but have been expropriated by the contractor-mining businesses, mostly outsiders.

The first major revolt was in 1765 by Baba Tilka Manjhi, a Santhali who was given the Divani of Bengal, Bihar and Odisha by the British. Soon after, the British began demanding lagaan (tax) from the Adivasis. Tilka Manjhi opposed this, and so the British began extracting the tax forcibly. He then organized the 'pahadiya' Adivasis and raised the banner of revolt. He formed an armed force to resist, and killed the Bhagalpur collector, Augustine Cleveland. As a result, the British sent massive forces to capture him dead or alive. He took refuge in the Tilabor Hills (between Latehar and Ranchi districts) where he was caught. The British dragged him (people say tied to a

169

horse) to Baghalpur and hanged him before a huge crowd in the town square. In the same decade there were other revolts too by these 'pahadiya' Adivasis, who two centuries later also supported Subhas Chandra Bose's INA. In the early 1770s the first 'pahadiya revolt' took place under the leadership of one Raman Ullhardi. Under him major parts of Jharkhand burned. After Raman's killing, his chief of staff, Kariya Pujjar, took charge and went underground. He defeated the British forces at Rajmahal at the famous 'Udhva Nallah' where many Santhali revolutionaries joined him. The next revolt took place in 1779 which was led by Rani Shiromani of 'Bagdor Chuar. She united 124 villages and attacked zamindar houses. A major clash occurred in Midnapore, now in West Bengal with British forces in which many British were killed. She was later betrayed, like many other leaders, causing her arrest and subsequent killing.

The Kol Revolt in the 1820s was spearheaded by Uraon, Munda and Ho Adivasis. The revolt spread from Chota Nagpur to the Kolhan region. It was also against British lagan. The zamindars assisted the British. In 1831, the revolt intensified as the British seized Adivasi land and gave it to outsiders. For example, in the Singhbum area they seized the land of 12 villages and gave it to Sikhs. The revolt covered a huge area and its main leaders were Buddhu Bhagat, Singra Manki and Bindrai Manki.

Next came the major revolt of the Santhalis in 1855 which was a precursor to the 1857 sipahi mutiny which had a major impact in the region. It was led by the four youngsters of just one family – the two brothers and two sisters, Siddhu, Kannu, Kanho and Chandbhairav. This came to be known as the famous Santhali Hul. Over 60,000 Santhalis took part in this revolt and in 1855 Siddhu–Kannu declared Santhali Raj. Siddhu–Kannu were later hanged and it is estimated that about 15,000 Santhalis became victims of British bullets.

In 1856 there was the 'Bhavan' revolt of the Santhalis led by Lubiya Manjhi and Bairai Manjhi which spread to neighbouring Purulia district. These all merged with the 1857 mutiny where the Ramgarh military cantonment saw major disturbance which spread to the neighbouring areas as well. Suraj Manjhi, a sipahi, was accused of giving provocative speeches amongst the troops and was sent to Kala Pani on 13 November 1857. Sona Manjhi was sent to Kala Pani on 15 October 1858. Kanchan Singh, a zamindar of Ramga and Chunmun of Hazaribagh, also supported the rebellion. In 1857 the most decisive battle took place in Chatra district where, in early October, 150 revolutionaries were killed. On 4 October 1857, Subehdar Jaimangal and Nadir Ali Khan were hanged and 77 were buried in a pit after being hung from a mango tree. After revolutionaries burnt down the Bangla Coal Factory in Palamu district, which produced very high-quality coal, the British hanged 500 people publicly at Rajghara village. During the 1857 revolt the entire Chota Nagpur and Santhal Parganas were burning in which the Gunju brothers were also involved – Nilamber–Pitamber. Others to be hanged in 1858 were the leaders Thakur Vishwanath Sahadev and Pandey Ganpat Rai from zamindar families. Rai's father was made the divan of Palkot in Chotta Nagpur.

In his youth he saw the close relationship between the British and the zamindars. This angered him as he found his own people betraying the masses, to act as dalals of the British. He led freedom fighters to burn houses of the British, the kutchery, treasury, etc. in Dovanda area. He released prisoners from Ranchi jail. For a full month all of Chota Nagpur was under his control. The British were terrified and moved massive forces against him. While fleeing he reached the house of zamindar Mahesh Shahi who kept him entertained and secretly informed the British. Afterwards he locked him inside his house...

Finally, there was the revolt by Birsa Munda who was arrested in 1900 and brought to Ranchi jail. He died under suspicious circumstances in June and the British disposed of his body secretively.

These heroic battles need to become part of our history textbooks on the freedom struggle.

It was in fact one of my aides in Hazaribagh jail, Narayan Ganju, who first introduced me to the two leaders of his community who raised an army against the British. Ganjus are a major tribe in this Hazaribagh–Chatra–Latehar–Palamu belt. They still revere Nilamber–Pitamber, the two brothers from their clan, who led an armed revolt against the British and zamindars and were finally captured and hanged.

Narayan recounted that the brothers were influenced by the 1857 revolt and fought using traditional weapons for two years. With their forces growing from strength to strength, the British sent massive forces against them from the Ramgarh camp under the top military officer Dalton (till today Daltonganj, named after him, is an important town in the area). They had a narrow escape along the Koel River and reached their sister's village in Latehar. As a huge award had been announced for them a relative informed the British. Too afraid to approach them in the house where they resided as they would have their bows and arrows with them, they waited till they went out to answer the call of nature unarmed, where they surrounded the brothers. Though they fought heroically they were overpowered and hanged publicly from a banyan tree on 28 March 1859. Narayan recounted these details with great pride and told me that even today their martyrdom is celebrated.

Now, before proceeding further we need to look at the lives of the two aides who assisted me during my stay in Hazaribagh jail as they throw much light on the socio-political situation in Jharkhand and bring out some ground-level aspects of the Maoists in the region. Narayan Ganju, who first introduced me to these Adivasi revolts, was one of the two aides who worked for me helping to bring water and other such tasks.

As the superintendent had agreed that I could keep a sevadar I was fortunate that Bajiram Mahato himself offered to do the work – being recently convicted he could get paid by the jail. Unlike undertrials those who have been convicted alone are allowed to work in jail, for which they get a nominal payment directly into their accounts. But he got bail within three months. Fortunately, it was Bajiram who found a replacement – the rare and excellent person, Narayan Ganju, a tribal from a village deep in the forests some 30 kilometre from Hazaribagh, who was serving a life sentence in a false case, due to lack of proper legal help.

Tale of Two Aides

First take the life and death of Bajiram Mahato. The Mahatos are the largest caste (Kurmis) in Jharkhand after the tribals. He was about 30 years old, illiterate and unmarried. He was from the neighbouring district of Ramgarh and was drawn to the Naxals in his childhood being part of the Jharkhand Avon (cultural wing) of the Maoist Communist Centre (MCC) from 1995 to 2002. He recounted that in those days there was a sweep of the then MCC. He said the MCC virtually captured support of all the tribal belts of the state mainly because they took up the anti-Mahajan struggles which the Jharkhand Mukti Morcha (JMM) had discontinued after entering electoral politics. As he grew up, he joined the squads and later rose to become the deputy commander in the Area Committee till 2006, after which he was section commander in the platoon till 2008. He maintained it was his obsession of wielding a gun that drew him to the Naxals. Though illiterate, he was very sharp and street smart. He could manage anyone and any situation, having few scruples. Yet instinctively, he was drawn to honest people and he disliked those who were crooked, however good they were at sweet talking.

He had apparently deserted the movement in about 2008 and formed his own gang. He left the Maoists with the complaint, like that of many others, that the leadership had become very bureaucratic and intolerant. The final straw that broke his conviction, he said, was that money that they themselves gathered in sacks and delivered to their leaders without touching a paisa; was not used in any developmental work in the village. What was worse, they felt, was that when they (or their families) were in need, nothing was given to them, even if they needed to rebuild huts broken by the police. He himself had asked for some money for his sister's marriage which was denied.

Once he started operating his own gang, it appears that he was betrayed by one of his gang members and it was a person whom they had kidnapped for extortion who gave evidence against him which landed him in jail with a life sentence. Though he had been about 6-7 years in jail, his single aim was to somehow get out and form a big gang. He had dreams of becoming Jharkhand's top gangster. In fact, his close friend, Rajan, who too was a one-time Maoist, and had earned a few crore with the sand mafia, used some of his money to get himself out. Rajan was a very social and helpful person (it was he who assisted me too) but within days of his release he was killed by the TPC gang (his own associates) who were after the money and the sand contract.

The trouble with these gangs is that however nice the person, the goal of each member is to make the maximum money. Survival is therefore extremely difficult unless one is ruthless and very alert, as one can be done in by one's right hand out of greed. At one level there is no job opportunity for the educated youth and being part of a gang can sometimes be the only decent source of income, giving one access to a reasonable middle-class life. Otherwise, survival for these youth is difficult, and that is why we see Jharkhand labour all over the country.

Yet such a life is dangerous and survival difficult unless one is big-time with all the political and police connections. The first threat is from one's very right-hand people who would like to take over the leadership of the gang. There are many such cases. There is also gang warfare over territory, which has led to the wiping out of many top gang leaders. The third threat is that the target and/or police can bribe one's own gang member, which seems to have happened in the case of Bajiram. Fourth, unless the person is very big, they are targets of the police as well. Besides, the bulk of these big gang leaders were either from Rajput, Bumihar or Brahmin castes. Those from the other castes, like Bajiram, seem to have little chance.

Bajiram got bail and within about one month was in the news for having killed the person who gave evidence against him and sent him to jail on a life sentence. Next, he gave an open challenge that he would target a notorious BJP minister from his area who was hated by the people for usurping their land for a private water project. By taking on such a big target he himself became targeted and within another month he was killed in what appeared to be a fake encounter by the cops – seemingly betrayed by his own people.

As far as I was concerned his sense of responsibility was such that before he left the jail, he made sure I had a good replacement in Narayan Ganju. When I had asked the Maoists, they claimed they knew no one who could help. Narayan Ganju was a totally different kettle of fish from Bajiram. He was about 35, with a wife and two little daughters – the younger one was hardly a few months old when he was sent to jail.

Narayan belongs to Neerie village in Hazaribagh district 10 kilometre from the Keredari police station. It is about 20 kilometre from the gigantic coal belt stretching from Barkagaon to Keredari and beyond (said to have the largest coal deposits in the world). Neerie was deep in the forests with about 40 huts (families) on the Hazaribagh–Ranchi–Chatra tri-junction and far from any other villages. He said when he was a child and the MCC entered this area in the early 1990s this village became a natural stronghold due to its location – it was on a small plateau and surrounded by hills and rivulets on all sides. It was also on the route to major Maoist strongholds like Buddha Pahar, Jumra Pahar, and others in the area.

In the 1980s there was a landlord with 14 acres – it was owned by the Maharaja (who had such land all over the region) – Yashwant Sinha's family – called Majhar land and worked upon by a Mahatao from Barkagaon 20 kilometre away. The then Maharaja of the Hazaribagh area owned and controlled several such tracts of land through which he took a tribute which he shared with the British. The Ramgarh Raj was a major zamindari estate ruled by the Narain dynasty. Territories which comprised the Ramgarh Raj presently constitute the districts of Ramgarh, Hazaribagh, Chatra, Giridih, Koderma, and Bokaro. The first king was Maharaja Baghdeo Singh (1368–1402) and the last king was Maharaja Kamakhya Narain Singh (1919–1953). The revenue of the estate ₹36 lakhs in those days and the first family were the only ones to use helicopters in their election campaign. People who worked on this land were paid 1.5 kilos of rice per day which was later raised to 5 kilos when the MCC arrived. In addition, there was a Rajput from Keredari who would come off and on and would forcibly take away crops, chicken, goats, from all. One day sometime in 1993–94, Narayan said, when he came the MCC cadre happened to be present. He was publicly flogged and humiliated. He never returned. The Raja's land, on the other hand, was distributed, with the understanding that a quarter of the produce would be kept for the party. Later, Narayan said, when the movement declined, as no official documents were made, though the land was being used by the villagers, they could not sustain it as the land was sold by the original owner in whose name the land had been registered.

With these steps taken against the Zamindar–Mahajans the villagers began to grow enough crops for the year, which was supplemented by labour and a lot of forest produce. According to Narayan, Neerie became a fortress for the Maoists in the late 1990s, where they would stay for months conducting their programmes. Yet no attempt was ever made to do any developmental work – whether in irrigation/ agriculture, health, medicine or education, nor fishery given the large number of ponds and streams in the area. Narayan and others would say that the MCC swept the entire area in the 1990s and built on the earlier movements of the JMM against the Zamindar–Mahajan combine. After the traditional Zamindars and Mahajans were uprooted, the party did not seem to have any new programme, and post 2002 the decline began. Also, arrogant with their successes, many wrong traits of domination, bureaucracy, arbitrariness, crept in according to Narayan and also many others. He would recount that when he was in school the cadres would come and mix with them. At that time, they had neither money nor guns. Yet, before their very eyes, as they grew in strength, and as the power they wielded grew, these same cadres, now leaders at different levels, would behave completely differently.

Hearing the accounts of the Maoists in this area I began to see the same story repeated that I had heard in Vishaka jail of the Orissa movement. The essence seems that power and money tend to corrupt, particularly under pressure. In Orissa it was the tribal leader Linga and his coterie, while here it was the very party cadres themselves, also mostly from tribal backgrounds, but non-tribals as well. The leadership, it seems, turned a blind eye to the faults of a mass leader like Linga, probably enamoured by his prowess in mass organization building. Here, they probably turned a blind eye as these cadre were apparently proficient in military matters. In both cases the limitations in the outlook of the local leaders was never considered or sought to be changed. Bhushanam had said that in Odisha the obvious faults of Linga were ignored like functioning through a coterie and pushing the non-class approach of attacking even poor non-tribals. More on this in the next section.

Narayan studied till the 5th standard and was associated with the Bal Sangam (children's organization) in the village but never joined the Maoists actively. He had to leave school after that, as economic conditions did not allow him to continue studies; besides the higher school was in a village quite far off. A few years later Narayan took his own initiative to form a committee of about 10-12 youth for developmental work. They first took up fish-breeding on a cooperative basis. Later, they took up developmental work approaching the local BDO, who was enthused by the young group, and allocated some projects to this committee. It was this that first irritated the dalals of the area seeing their source of income threatened. By 2006–07, with a school being built in his sister's village through shramdan at his initiative and numerous other developmental activities, Narayan's rising stature in the entire area, was noticed by the dalals who

178

decided to take action. In 2008 they schemed, not only beat him up, but also involved him in a murder case, allegedly committed by themselves to settle a land dispute. With their money and influence in the corridors of power they managed the police, lawyers and court staff, dragging the case on for ten years until finally he was given life imprisonment. Till recently he was in his thirteenth year in jail. His only crime: he attempted genuine development in the area cutting off the potential funds to the corrupt and dalals. Fortunately, when I was released, I requested my high court lawyer to take his case up. In spite of the lockdown, in September 2020, Jitendra Singh was able to get Narayan's life sentence reduced to ten years and he was finally released.

Apparently, getting innocents stuck in false cases is rampant in the villages of Jharkhand. I will give just one more example. Another young tribal was in jail on a murder charge. The story went that he had taken the village cattle to the forest for grazing. While returning in the evening he saw a cycle lying on the ground unattended. Thinking it must belong to some drunk from his village he took it along, but no one claimed it. On the third day the village chowkidar, a non-tribal, came with the police and had him arrested for murder, as the owner of the cycle was a cloth trader whose body had been discovered a few kilometres away. Though the trader was from a far-off village, some phones were planted in his house which they claimed belonged to the man killed. The trial went on for two years without him getting bail. Finally, when it was shown that the phones did not belong to the trader, he was granted bail. Obviously, someone had a conflict with the trader and killed him and using the services of the chowkidar and police they implicated an innocent tribal. As it was a clumsy job he came out, but if the genuine phones had been planted, he would probably

179

have been given a life sentence. As it is, he wasted two years in jail and paid enormous fees to the lawyer, in which too he was duped. Such stories were sadly very common inside Hazaribagh jail.

Having viewed a wide spectrum of political activists who were in jail, now for the big-time dons of North India.

Dons and Others

Several Bollywood films have been inspired by the Chambal Valley dacoits and the dons of Dhanbad, most recently the film *Sonchiriya*. Most of them romanticize the lives of these 'rebels' which are, no doubt, quite colourful. I met quite a few of the major dons of North India in Tihar and Jharkhand jails and got an insight into their lives and the conditions that drove them in this direction. Fortunately, I was able to see them from close quarters. What I could gather was that they were part of, and also victims of, the prevailing feudal ethos in the Hindi belt where feudal authority, backed by arms, reigns supreme. Most were victims of this power equation, and then they themselves acquired feudal authority of their own, based on their gangs and fire-power.

When I present them relatively positively it is only in comparison with many a politician or bureaucrat/official. While the former make no claims of advancing the nation or improving society, the latter do, so one would have expected greater decency from them, but I found most of these dons had healthier ethics than most of our public servants.

The Dons

There were two big dons – Delhi's notorious Kishan Pehlwan and one Fazlu Rehman – in my ward in Tihar, and I happened to be put in a cell with the former on my very first night in jail.

Kishan Pehlwan (KP) was famous for the many murders he had reportedly committed and his close connection with the Chautala political family of Haryana. He was feared by all and was said to own large amounts of land, mostly believed to be seized from others, and wealth worth over ₹100 crore. He was said to be implicated in over 80 murder cases. He belonged to Dichau village on the Haryana–Delhi border.

Kishan Pehlwan had a running battle with one Uday Vir and his family, who were the richest people in the neighbouring village. They were more educated and social and linked with the Anna Hazare movement. The latter made many attempts on Kishan Pehlwan's life to revenge the many killings in their family, and finally in 2015 they killed KP's brother and MLA of the Indian National Lok Dal (INLD), in his office in broad daylight.

I met KP and was with him for about a month when I entered jail in 2009. He then went out on bail. Apparently, the war between the two families was still on at the time I left Tihar in June 2016 when Kishan Phelwan had again come to jail, where I met him briefly. By then Om Prakash Chautala and his son Ajay, were serving an eight-year sentence on corruption charges, and their clout outside too had reduced so they had become a relatively weakened force.

Also present at the time of entry into Tihar, in another cell, was Fazlu Rehman, who attained notoriety for a case involving the Bollywood star Shilpa Shetty. As the story goes a Surat business house had refused to pay Shetty ₹2 crores for modelling work she had done for them. So she hired Fazlu to retrieve her dues. Fazlu was soon transferred to Gujarat jails from Tihar, as it was there that he had most of his cases.

With KP there was nothing much to talk about, as he was a typical Haryana Jat who was least interested in the world outside and secretive (as they all are) about their activities. I got to know more about him from others. Others would fawn over him as he was the biggest don at that time in the Delhi–Haryana region. Fazlu, on the other hand, was quite the opposite. Unassuming, not throwing his weight around and interested in other matters. I remember him spending enormous time collecting jamuns from the trees in the compound, drying the seeds and crushing them to make a powder which he said was very good for his diabetes.

Besides these two, there were two others I met in the course of my stay in Jail 3 before transfer in 2013. One was from U.P. who I got to know well, the other was from Haryana.

I spent over one year from mid-2013 to mid-2014 living with UP's (and probably India's) top-most don, Brijesh Singh, and his close associate, Tribhoovan Singh, both originally from the Benaras area. It is said that he was transferred from Benaras jail to Tihar at the behest of his main rival in UP, Mukhtar Ansari on a vague MOCOCA case (a Maharashtra law against organised crime). When Jail 3 HRW closed down for repairs we moved together to Jail 1 and occupied a ward together, as I've described earlier.

Though roughly in his late forties, Brijesh Singh was very fit and every morning would do four rounds of 80 press-ups (dips). Tribhoovan and myself would do a combination of yoga and exercises in the block. Brijesh was aloof by nature, yet cordial, while Tribhoovan was warm and friendly. The five of us would have lunch together ordered from the canteen. The two were very close, like brothers. I gathered from others that Tribhoovan was so close to Brijesh that he got himself arrested after the latter was jailed in order to assist/protect him. Both appeared very polite and one could not imagine that Brijesh was worth thousands of crores and had an empire stretching from UP, to Bihar, Jharkhand (Dhanbad), Chhattisgarh and beyond. In fact, Brijesh said he stayed incognito in Odisha for 22 years, before getting caught. Information that his children were studying at Welham School was leaked, and he was apprehended as he went to meet them. This was many years ago, as he had been in jail for some years now. At the time he came to Tihar, they were grown up and studying at Mithibai College Mumbai, while his wife was an MLC on a BSP ticket from Benaras. It was 2014 and the Modi wave was sweeping north India; like most of the big dons Brijesh and family too were Modi fans, however they were not in the least bit communal. Both were quite superstitious and god-fearing. On his way to the court hearing there were many things he would do to avoid invoking bad luck.

It is said that whenever they went to court, not only did they have a huge posse of police, but also a bus load of his own people who came from UP for his protection. Such were the threat perceptions around these big dons.

Brijesh entered this world of crime to take revenge for his father's killing, as the police did little to bring the guilty to book. This is quite common in UP (and Bihar) where feudal elements crush those perceived to challenge their unquestioned authority. Most stay quiet and accept their domination, some retaliate. To survive in the bad-lands of UP Brijesh had to form his own gang. The rest, of course, is history.

The other big don from UP whom I had briefly met in the Tis Hazari lock-up, was Munna Bajrangi, the right hand of Mukhtar Ansari, and a top don (sharp-shooter) of UP in his own right. He was quite a knowledgeable sort. In 2018, Munna Bajrangi was shot dead in Baghpat jail, with the authorities turning a blind eye. Revolvers getting into UP and Bihar jails is not uncommon, I was told.

The person who allegedly shot him was one Sunil Rathi who had been in the same HRW as me during my last four months at Tihar. Rathi was probably one of the most socially conscious dons I met from north India. He belonged to the West UP Mahendra Singh Tikait belt, and his village was near Meerut. His father was a close associate of Charan Singh and a kisaan leader. He had a good knowledge of the kisaan movement of Tikait and their problems. His father too was killed by landlords and the culprits were soon roaming free after a brief stint in jail. Rathi was still young but he took revenge and killed all three, and later formed a gang in order to survive. He was soon arrested and sentenced to life imprisonment. He had come to Tihar from Uttarakhand jails where he had been lodged for the past thirteen years, as he was allegedly involved in the killing of two oppressive jailors there.

Though West UP had become the major school for the promotion of Hindutva and was used by the BJP to launch itself in the entire state, Rathi was not at all communal and he said in fact his Jat-dominated village had protected Muslims escaping mobs. During the days we were together, in mid-2016, elections were being held in UP and Rathi was desperately gathering money to get his mother a BSP ticket. (Later while in Hyderabad jail, I heard she had got a ticket but lost in the BJP sweep.) His calculation was that a 20 per cent Dalit vote, plus half the Muslim and Jat votes, was a sure-shot winning formula. Rathi shifted into my cell at Tihar when I left for Hyderabad jail. He gave me his new Adidas sandals and slippers when he saw mine were torn. How he was involved in the Munna Bajrangi killing one doesn't know. He would recount nostalgically about the Tikait Kisaan movement and how his two sons were relatively ineffective, unlike their father. Though, in present farmers' agitation they seem to have regained the status of their father.

In all these cases it seems the ruthlessness of the feudal elite had pushed people into the underworld to survive against the lawlessness of the region. When they become a power unto themselves, they seemed to take on a feudal authority of their own, with a sort of Robin-Hood type image – popular folk heroes in their own right. Though they don't necessarily give to the poor, they are said to spend on people's weddings and also on religious functions in a big way. They are feared, yet respected, and most politicians, I was told, depend on them to gain support amongst the people, particularly during elections.

If we now turn to the Haryana Dons the most famous was what was known as the Jajjhar gang from Rohtak, led by Raj Kumar (RK) and Kale. They too came to the crime world to fight the terror of a local sarpanch of RK's village who was backed by a senior police official and the then ruling Congress party. It was to retaliate against the terror of this sarpanch's family that they formed a gang and began eliminating rival members. They got their name from the famous attack on a police van near Jajjhar, in which the three brothers inside were killed but not a single policeman harmed. There were other Haryana dons like Bawana in the jail too, but these were more lumpen elements, not worthy of comment.

The Dons of Jharkhand

Jharkhand state is rich in natural resources and has huge deposits of minerals; not only coal and iron ore, but also mica, limestone, precious metals, uranium, stone quarries, besides sand mining. All mining is now done through contractors who hire sub-contractors who further hire contractual labour. This applies to the public sector companies and the private ones. With such huge contracts in mining, a mining mafia is born which generates massive amounts of black money. This contractualization is not just limited to mining, it is seen in all spheres of industrial as well as service activities. It is to be seen in the railways (loading, construction, repair, servicing), road, irrigation and other construction, also in education, health care, every sphere of economic activity the same story is repeated. A large proportion of the money generated is thus black, with the paradoxical result that Jharkhand is one of the wealthiest and one of the poorest states.

For example, Vaidyanath Mahatao, brother of a JMM MLA, who was with me in Tenughat jail, estimated that over 40 per cent of coal production gets siphoned into the black market. Subsequently, this black money goes towards bribing one and all, bureaucrats, politicians, police, village-level officials, and the Maoists too. It results in a de facto criminalization of society and people's values. Not surprisingly over 50 per cent of jail inmates are dowry death and women-related cases. Quite naturally, in such an atmosphere, dons flourish. In fact, it is difficult to tell where business ends and crime begins. The line is thin.

Here in Hazaribagh jail my neighbour in the hospital premises was Titu (Amit) Sharma, one of Jharkhand's biggest dons after Akhilesh Singh (who was in Dumka jail). Like the dons of Tihar, Titu seemed a more pleasant sort than most politicians and certainly, ten times more so than many of the Ravani-types (jail mafia) or even some of the Maoists.

Being neighbours and finding him a pleasant jovial sort I enjoyed his company. He would also give me a picture of life in Jharkhand and how business operated. He was also very helpful when he learnt I did not know anyone in Jharkhand. He had very high BP and back pain and I taught him yoga which helped his pains immensely. In the later stages we would do it together. It was he who in the winter gave me some warm clothes and made arrangements for hot water when the solar heating system collapsed.

His main areas of operation were the railways, mostly in Odisha, taking contracts. Apparently most contracts in this region were given at gunpoint and/or with heavy bribes. I call him a 'gentleman don' as he has a wife and two children and is a dog/animal lover. He apparently has a huge home in Jamshedpur which has dogs, cats, pigeons, and monkeys. His support base is in the neighbouring railway colony where people are said to idolise him, particularly the women, as he has a reputation of keeping the loafers away and protecting young girls. Many mothers, he said, turn to him, and not the police, when their college going daughters are being harassed. Though he is a Modi supporter and his right hand an RSS supporter he too was in no way communal. Of course, being a Bumihar, originally from Bihar, he has intense religious feelings with a strong Bumihar identity. He would say that if the police officers who arrested him were from his caste, they would invariably take a soft approach. He was a happy-go-lucky type who loved his drink. His close associate in jail was one Vickey Sharma serving a life sentence, a quiet and helpful person. It was a real advantage to have them as neighbours in the jail. If it hadn't been for Titu my Hazaribagh jail stay would have been terrible. In him I not only had good company but also lot of assistance and sometimes good food as well.

Lastly, we have the numerous groups that broke away from the Maoists around 2008 and became part of the underworld, extorting money. The biggest and most notorious was the TPC (Tritya Prastuti Committee), Chatra-based, but wielding influence in the entire region. It comprises mostly Ganjus and, as I mentioned earlier, many of the top leaders were relatives of Narayan. It is led by one Brajesh Ganju whose brother was a BJP MLA. While speaking to them in jail they said that during 2003–04 one top leader of the MCC, Bharatji, broke away and formed a legal organization in Chatra district. But the then MCC) there apparently wiped them out. It was then that they formed the TPC, built basically along the same military lines as the Maoists, by those earlier arrested when released from jail around 2008. They are known for their ruthlessness not only against the Maoists but also against all other groups or anyone who disturbs their fiefdom.

A particularly notorious incident people recount was the killing of 10-12 Maoists, including many leaders around 2013. Apparently the two groups had just agreed to a ceasefire. Maoists had been called by the TPC for talks, and during that they were disarmed and ruthlessly gunned down. Others would say that they acted as the front paw of the big coal contractors of Chatra – Amrapalli and Magadh (contractors for CCL) – soon spreading their tentacles to the notorious Triveni Sainik (contractors for NTPC) in the Barkagaon area of Hazaribagh district. The TPC had control over all the coal activities in the area, whether railway sidings, coal transport, or other key money-spinning activities. Lately, some of their top leaders have been targeted and brought to jail, surprisingly by the NIA. The reason is unknown but may have something to do with conflict amongst the contractors; besides, the Maoists are no longer a force in the area and therefore not required for that purpose.

The TPC is just one such group; there are numerous smaller ones like JPC, JJMP, and others. There was a world of difference between the gangsters/dons and these TPC-type groups. The former were gangs formed by individuals who faced, at some time in their life, atrocities to which the state turned a blind eye. Many had lost their close relatives to feudal terror which remained unpunished. To avenge the killings, they would retaliate, and survival thenceforth depended on the formation of gangs and living life on the fringes. On the other hand, the TPC-types were mostly tribals, disillusioned by the revolutionary movement, who de facto became vigilante groups acting at the behest of the police to counter the Maoists, as well as hatchet-men for the mining contractors. Though both groups tend to be ruthless in dealing with those they are threatened by, the former seemed to have some ethics of their own, whereas the latter were utterly unscrupulous.

The proliferation of such elements in the bad lands of the Hindi belt can be a subject for sociological study. This becomes more relevant in the light of the Dubey encounters in the Kanpur region. In this case too, Dubey seemed to have top connections as he had prior information of the police raid. As the government would have had to act as so many policemen were killed, this could have resulted in him opening his mouth and indicating his links and connections. The government was stuck, as in many of such cases – if they did not act harshly the police force would be discontented; if they did act, he would squeal. Best alternative was therefore probably to act as they finally did – eliminate him. Most of the big dons that I met are also said to have top political connections, but they would not speak about it.

Judicial Procedures and Lawyers

In most democracies, people are jailed only after conviction but here in India, the jails are packed with undertrials more than convicts; people imprisoned even before they have been proven guilty. And because the judicial process is so slow, many of them end up spending years in jail. This is the starting point of the injustice in our legal system.

The fact that judicial procedures are so slow and long-drawn-out was the main reason for my lengthy incarceration. Moreover, as an undertrial getting bail in UAPA cases is extremely difficult, even though I was eventually acquitted in case after case. And this was in spite of my having good legal advice, and on the whole reasonably fair judges.

Of course, the judiciary also entails the bulk of the legal profession, many of whom, according to inmates, would cheat their clients even after taking fabulous fees; often consciously delaying cases in order to retain their regular payments. With cases dragging on endlessly due to lack of proper legal assistance, often resulting in harsh sentences, the system is a veritable nightmare for most inmates, who have little access to the legal resources. Even with the good legal resources and fair judges I was fortunate to have, there was one case in Delhi (out of 18 in the country) that dragged on for nearly seven years. What others face can well be imagined; of course, conditions in the South were generally somewhat better.

My lawyers in Delhi were a team led by the senior advocate Rebecca John, who normally does not practice in the sessions court. She and her juniors were extremely professional and did a thorough job in their preparations and arguments, all pro bono. Also helping out at jail visits and coordinating with this team were first the Andhra Pradesh lawyers who had settled in Delhi, advocates Dashrath and advocates K.D. Rao. Particularly from Mumbai there was the highly committed lawyer, the late P.A. Sabastian, who took a leading role in organizing advocates for my release. He gave up an elite existence in Kerala and became one of the most committed human rights lawyers in the country living a frugal existence in the YMCA hostel, though he had polio in both legs. Some of his arguments in the Mumbai courts make history. They were not only advocates, but also personally helpful in every possible way. They were human rights lawyers who never considered charging fees. Both were a real godsend and have continued helping in the Andhra Pradesh and Telangana cases. After they returned to Andhra Pradesh, advocates Sandeep Vishnu and his team (advocates Anilji and daughter Mahek) took over and continued while I was in Delhi, very systematically coming to the jail and coordinating with the senior lawyers. At a later stage of the case when we had some problems with a lawyer arguing for my co-accused, Rajender Kumar, advocate Priyanka Kakkar, offered to take up the case and it was she who actively intervened in the court when I went on a hunger strike. At that late stage she played an invaluable role as the earlier lawyer was dragging the arguments unnecessarily and had already set the case back by months. The co-accused, Rajender Kumar (who had rented the room at Molarband Extension, Badarpur), only had 420-related charges on him with UAPA being dropped, had already served the maximum possible sentence so there was no point in the lengthy arguments.

As already mentioned, the judges too were basically fair. They were also sensitive to my health needs. Take for example when I needed a cataract operation. It was judge P.K. Jain who showed concern. As I had heard some in Tihar had lost their eye sight in the process of surgery, I requested for a private hospital. He said that was impossible and he could order that it be done at AIIMS; which he did. After the operation was over, he enquired how it went and who the doctor was. When I mentioned Dr. Tityal, he responded 'Oh, you are in famous company, he also did the operation of Vajpayee'. It was true Dr. Tityal, was extremely professional, and completed the operation in a matter of minutes.

When all the cases of the Special Cell were shifted to a special court (earlier they were spread out in various courts of Delhi) at the Patiala House Court, a judge was appointed who had a terrible image. The Special Cell (like ATS, etc in other places) is a special police force in Delhi to deal with terrorist-linked cases and those of high-profile organized crime. Suddenly, within six months this judge died of a heart attack and Judge Reetesh Singh was appointed. He was also equally sensitive and would often notice I was unwell and unsteady on my feet and would go out of his way to enquire after me. He would sometimes scold the inspector when they would not allow me to speak to relatives or the lawyer. On one occasion I remember he told a particularly nasty inspector, 'You allow Bawana (a don) to speak for hours sitting at the back of the court and you are not allowing him even five minutes.' When all the witnesses had been examined, he went to the extent of granting me interim bail of three months on health grounds though this was a UAPA case. Finally, he acquitted me of the main UAPA charges while finding me guilty of the 420-related charges of impersonation. The decision came very suddenly. I was not expecting it, and on hearing the acquittal on the main charge I smiled, looking pleased; he said, probably feeling bad, what are you smiling for, it has taken so very long. I replied that the acquittal could help my cases elsewhere.

With the main Delhi case over I was immediately shifted to Cherlapally Central Jail in Hyderabad, Telangana where 11 FIRs against me were pending.

In early 2010, soon after my initial arrest at Delhi, the Andhra Pradesh police took me from Tihar on a production warrant to the Karimnagar court in Telangana in a general conspiracy case. There I was given a day's police custody. I was kept in a police guest house and spent the day watching TV. In the afternoon two men came in civilian dress and began asking me questions. When I demanded that my lawyers be produced as the court had mandated so, they immediately disappeared. Next day in the court a 'confession' statement was produced in Telugu (a language I do not know) with those two signing as witnesses. I immediately denied in the court having made any statement and also put it in the court records. Yet no action was taken for contempt of court, on the contrary this statement was used to add my name onto 12 ongoing cases, some going as far back as 1996. Though this is illegal as per the Evidence Act (statements in police custody cannot be used in court), it was this statement that was used to make cases in all the 12 cases.

Later I was again brought to Andhra Pradesh and produced in two of these cases – one in Mehboobnagar district of Telangana where 10 people were killed including an MLA on 15 August 2005 by alleged Naxals. In the charge sheet it is mentioned that the case relates to the killing of Narsi Reddy (MLA) and nine of his bodyguards while he was inaugurating a new road. The CPI (Maoists) cadre allegedly came on

194

two motorcycles and fired at random. The other was a case in Srikakulam, about 100 kilometre from Visakhapatnam in present-day Andhra Pradesh, which is still ongoing.

On my return trip I was surprised I was taken to Hyderabad Airport, considering that all the three earlier to-and-fro trips were done by train. When I enquired as to the reason the inspector informed me that today's Telugu papers carried a news item that there was a plan by Naxals to rescue me, while the train passed through North Telangana on its way to Delhi. As far as I knew the movement in North Telangana had totally collapsed and the police had, for years, been taking credit for it. The inspector, who was friendly, said he knew nothing else about the issue. When we went to the airport the authorities demanded the ministerial permission which is mandatory while taking a prisoner. Many hours were spent in somehow making it to the aircraft, as the airport authorities were adamant on a written permission, particularly given the newspaper headlines. We later parked the van in a public ground while the police sought to get the permission hoping to take the evening flight. In the hours we spent together the inspector asked at length about the state of the Indian economy and investment opportunities and requested me to talk to his wife on the phone on the issue. Finally, when they could not organize it, I was taken back to jail and we took the next day's flight back. Being surrounded by police personnel during these flights was very awkward as most of the onlooking passengers tend to connect police with dangerous criminals. Fortunately, I was never handcuffed.

That was in 2010, but I could not be produced in these cases again as by then 268 of the CrPC had been put on me which states: that I cannot be produced in any other state until the Delhi case gets over... apparently due to the threat of escape.

For this a similar drama was repeated, on a far bigger scale during a production at Midnapore in West Bengal. In this incident I was in fact offloaded from the train at Allahabad, and taken to a police station under massive security. I could not understand what was going on. The next day I was flown back to Delhi, without being produced, and at the airport there was a massive posse of police with all the top officials of the Special Cell present. I was driven back to Tihar under huge police escort. It was only the next day, on reading the newspapers, that I realized this same drama had been repeated – that there was a plan to hijack the train and release me. Soon after, not surprisingly, the same 268 which prevents my attending cases outside Delhi as long as the Delhi case is on, was clamped on me. Yet another scheme to delay my court proceedings. I complained to the NHRC about this stage-managed reason to clamp 268 on me, thereby denying my basic right to a speedy trial, but there was no response.

By mid-2016, not expecting a quick order in Delhi, the judge and lawyers had said that I was free to go to Telangana (268 imposed by the Delhi government had also been lifted in October 2015). Given that all the witnesses had been examined and even the 313 statement (i.e. my answer to the judge's final queries) was over, the judge said as I was no longer needed in the Delhi case. The judge had said that the order could even be given in my absence. Imagine my shock when, on 9 June 2016, just a few days before the courts were to close for the summer vacations, the Honourable Judge issued his order, acquitting me of all the UAPA charges which were Naxalite related and finding me guilty only on the 420-related charges of impersonation: of using a fake voter ID card and a false name while visiting doctors for medical treatment. He also stated in the order that the two – UAPA and the 420 charges – were in no way linked.

So, it was only in June 2016 that I was finally produced in the Narayanpet court in Mehboobnagar district (I had never heard of the place Narayanpet). The judge was very cooperative when I mentioned that travelling such distances would further damage my slip disc and spondylitis. He very kindly said there was no need to come and, if necessary, he would speak to me by videoconferencing. He disposed of the case in eight months and did not once call me to the court. He did speak to me through videoconferencing twice, but more to enquire about my health. Even the 313 statement was taken that way and finally in February 2017 I was acquitted.

I was also produced in the far away courts by the police in FIRs lodged on me in Karimnagar, Bellampalli, Adilabad and Achampet with none of the commando type paraphernalia used in Delhi. Except for the two cases in Adilabad (where the magistrate refused to issue the production warrant as the case, which he felt, was ridiculous) in all the other seven cases the police did not file charge sheets so I was given default bail after 90 days. In the two Adilabad cases the police challenged the dismissal in the sessions court but this too was dismissed in February 2017. The Adilabad cases (Sirpur) pertain to an alleged confession by a CC member, Malla Raji Reddy, who allegedly just mentioned my name in the list of politburo members during the police interrogation where they claimed the plan to attack the police station was hatched, without any evidence of a resolution or statement by the CC to that effect. The case entailed attacks on police stations by Maoists in 1996 and 1998, both of which years I had travelled abroad to attend conferences. The Achampet cases are of a similar type; where my name has merely been added to four ongoing cases dating back to the early 2000s.

Amidst these cases the Patiala court in Punjab had sent a number of production warrants to Hyderabad jail. As my cases were proceeding in Mehboobnagar, I was not sent there. In October 2016, the honourable judge sent a stern note that if, this time, I was not produced the superintendent should appear in person. I was taken all the way by train, expecting to return immediately after production.

At the court, human rights activist lawyer, advocate Aarti was present from Chandigarh who had requested Patiala's senior most advocate, Brajendra Singh Sodhi to do the arguments. When I offered him money, he said he had a strong belief in the Guru Granth Sahib and the work we were doing was similar to that of the Gurus, so how could he possibly take money. We had expected to be merely presented in court and immediately return to Hyderabad. We were, in fact, quite shocked when we found the judge insisting that we remain there in Patiala jail and the case be completed. I conjectured up a nightmarish situation of the case dragging on and on, with all my Telangana cases held up and in a totally alien atmosphere. I was sent to Patiala jail with the judge instructing that my health was bad and I be given proper facilities. I was taken to the hospital which had excellent facilities.

To my utter surprise the judge gave daily schedules and Sodhi saheb tried his best to be present in spite of a heavy burden of other cases. The normal routine was that I would be brought in the morning and stay till about 4 p.m. waiting either for a witness or advocate Sodhi to come around. The judge did not relent with any of the witnesses and if they did not come scolded the police and passed on giving them one more chance. He wrapped up the case within a month.

The media in Punjab were particularly interested in the case. On the very first day there was a pack of journalists waiting in the court so the police tried to take me through the back staircase, but they were everywhere. They were also present on the final day in large numbers. I normally avoid the press as my case has had the aspect of a media trial where it was propagated that I was a big Maoist leader. As mere membership entails life imprisonment, what would be the sentence of a 'leader'? On this occasion, on our way out of the court I did speak to the journalists present asking them to at least now print how I was time and again being vindicated of the charges against me. Till then there was a veritable media trial accusing me everywhere of being a top leader of the Maoists despite my acquittals in all Maoist charges. Later, I gathered they presented the facts as stated in the court.

Back in Hyderabad jail all the cases were completed by February 2017 but it took two months to shift to Visakhapatanam. In all jails one is at the mercy of the authorities and even in the more efficient state like Telangana it took two months to organize the shift. That de facto meant two extra months in jail for no reason. Though I already had bail in this case (upheld by the Supreme Court), as I did not fancy travelling regularly from Mumbai for the hearings, and the lawyers there assured me it would be completed in a couple of months, given that all others had been acquitted, I thought to complete this while in jail. Besides, the conditions in jail were a replica of Hyderabad and the superintendent turned out to be an extremely progressive and honest person.

As it turned out the judge was hell bent on delaying the proceedings; first re-calling all the 60 witnesses (most of whom did not turn up), and spending over two months tracing the I.O. (Investigative Officer), who had retired and settled in Visakhapatnam itself. When, even after the IO was examined, he continued calling witnesses, I felt this could go on endlessly and decided to take the bail, especially as my prostrate/ urinary problem was aggravated. For each hearing two very committed advocates would appear at no cost. Advocate K.S. Chelam worked full time doing all such cases free while his wife earned an income working as a clerk in the court. The senior advocate Appa Rao, was a retired Dock employee and a very committed lawyer. I finally took the bail and was released from jail on the evening of 12 December 2017.

Re-arrest and Unconstitutional Methods of the State

While in jail there were still two FIRs pending for which production warrants had not been issued. The background to these FIRs was that they had been served when I was in Tihar and 268 CrPC was still applicable (the law forbidding a person from being moved from the prison where they are as long as order is in force). After it was vacated in October 2015 all courts issued production warrants and all cases advanced, except those from Jharkhand and Surat. In fact, it was only when I was awarded three months interim bail in the Delhi case that the Delhi government and police withdrew the order.

When I came to Hyderabad jail, I waited six months for these production warrants, but neither of the two came. As nothing arrived, at the advice of the lawyers, a legal notice was sent through the Cherlapally jail superintendent in November 2016 to the magistrates of the two courts in Jharkhand and Surat, which stated to either take KG's production or else he will have to be released as all cases were fast concluding. As there was no response, in March 2017 the superintendent sent another reminder putting greater emphasis on the issue. Still no reply.

Meanwhile, I was transferred to Visakhapatnam jail where the lawyers advised that as the two courts were not responding to our appeals for production, they, most probably, were no longer interested. Yet, as a precautionary measure I went to the Supreme Court to prevent possible arrest later. Though the case was argued by India's top advocates, Fali Nariman and Colin Gonsalves, the bench headed by Justice Arun Mishra was not inclined to accept the Appeal so the SLP (Special Leave Petition) was withdrawn. Fali had himself offered my family to do the case while Colin was a friend whom I knew from the time he was in Mumbai. Though the appeal sighted old age and health conditions and also gave copies of the applications to the courts for production which were ignored, and, in addition sighted many other similar cases, and Fali Nariman himself argued in person, the judge was not prepared to listen. All that was asked for, was that if in those two FIRs the warrants have to be served, they should first come through the Supreme Court. The court rejected this appeal and said to first appeal to the lower courts and later come to the SC if rejected. I felt terribly disillusioned by the attitude of the highest court when at the lower levels I found much greater humanity and fairness.

In fact, what transpired later is exactly what I feared, the Jharkhand police came all the way to Telangana soon after my release from Visakhapatnam jail. If the Supreme Court had granted relief they could not have done that and would have had to apply in the Supreme Court itself before any action could have been taken.

We subsequently let it lie, thinking, the two courts were probably no longer interested in my case. Suddenly, in August 2017, another person related to the Surat case, who had been living legally for years in Nagpur, was arrested by the Surat police. We then realized that the Surat police were not going to remain quiet in my case as well. As a result, the Visakhapatnam jail superintendent sent three more official letters to the Surat court to send the production warrant. Still there was no response.

Finally, when I took bail in the Visakhapatnam case the jail

201

authorities released me as there was no other pending case. Regarding the two pending FIRs they made me sign a bond that I would attend the court in case I was ever needed.

I finally breathed freedom after over eight years in jail as an undertrial. It was late evening by the time I was let out and my lawyers immediately put me on a bus to Hyderabad. They were afraid that, as happens very often, I may get arrested in another case.

I remember the night journey to be quite traumatic as my urinary/prostate problem was acute and the driver was uncooperative and not prepared to stop when asked. I somehow made it to Hyderabad by early morning and the two lawyers, Dashrath and Ravindran, warmly greeted me there. The lawyers had kept a week to attend to the cases on which I had been granted bail, as also attend the police station in the Achampet cases which had imposed a condition for the bail. Only after that would I be free to go to Mumbai, urgently needed, particularly for the medical attention.

It was only after reaching Hyderabad that I contacted family and friends who too could not believe that I was out, as it had all happened so sudden. Some in fact first thought I was speaking from within the jail. Reetha suggested I buy my own phone so that I could keep in regular touch, which I did, but, of course did not know how to use.

Though at the back of my mind the fear of re-arrest was there, it was not expected by the lawyers as there were no more cases against me. I was immediately driven to Varavara Rao's house where I was greeted by the poet and Hema, his wife. We spent the day recapitulating the past, met some other acquaintances who came to the house to meet me, and since my health was poor, he organized a visit to a doctor at the Apollo Hospital.

I knew VV from the time of the upsurge in the civil

liberties movement during the days of the Janata Party rule in the late 1970s, when we had both been active members of our respective state human rights organizations – APCLC and CPDR. Though I had not met him often, it was he who translated my speech at the gigantic RYL (Radical Youth League) rally in Warangal in 1979 where I had been called as the chief guest.

The next two days I spent with my Telangana advocates, Ravindran's family and Dashrath, before going for the court date at Achampet on 16 December. I was warmly welcomed by his wife Savithri (also an advocate activist) and their two beautiful children – daughter, Koumudi, about 13 and son Saumil, about 10. Dashrath though a reputed lawyer is the simplest of persons totally dedicated to serving the oppressed. When in Delhi, and helping in the jail visits, he was working in the office of senior advocate Ravindra Bhatt, now a judge of the Supreme Court. He could have earned a fortune but due to his commitment lives very simply. He is from a village background and the famous lawyer, the late K.G. Kannabiran is supposed to have said that if it was not for his difficulty with English, Dashrath would have been one of the top lawyers of the country. He has been a constant throughout my jail journey, first coordinating with the Delhi lawyers and making regular jail visits to Tihar for the first two crucial years, afterwards, during my entire stay in Hyderabad, and finally even visited me in Tenughat jail in Jharkhand and guided the local advocate on how to initiate my case.

Ravindran, though much younger, is more an activist and helped coordinate my cases not only in Andhra Pradesh/ Telangana but throughout the country. He too made a number of visits to Delhi. This was the first time I met his entire family. Savithri cooked the most exquisite food, the type of which I did not have for the past eight years. I spent much of the time

203

with Koumudi trying to learn how to use the new cell phone that I had bought. She was a patient and good teacher; I was a terrible student. Saumil would also help out now and then.

It was a very relaxed atmosphere for those two days like having reached home. On the second day there, Uma Vishnu of the Delhi *Indian Express* took a lengthy phone interview, which I later learnt was published the next day.

The following day, on 16 December, Dashrath came over and in a friend's car we all (two advocates and myself) went to Achampet court and police station about 150 kilometre away. Savithri said that when we returned home, we could eat Hyderabadi biryani ordered from the famous Paradise. This, of course, was not to be. Dashrath was his jovial and responsible self, and he remembered to give me a book Fali Nariman had given him in Delhi for me a year back. This was at the time he was helping with my case in the Supreme Court. The book was a translation of the Zoroastrian religious texts, the Gathas, by his son Justice Rohinton Nariman, a sitting judge of the Supreme Court.

Hardly had Dashrath handed this over to me, and with all court procedures being over, we began leaving the court premises when, in filmy style, our car was intercepted by another car and a person in civil dress jumped out and said he was from Jharkhand police and that they had a warrant for my arrest. The advocates looked at it and said we could drive back to Hyderabad together in our separate cars. The officer, though very polite, insisted I come in their car, being driven by Andhra Pradesh IB personnel. At that juncture, the lawyers said that they too would like to come in the same car to which he agreed.

In the car I wrote a press statement which was immediately circulated through the mobile phone. Also, Ravindran, through Savitri, had made arrangements for warm clothes, as Jharkhand would be much cooler. The police said they would

204

have to go to the court first for a transit warrant and that a flight had been booked for 7 p.m. That did not leave much time considering we reached the court only at 3 p.m. and had to go to Ravindran's house to pick up my luggage and the clothes Savitri had bought. Hyderabad's traffic is quite bad. At the court the IB fellows refused to help the Jharkhand police in getting a transit warrant, so they had to turn to my lawyers for help. As it was taking too long, they skipped the procedure and we went straight to Ravindran's home where that sumptuous Hyderabadi chicken biryani was awaiting us. We all ate a little, and with the atmosphere entirely changed, left for the airport.

This re-arrest shocked me as the lawyers said it was unlikely to take place. Yet the fear was there knowing the ways of the state which was the reason why I approached the Supreme Court. But then I thought if it was to take place better now than later. It would, for example, be much more difficult to adjust to jail life after being at home for some time. As I was picked up before reaching home it was as though there was a continuity. All through the journey the two police officers (one was the Investigating Officer of the case) were very civil and had repeatedly said their SP (Bokaro) had specifically instructed them that there should be no inconvenience to me, and was regularly in touch on the phone to see that all was fine. They were exceedingly polite and sensitive, knowing that I was unwell and on my way to Mumbai for medical treatment. The police were not armed so the procedure at the Hyderabad airport was not complicated and we could board the plane easily as I did not appear as a prisoner. We landed at Ranchi airport around 9 p.m., and immediately drove for about three hours to Tenughat, where the case was registered.

By about midnight we had had the medical check-up (my blood pressure was very high) and I was handed over to the young officer in-charge, Jaat saheb, who was also extremely helpful. As the magistrate was away at a party in Bokaro we had to await his arrival before formally completing the arrest. For some time, I sat out in the cold in the car, but later the officer called me into his office and we all had tea and snacks. Knowing that I was knowledgeable in economics, we had a long discussion on the economic state of the country like the huge NPAs, the low growth rates simultaneous to the high stock market prices.

Finally, at about 2.30 a.m., the magistrate turned up and it was 3 a.m. when I was admitted into Tenughat sub-jail, exhausted as we had been travelling since six in the morning. That made it a good 21 hours on the move, that too when I had specifically come out for medical treatment. This once again aggravated all my orthopaedic problems, particularly as it was cold.

This was the first time I had been to Jharkhand in my life and the police said that they arrested me in a case where a police camp had been attacked by a mob of about 500 alleged Naxals in 2006. I had never heard of the place Tenughat before, let alone of this alleged incident. Generally, in the charge sheets made out, there is a clause 'and others' to which they can add any name. They claimed that in the 'confession' before Delhi Special Cell during the period of police custody in 2009 I had confessed to being part of this action. Surprising, as neither had I signed that statement, nor did it stand in the main case in Delhi which was primarily based on this statement, where I was acquitted of all Maoist charges. As it is, it is not admissible as per the Evidence Act even if it were signed, yet cases continued to be put on the basis of these fake confessions.

Jharkhand was the only state in which I saw that no one was taken to the courts denying one a basic right. During the trial as well, I observed inmates entire process being done through videoconferencing. This is unheard of in other states. It also cut out our ability to meet the lawyer and as far as jail visits were concerned, this was the first jail where lawyers' visits were included in the mulaqaat and not treated separately. Like the other visitors, lawyers too had to speak through the mesh in the midst of shouting and chaos. No documents could be passed either way unless the mulaqaat sevadars and staff, both inside and outside, were taken care of.

Not only that, even on a new production warrant they produce one through videoconferencing, which again is unheard of in other states. In fact, on this basis I requested that in the Surat case I be produced by videoconferencing so that the case could proceed while I was in Jharkhand jail but the local court refused. As a result, nothing could proceed until I reached Surat. So also elsewhere; if one could have been produced by videoconferencing all my cases in the country could have proceeded simultaneously despite the 268 imposition; but I had to face a serial trial, one case after the other. Such is the arbitrariness of the legal system. So, when a totally new case was foisted on me in February 2018, of which there was no earlier record, I was produced through videoconferencing, though the court was just 5 minutes away. It's incredible that in backward Jharkhand the videoconferencing system is more sophisticated than what I saw anywhere else – be it Delhi, Gujarat, Andhra Pradesh, Telangana, or Punjab.

Though the police in Jharkhand did not add any new evidence to my case, and what existed was merely the so-called confession before Delhi Police, and though an excellent lawyer in the high court, Jitendra Singh, took up the matter, merely getting bail took nearly two years. The time taken to get bail in these two cases was more than that taken for 11 cases in Telangana, including three acquittals. I did not see anyone getting bail in the sessions court even for the flimsiest of charges... all had to go to the high court, putting an enormous burden on it.

In addition, after getting the bail/release order it took over a month to send me to Surat, due to the inefficiency of the escort system. Even after a court order, more often than not, the police would just not bother to produce the inmate, and the courts too would turn a blind eye. So, often cases were delayed inordinately, particularly for those with little assistance outside. Take the case of Narayan Ganju (who helped me in the Hazaribagh jail): there were barely five witnesses, yet the cases went through all the nine judges that sit in the Hazaribagh court, switching to a different court practically every year and taking nearly ten years to conclude. This is just one example; there would be hundreds like this.

As it is, in the entire country the jail and criminal-justice system is anti-people, but Jharkhand can be considered an extreme example for arbitrariness and dysfunctionality. No wonder the jails are full and new ones are being built continuously. Besides, with the contract raj dominating everything, from mineral production, railway loading and servicing, all construction activity, also education and health care, the gigantic black money generated tends to criminalize all activities. So, the rapid growth of jails.

I was finally given bail by the Jharkhand High Court with severe conditions for the sureties. It was due to the tremendous courage and effort of local social workers Bikash Singh and Alka Mishra that the sureties were finally organized with the help of another individual, Lix. Bikashji is a well-known social activist who was active with Jayaprakash Narayan during the movement in the 1970s and has continued his activities at the local level and is a person of high principles and honesty as is Alkaji. Both are locals in the Tenughat region, with homes in Bermo. During my court dates all three have been extremely helpful, and without them even movement would have been difficult, given that Tenughat is over 100 kilometre from Ranchi. Their warmth and affection have been particularly touching as it was a place I knew no one.

Finally, I left Hazaribagh jail for Surat on 24 August 2019 and once again the Jharkhand escort authorities messed up the procedure. Normally, on arrival at our destination the local police have prior information and they are waiting to take over the security and transport. But this was not the case. When we reached Surat station, the Jharkhand police escorts were running from pillar to post to get help and transport to the Kathor court. All in vain as no one had been informed, and without instructions the police never act. Here I was, a supposedly high-security prisoner travelling with seven police escorts in two autos to the court 18 kilometre away. When we reached the court the magistrate was astounded, and asked where the Gujarat police were. No one knew. While asking me to sit down, he called for them. Naxals are hardly known in Gujarat and a supposed top Naxal coming in this manner, seemed rather strange to all.

The FIR in the Surat case was filed nearly five months after I had already been in Tihar. How could I commit a crime while being in jail, I could not understand? The absurdity of the case became more apparent given that I had never been to Gujarat in my life.

These unconstitutional methods continued. While the Surat/Kathor court/police did not respond to five letters for the production warrant sent from Hyderabad and Vishaka jails, once I was granted bail in the Jharkhand cases on 3 April 2019, forthwith a production warrant was sent to Hazaribagh jail on 22 April, before I could avail of the bail. This was just to make sure that I was not released and that my incarceration would be guaranteed as long as possible.

As per Gujarat procedure, the magistrate gave the police one day for investigation before the official arrest. I was taken to the police station and the next day I was produced in court and officially arrested. I was given four days police remand and taken back to the police station which was just 3–4 kilometre from the court.

I was finally sent to Lajpore Central Jail when the bail came through after one and a half months on 16 October 2019. The sessions court gave this order on the basis of arguments by advocate Panwalla – Surat's senior advocate who had earlier taken the bail for all the other 25 co-accused and is conducting their trial. It was my sister who came all the way from Mumbai, took the bail from the court and rushed to the jail 25 kilometre away with the release order just in time before the jail closed. The superintendent and jailor were very cooperative and within an hour all the formalities were completed and I was finally free. Two journalists were waiting outside, but there was no coverage of my release the next day. From jail we drove straight to Mumbai and reached her home at four in the morning.

~

I was finally released after ten years and one month on 16 October 2019. It was an arduous journey through seven jails in six states for trying to help the poor of this country stand on their feet and get their due. What was worse, the jails were in some states I had never been and cases in places I had, till then, never even heard of. Such is the nature of the criminal-justice system in India. In such alien places it becomes very difficult to organize anything from clothes to lawyers as there is no local acquaintance. But probably this is done on purpose to harass in various ways.

It was not what one would expect in an independent country where the future of citizens should be the chief focus of government policy, irrespective of the parties in power. I was arrested under Congress rule when P. Chidambaram was the home minister; re-arrested after release in 2017 when BJP was ruling at the Centre and TRS in Telangana from where I was picked up.

While on the long journey from Surat to Mumbai, there was some relief, at finally being released, but I could not fully relax because of the recent string of arrests of so called 'Urban Naxals' that had made national headlines. Some of them from Nagpur and Mumbai were people I had known a long time ago, and were well-placed social activists and professionals. All were intellectuals with no known Naxal link as per the reports. All these arrests happened just before and even after my release. This made me uneasy about my own security as well.

Getting Back to Society

On the long journey back with my sister and Vaibhav in a cab, I began to reflect on the future. With Anu gone I had no real home or family to go back to and settling back into society after so many years would be difficult; even small things like getting a mobile, Aadhaar card, re-opening bank accounts, getting a legal identity and address. How would my health stand up, and what about the medical treatment? How would I manage my expenses and find a source of income at this age? Regarding what I wanted to do with the rest of my life I was clear – to write on my half century of experiences, based on studies I had done in jail and would continue after release – but how would I organize this? Where would real assistance come from? Last-but-not least there were still the ongoing court cases to attend, and the Delhi Police had just challenged my acquittal in the high court.

All such thoughts and more raced through my mind, letting me know that life after release would not be a bed of roses. There could be thorns all over, but Meenal's energy practices helped me relax in the face of these unknowns. Being out finally after over ten years was a huge relief, the future would no doubt look after itself. In fact, when we reached Mahrouk's house at four in the morning in Mumbai, Meenal, who stays a few floors below, received me with a bouquet of flowers, having kept awake the whole night.

By ten in the morning Anu's entire family came over and we immediately went to Sunil's place to see Anu's mother. Sunil had planned it as a surprise. She was so astonished to see me she just could not believe it was me. We chatted a long time and she remembered Anu a lot and tears would come to her eyes. Before Covid, I would visit her once a week but her condition kept deteriorating. At least we were able to have a small celebration on her 92nd birthday in September 2020. When I visited her last in December she had had a mild stroke and her condition was critical, though she recognized me and held my hand for long. Two days later she passed away.

Surprisingly, the same media that had highlighted my case while I was in jail was completely silent on my final release; so much so that even after a month when I rang up journalists who had been in regular touch with me while in jail, they were not even aware that I had been released. I preferred it that way and avoided any interviews which some had asked me to give.

It has now been over a year and I have been fortunate that my sister who helped throughout my incarceration and brother-in-law have welcomed me to stay at their place in Mumbai. Quite naturally I have been getting a surfeit of lovely Parsi food. And it was Reetha from day one who helped me get all my documents in place, not knowing the ropes due to so many years of being out of touch. As far as medical issues, being introduced to a Jaslok Hospital doctor by a friend, I was able to get an entire check-up done.

Since then, much time has gone in attending cases in Jharkhand – once every month for four months until relief from attendance was given by the high court – and the Visakhapatanam case in March 2020; fortunately, just before the lockdown. Fortunately, during the four trips to Jharkhand, I utilized the opportunity to arrange to take up Narayan Ganju's case which I had promised while leaving Hazaribagh jail. It was a real pleasure to hear that as a result, in September 2020, he had been released.

Back in Mumbai, there tended to be fear all around with the continuing arrests of progressives in the Pune case even those over eighty and probably not even remotely associated with the issue. Anyhow, I preferred to catch up with new friends/relatives in the community and class/school mates both of whom had been quite supportive during my incarceration. It was very interesting to find that even in these elite circles these days there is so much sensitivity where most seem to find the existing atmosphere claustrophobic and are keen for a more humane environment. I was able to find this even amongst relatives with whom I was really interacting for the first time.

I realized from all these interactions that I had myself become rather closed with no relation to fresh and different ideas. And being only associated with a limited stagnant left circle, ideas and relationships tended to fester, often leading to bitterness, pettiness and lack of creativity. Unnecessary energy would get expended in unimportant matters, and tensions would arise, further debilitating one's creative abilities. Now, one is free to get new and contrary views which provoke thinking and prompt new ideas to evolve.

Finally, when my court attendances were reduced and my running around to get all my documentation in place, I began to concentrate on getting this memoir out and contacting publishers. In this, major assistance was given by journalists, including *Parsiana* editor, Jehangir Patel, *Mumbai Mirror* editor, Meenal Baghel and Sunetra Choudhury. Of particular assistance were Simin Patel and advocate Xerxes Ranina who have been a great support throughout this entire process, both very sensitive individuals. Not to mention my one-time neighbours and long-lost friends Govind and Roshan Shahani, whose extensive knowledge of English literature helped improve this manuscript no end. The food Roshan cooked with so much love and care was particularly rewarding.

But then came Covid and the lockdown, just as I was planning to go to Delhi and meet all my class friends at a get-together organized by Gautam Vohra at his home in Vasant Vihar. I had also planned to meet all those who had assisted me during my long stay in Tihar, like Professor Moushumi Basu, and the many lawyers who took up my cases and potential publishers that had shown interest in this book (all of whom happen to be in Delhi). But this was not to be, as on the very day of my scheduled departure for Delhi, 20 March, it was being estimated that Covid was spreading fast, and even if I did go, few were likely to meet. The Delhi High Court date was also fixed for 24 March. At the very last minute I unpacked my bags and cancelled the train journey on the suggestion of my advocate Rebecca John and other well-wishers.

Once conditions ease not only is this visit pending but those to Visakhapatanam and Tenughat to finish the cases there, where the courts are still non-functional. Also, in the Surat case the charge sheet has just been filed which means one more regular trip. Fortunately, a very active class of '63 WhatsApp group has facilitated my bonding with my Doon

School classmates. The group comprises individuals of varied views and all seem particularly well read and interventions are not only filled with humour but in-depth analysis.

Another great get-together was with my classmate and closest friend in school, Ishaat Hussain. We had lunch a number of times at his flat at the NCPA complex at Nariman Point recollecting old times and discussing present conditions and many aspects of philosophy and history on which he is well read. He was extremely knowledgeable, and though our meetings in person came to an end with Covid, we often talk at length on the phone.

With the lockdown, I was faced with a new form of confinement – from ten years of jail, hardly had I been out six months when this was clamped on the entire population with paranoia all around. But with this confinement I returned to my jail routine of yoga in the mornings, exercises in the evenings, spending more time on house work now, and focusing on the writing of this manuscript.

No doubt the decade long jail journey was harsh and took its toll, but any situation can be educative. Much of what I recounted above was absolutely new to me, though I had spent four decades in social activities. As this was mostly in Maharashtra there was little knowledge of the North. One thing that struck me about the North was that attitudes and culture is far more feudal than the South and even Maharashtra. Like attitudes of patriarchy, caste, superstitions, religious practices, etc. My assessment was that this was probably because the Hindi belt never went through social reform movements as did most other parts of the country. Besides, jail life gives a totally different picture of the world outside; many nuances were brought into sharp focus which often one doesn't notice or see. When I was outside there was no time for anything, just running from one activity/meeting to another. Here, at least when things were peaceful and tensions were not high I was, to some extent, able to focus on study and writing. Most important, I was able to reflect, examine the past, become more aware of myself and my shortcomings, try and understand the causes for the reversals in communism the world over and its stagnation in India, and particularly look into the future, not just pessimistically, but with a new hope.

Reflecting on these movements, I began to see more clearly that similar tendencies seem to afflict the African-American movement in the West and the Dalit movement in India. Some seek to turn it into a black vs white issue so that the people are divided and the poor attack each other, while the real perpetrators of racism – the ruling establishment and the KKK types – get off the hook. Also, on the Dalit question in India the target is sought to be diverted towards the upper castes again pitting poor against poor, while it should be against the perpetrators of Brahminism. To target whites and upper castes are easy as they do have inclinations towards racism and Brahminism due to their childhood upbringing; they tend to become soft targets, but these people are being misled by the real perpetrators and need education rather than targeting. Besides there are many whites and upper castes who are liberal and not racist or casteist. The approach should be that progressive forces unitedly fight against racism and casteism focusing on the real perpetrators of these evils. So also on the question of the Sikh and Islamic issues, it should be of federalism and anti-communalism, not Sikhs/Muslims vs Hindus which only divide the people.

All these thoughts and more, particularly the setback in communism the world over, were racing through my mind. Particularly with conditions getting worse and worse I continued to reflect on the future, and what could be a better and more effective project for change.

216

SECTION III
REFLECTIONS AND RELEVANCE

After getting over the initial shock of the sudden arrest I tried not to let the jail system break me. Though already a senior citizen at the time of arrest with numerous ailments, I tried to maintain a strict routine of yoga and exercises, and when possible would take the health foods and vitamins sent by my sister. Yet the chronic problems kept aggravating with age. Mentally, I sought to keep myself preoccupied in studying, making notes and jottings from newspapers and magazines and utilizing all these to write articles. Fortunately, *Mainstream Weekly* published most of what I wrote. This encouraged me to do some creative thinking and writing. The main topics that I would touch on were economic issues of our country and world, which included budget analysis, development issues and GDP growth, demonetization and others; then on issues of democracy and freedom; on the issues of corruption and real nationalism; and finally, on issues of a new value system modelled on the example of Anuradha.

In the first four years of my time at Tihar, before I was put on the 3-monthly transfer routine from one HRW to another, I could focus better and, once I became mentally attuned to the fact that the court procedures were going to take a long time. Of course, I hoped that matters would proceed more quickly, but for a while I was resigned to the fact that there would be delay. In a way on some aspects these writings represented my reflections during this period as did my letters to my classmate Gautam Vohra. But what needed to be reflected on most was the relevance of my four decades of activities as a communist in India.

On this question of relevance, the issue arose as to the question whether the communist project was relevant to solve the ills of society. It has been clear from the start that the existing system is untenable and getting more and more unjust; more and more inhuman; more and more unequal; more and more destructive of everything; with the political class becoming increasingly uncouth, vile, uncivilized and fascistic worldwide. The horrors likely for the people in the coming days are unimaginable. There is no doubt a need for an urgent change; but no alternative is visible on the horizon. Also, the hope communism gave to the world in the twentieth century no longer exists, with the main socialist states reverting back and major socialist/communist movements around the world in limbo.

What then is the alternative? Sitting in the grounds amidst the trees in Jail 3, I began thinking that till today no other economic system has appeared that is more just and sustainable than the communist project. Yet, due to its failures worldwide there is need for some rethinking. I felt that no doubt the seeds have to be maintained, but one has to ensure that the flowers don't wilt and fruits don't turn sour. For that, the seeds probably need to be nurtured with much greater care than they were in the past. Primarily, the saplings, I concluded, should be nursed:

Firstly, in an environment of freedom.

Secondly, it should be built with a new set of values, as, say, epitomized by the Anuradha-model.

Thirdly, it should have as its goal universal happiness.

Sitting there in the quiet of the ground I thought that it is these three aspects of life that have to be woven into any project for change – any alternative, the shell of which I shall outline below.

Reflections of the Past

I began to reflect on what had been achieved over my past 40 years of activism. Internationally, communism, which swept the world in the late 1960s when I was drawn to it, has declined to become an almost spent force. In India, too, the movement does not seem to have moved forward in a dynamic fashion; it seems to have reached a dead-end. In my own areas of work too, there was little growth, this indicated both my limitations and my inability to sufficiently impact the situation. Also, the conditions of vast sections of the people are probably worse today than when we started our work. Certainly, the gap between the rich and the poor is far more now than it was when we started. Let alone the visualized revolution, there has been little reform, probably retrogression, a situation worse than what I saw in the 1970s and 1980s. Now, nearly all private employment is contracted and sub-contracted, while in the earlier days we saw permanent workers with reasonable salaries and amenities who were easier to organise than contract workers who are dispersed. For example, in place of the textile mills where permanent workers earned around ₹30,000 per month with other facilities and had powerful unions, we now have the power loom workers working 12 hours per day for a pittance, with no facilities and no unions. A similar situation exists in most manufacturing, mining and even services; a crude form of which I witnessed in Jharkhand. All this required deep reflection.

Of course, I had the example of Anuradha before me. A source from which one could learn many things about social activists. Also, her experiences in Bastar, and the way she recounted how they built the individuality, personality and self-confidence of even the most backward Adivasi women were no doubt enlightening.

In addition, I searched deep into Indian tradition, to find what could be found on the issue of our values. I discovered beautiful writings like the Panchatantra and Jataka stories and also the Hitopadesh tales, all based on animals and birds, stretching back 2,500 years. Of course, there were my additional studies in jail and the writings of the giants of the West and Russia whose pain and agony was reflected in their sensitivity and deeply emotional writings. Finally, the interaction with Afzal was intellectually stimulating as it introduced me to many new ideas of Rumi, Iqbal, and aspects of Islam that were all about love and freedom; issues that interested me. All this gave me a wide compass to reflect on our four decades of activities and the ideology associated with it. After all, the Panchatantra and other folktales are all simple stories through which one can imbibe the best of the values which no doubt need to be promoted not only amongst activists but in society generally; while Rumi's philosophy encompassed the importance of love in our lives to help promote universal happiness.

My reflections were derived from the interweaving of three main factors: first, an assessment of my 40 years of experience in the movement; second, the evaluation of the value-system of people like Anuradha; and third my extensive studies and observations and reflections within Tihar. All this was woven into a mosaic of a possible alternative which could be more sustainable and humane.

First, if I look at our experience over the past 40 years, we seem to have had limited success in our trade union and slum work; though there had been many immediate victories, little has been sustained. The only sphere in which there has been some amount of sustenance it seems is in the work among Dalits. I feel we, together with others, have played, to some extent, a role in creating a new consciousness. This new awakening has in part been made possible by working with them and living in their midst. Moreover, writing on the caste issue and bringing it to the forefront of the ideological debate among leftists, has helped bring about some shift.

This is reflected in the growing, though limited, trend for unity amongst the Ambedkarites and Marxists (best reflected in the book *Republic of Caste* by Anand Teltumbde) as also increasing assertion amongst Dalits for their rights. Actually, there should have been no real dichotomy between the two trends as Ambedkar's thoughts are particularly democratic, especially in the Indian context; while the communists speak of a democratic revolution.

Regarding the long-term aims of building a democratic and just society, one may not have advanced even a step further, in fact, there has probably been a certain regression. We see how democracy has taken a backseat in practically all spheres of life and not just in politics. In the absence of democracy there is more intolerance; be it in caste equations, communal relations, political and religious discourse, within the family, in our right to love the person of our choice, or even eat the food of our choice.

In fact, the situation may have been better centuries back if we look at the history of the Bhakti tradition of the thirteenth and fourteenth centuries, initiated by Chakradhar Swami who launched the Mahanubhav movement. At least then, even in the extreme feudal conditions (much worse than that of today), there was continuous upheaval against the oppression of the caste system. Though Chakradhar Swami was killed by the more orthodox Brahmins who wielded power, the Bhakti tradition evolved through the 12 saint poets and reformers who followed – mainly Jnandev, Eknath, Bhinabai, Namdev, Tukaram and finally Kabir and Guru Nanak stretching into the fifteenth century.

Even before this, there was also the famous twelfth-century reformer of North Karnataka, Basavanna; though a Brahmin, he vehemently opposed the caste system. This period saw a boom in Kannada literature by the lower castes, unheard-of in those days – a shepherd, a woodcutter, a washerman, a cobbler, and a toddy tapper. Many were brutally killed by the orthodoxy and it is not clear whether he too was murdered or died a natural death. This Bhakti tradition of reform, which was further advanced by Phule, Periyar and Ambedkar in the last century, seems to be lost in today's India. In fact, for the further democratization of society it would have been necessary to take forward the traditions of the Bhakti movement and the twentieth-century reformers.

All these movements and sages as also the earlier communists gave India a strong democratic tradition in general; against casteism and patriarchy in particular. Yet, where is their impact to be seen today? One would have hoped we could have drawn from our past history which evolved so many centuries back, and over these years India could have slowly, but steadily, evolved into a vibrant democratic republic. Unfortunately, today there seems little impact of these historic movements through the centuries. On the contrary there appears retrogression and decay.

British-era sedition laws are still followed, used with such impunity for minor statements on the social media, unheard of in independent India. We see the distinctions between the three anchors of a democracy slowly being eaten away with the judiciary and press more and more in tune with the executive. Political parties are dominated by a handful of individuals and/or their families. Labour, land and forest laws are undermined as never before. Vigilante groups interfere in legitimate business and food habits, not to mention peoples' personal lives. There are increasing levels of patriarchy and caste discrimination in social life itself. What is worse, we see greater intolerance within families and friends and in various other spheres of civil society.

So where did we, or for that matter the communists throughout the world, go wrong. No doubt, the conditions are depressing all over with a crude form of capitalism ravaging the world – both people and environment – destroying anything and everything in its path. Even human nature and sensitivities are being distorted. Probably never before in history has humanity and nature been so ravaged. The situation is crying out for a change. Yet there appears no alternative on the horizon. Still one maintains hope, drawing inspiration from the writings of the past where people have been continuously searching for happiness, as also from the common folk who are, in the main, honest and decent.

If we look into past history, we see a continuous search for happiness, freedom and the good values cherished by philosophers and sages from yore. Some of these were recounted in my articles in *Mainstream*. In these articles I have tried to trace man's search for happiness, freedom, and a new set of values through history – from the ancient prophets and philosophers, through the Middle Ages, through the period of the Renaissance (1300–1600) and to the Enlightenment (1600–1800). In the last period the search for freedom was most intense with the evolvement of man's individuality from the earlier clan structures.

Take happiness, its search is as old as humanity itself. Five thousand years ago in 3000 BC, the I Ching philosophy of the Chinese first put it forth. In it Tao Te Ching explained 'Embrace simplicity... be content with what you have and are, and no one can despoil you'. In other words, it says: be happy with what you have; i.e. avoid greed. Coincidentally, when Marx was asked which quality he admired most, his reply was 'simplicity'. So also, there were many other Chinese philosophers like Lao Tzu and his ancient classic *Tao Te Ching* written 2,500 years ago which explored a similar theme.

Happiness, though, should not be equated with pleasure, though the latter could be a part of it. Pleasure can be abandoned after it is achieved, as its attainment marks the end of the quest for it. Happiness has no end. It is a continuous, never ending process of destroying pain and suffering, both physical and mental.

The Charvaka's materialism, going as far back as the seventh century BC (i.e. pre-Buddhist) while denying god, sought happiness only in pleasures associated with food, sex, fine clothes. Charvaka, also known as Lokāyata, is an ancient school of Indian materialism. Charvaka holds direct perception, empiricism, and conditional inference as proper sources of knowledge, embraces philosophical scepticism and rejects ritualism, and supernaturalism. Charvaka was a response to the accepted religious vision of India at the time based on the Vedas. Charvaka's primary objection to the Vedic vision was that it could not be proven; it had to be accepted on faith and that faith was encouraged by a priestly class which was clearly benefiting from it at the expense of others. Sacrifices, gifts, and penitential gestures enriched the priests while contributing to the poverty of the lower class. The Charvaka vision rejected all supernatural claims, all religious authority and scripture, the acceptance of inference and testimony in establishing truth, and any religious ritual or tradition. The essential tenets of the philosophy were:

- Direct perception as the only means of establishing and accepting any truth;
- What cannot be perceived and understood by the senses does not exist;
- All that exists are the observable elements of air, earth, fire, and water;

- The ultimate good in life is pleasure; the only evil is pain;
- Pursuing pleasure and avoiding pain is the sole purpose of human existence;
- Religion is an invention of the strong and clever who prey on the weak.

Here of course no distinction was made between pleasure and happiness; but, no doubt, pleasure is an aspect of happiness.

Other religious sages saw happiness achieved through union with god. As far back as 350 BC Aristotle spoke much about happiness. He said, 'Happiness is not a natural state of mind. We have to strive and make a conscious effort to achieve happiness. Happiness is not a means but an end in itself.' The Western philosophers of the Renaissance and Enlightenment also searched for their heaven on earth, like Thomas More's book *Utopia* written in 1535.

If we turn to the questions of the value systems required, not only do we find it portrayed in the writings of the Western philosophers but strongly represented in the Indian tradition as well. As far back as 2,300 years ago the Panchatantra is the best example where children's stories on animals and birds impart excellent values which can be inculcated from childhood itself. Instead of fairy tales, parents can tell their children these stories. While putting a child to sleep the parents can recount each night a different story as there are so many. They could also be used to convey simply to the illiterate masses what values communists – or for that matter, any decent human being – should inculcate. Take some of these stories, put forward by the writer of the Panchatantra tales, Pandit Vishnu Sharma as far back as the third century BC: There is the story of the three fish, moral: those who depend on fate perish; next the story of the owl and the swan, moral: false pride leads

227

to downfall; then numerous stories on unity is strength: like those of the python and ants, pigeons and the bird catcher, rogue elephant vs the birds and the bees; also the story of the dyed jackal, moral: you can't fool all the people all the time; the story of the lion, jackal and ass, moral: do not be taken in by cunning sweet talk; story of the greedy jackal, moral: greed is no good... and eighty more.

In addition, well before the Panchatantra we had the Jataka Tales told by the Lord Buddha in 600 BC. These stories were messages used to narrate tales of compassion, love, friendship, brotherhood, and moral values. There were also the Hitopadesh Stories of the ninth century AD, which built on the Panchatantra stories. With such a rich storehouse of writings to promote the good values in our cultural history that goes back over 2,500 years, why is this such a neglected sphere in our country and even among communists.

Finally, when we turn to the question of democracy and freedom, we find this too was referred to as far back as 1500 BC by the prophet Zarathustra when he says:

> With an open mind,
> Seek and listen to all the ideals.
> Consider the most enlightened thoughts,
> Then choose your path,
> Person by person, each for oneself,
> Turn yourself not away from the three best things:
> Good Thoughts, Good Words, Good Deeds.
> (Mansahani, Gavshani and Kuvshani in the original)

This short stanza not only pictures a democratic approach but also presents, in the last two lines, a need for good values.

Of course, the concept of 'freedom' is closely linked to the assertion of the individuality of the person and its promotion amongst others. And the evolving of the individuality of the person is, in turn, closely associated with one's freedom from alienation. These concepts particularly came to the fore in the present era once the feudal clan structures crumbled. We see it strongly presented in the writings of the Western philosophers of the eighteenth century onwards – in those of Goethe, Chekov and coming up to the more recent existentialists. In fact, it was Marx who showed scientifically how the capitalist production process itself alienates man not only from his product but from other men as well.

In India, unfortunately we have not seen an industrial revolution like in the West, and so feudal/clan systems continue in spite of modernism, in the form of caste and patriarchal relationships. Only a section of the urban population, that too the westernised, may, to a limited extent, have come out of these caste and patriarchal tendencies. Alienation no doubt does exist, but here it is not so much linked to the production process as it is associated more with our desires and aspirations – much of which is created by the media, films, internet – and our inability to fulfil them due to both childhood conditioning and social mores.

Of course, when you lose every aspect of freedom as I did behind bars, I began to value it, to want to be once more in a world I could call my own. Yet, precious though that freedom is, I began to reflect on its significance in any model for change.

As Albert Camus once said: 'The only way to deal with an unfree world is to become so absolutely free, that your very existence is an act of rebellion.'

Easier said than done, particularly if one is without resources in this society. Yet, it was in this spirit, that I stared working on my articles on 'freedom'. Not in any particular circumstance, but reflecting on its importance in any model for change. Not just freedom from want, not just freedom in the political/governmental sphere, not just freedom on how the term is used today (i.e. democracy vs autocracy), but freedom in all spheres of human existence – in our daily interactions with others, starting right from the family, friends, organization and further to the party, government and power. In fact, first and foremost, starting with freedom for oneself.

Thoughts for the Future

In that six-piece article in *Mainstream*, I had tried to touch on some of these main themes. Ironically, the series was completed with the hanging of Afzal Guru in February 2013, the most unfree act possible.

What provoked me to reflect deeply on the past, try and understand the present, and look into the future, was that not only in our activities was there little success, even in the world that existed when I was drawn towards communism in the late 1960s, little remains today, just in my life span. Why?

As I say in the very introduction to those articles itself: 'Why such a devastating reversal? What happened to our hopes and dreams for a better future? Forget the autocratic rulers, why did the masses so easily choose a free market over real freedom, as also freedom from want? If there are no clear-cut answers and also solutions, the communists of today may continue to live ostrich-like in their make-believe limited worlds; but the future will pass them by.' Look at India, for example, not only are the parliamentary left in stagnation, but so are the varied Naxal factions. Let alone growth, both trends have declined from their peak years in the 1990s and early 2000s, and that too just at a time when the neo-liberal economic policies have hit the masses the worst, and they needed socialist policies the most!

In these essays I outlined that 'freedom' should be intrinsically interwoven with 'good values' and the goal of 'happiness'. That in any project for basic change, together with the economic agenda, all three must co-exist with universal happiness being the goal. Questions of freedom and good values need to be a part of it, which I felt was best reflected in Anu. Freedom started from within herself – her naturalness and straightforwardness; it was reflected in her relations with others in respecting dissenting views, while being firm on her own; it was further seen in her intolerance of any form of injustice; it was seen in her attitude toward social institutions; and most importantly, though a leader, it was reflected in her simplicity and lack of ego.

In fact, in that article, giving the example of Anuradha I wrote: 'So lively and chirpy, like the little squirrels, she was straightforward, simple, with few complexes, and her reactions were so spontaneous and child-like (not calculated and cunning). My impression was that probably her inner feelings were very much in tune with her outward reactions; as a result, she was closest to what we may call a free person.' Yes, here we have the naturalism Marx referred to: 'Communism as a fully developed naturalism, is humanism; and, as a fully developed humanism, is naturalism.'

No doubt, as outlined above, the issues of Happiness, Freedom and Good Values have been discussed time and again by great philosophers, sages and social reformers. These issues are nothing new, but they have remained in the realm of dreams not turned into a reality. The importance here is to evolve a beautiful mosaic of the three interwoven into the fabric of a just economic order. This, in fact Marx, sought to do, but somewhere in the stream of the practical movements it got lost, or, at least took a back seat. The point here is to bring it to the forefront, using the rich experiences of the past.

After all, it was none other than Marx himself, in his concept of communism, who pictured an ideal society, a veritable Utopia, filled with happiness, freedom and good values, when he said:

Communism is the return of man himself as a social, i.e. really human being, a complete and conscious return which assimilates all the wealth of previous development. Communism, as a fully developed naturalism, is humanism, and, as a fully developed humanism, is naturalism. It is the DEFINITIVE resolution of the antagonism between man and nature, and between man and man. It is the true solution of the conflict between existence and essence, between objectification and self-affirmation, between freedom and necessity, between individual and species. It is the solution of the riddle of history and knows itself to be this solution.

Let us see how to realize this utopia in the future, taking lessons from the past. Here I will not dwell on the economic aspects as that requires an independent in-depth analysis, taking both the Russian and Chinese experiences into account as also environmental concerns. Besides, the economic structures must facilitate the evolution of happiness, freedom and good values in the superstructure; while the latter must promote an economic base built in their image. It is a vast subject to be taken up separately.

I will instead focus on the social aspects related to the building of the new order, reflected in organizational work – whether mass organizations, cultural organizations, trade unions, any other organization, and most important, the party organization and the structures and organs of state power when they arise. In all these activities, relationships and organisations the three aspects of happiness, freedom and good values need to be interwoven. After all, our goals should be reflected in embryonic form throughout the entire process of its achievements. Only then will the final outcome not get reversed and sustain after the seizure of power as well. Unfortunately, I don't see such a process in India.

Where in our activities, did we even remotely seek to achieve this? Though we did not, one positive aspect is that an Anu-prototype could gain recognition and also a leadership role in her organizational environment, which may not have been possible in other organizations. It was therefore a tacit acceptance (though not vocal) of these positive attributes. There were no doubt others who had shades of Anu, particularly from many of the Andhra and tribal cadre but our relationships were not deep or close, and from a distance one does not get to see the intricacies.

～

Sitting in the serene atmosphere of the ground in Tihar's Jail 3, watching the squirrels prancing around, I began to review my past experiences that spanned four decades making the following jottings of which I produce the essence:

Questions of Happiness

To start with, the goalposts have to be changed from fighting inequality to happiness for all. In this, no doubt, a decent standard of living would have to be a starting point (but should not be an end in itself), as a hungry person cannot be happy. Of course, seeking happiness not in some esoteric

233

form, but concretely in our lives and our relationships, which includes family, friends, organization, party, nation. For, if the goal is to spread happiness while building a more egalitarian society, one would not act to curb others' freedom and/or democratic rights in organizations/parties; one will seek the flowering of the individuality of all; one will try and act from the best of the values outlined.

Then again, only if happiness is the goal, all evils like ego, domination, servility, manipulations, etc that arise in the course of organisational work and social interaction can be countered. If the organisation seeking radical change keeps 'happiness' as their central goal, it will get reflected in day-to-day associations, in leaders' attitude to cadres, in approach to the masses, women, Dalits, everywhere; bringing with it a fresh breeze of freedom, democracy and the good values. Besides, in any other social interaction if happiness is the aim, not just for oneself, we would then act with the good values with one and all.

If happiness is nowhere on the agenda, inevitably all the negative values will tend to creep in. If we merely limit our goal to the economic sphere without thought of the entire project, the tendency may be to achieve that as the sole goal negating these other aspects. Invariably that is short-sighted as we have seen in Russia and China where the new rulers become the new lords, though there is no denying the economic gains made.

Question of Democracy and Freedom

Having stated what the objective or goal of all activities should be, there is need to remember that happiness is inconceivable without freedom, democracy and a new value system. Any form of domination and the restriction of freedom usurps

234

others' happiness and is a cause for much agony. In addition, unless it is linked to the values of love, truth and honesty, straightforwardness and compassion, happiness will remain an abstract term.

Now, given that happiness is inconceivable without freedom, the path one treads must be paved with the cement of freedom. Freedom itself comes from countering individualism/ ego and allowing the individuality of each person to flower, countering alienation, resulting in social interaction with ease of mind and none of the negativity, generally associated with all relationships today, in both organisational and personal matters.

Freedom and democracy are not just for governments and countries, but primarily starts with oneself and our immediate circle. Normally when it is taken up it is mostly discussed at the structural level – country, organisational (democratic-centralism, multi-party democracy). In fact, democracy operates at many levels, not only the structural. It is there at the individual level, at the family and friendship level, at the institutional level, at the social level, and, in fact, all levels of social interaction. It will get reflected in one's personal behaviour to others, in leader-cadre relations, in boss-employee relations, in man-woman relations, in upper-caste/lower caste relations, in fact, it will be reflected in any and every form of human interaction – which will be either democratic or autocratic; humane or intolerant.

The starting point of democracy is not, structural, but human. If the individuals (particularly leaders) who comprise the state/party/organisation are not democratic, how can the organisation be democratic, whatever its structure? A change of form cannot change the content. Take the communist concept of organisation of democratic centralism. In theory, nothing could be more democratic, as, by this principle, the majority decides, which is then binding on all. In practice, of course, mostly the leader and her/his coterie decide and others are forced to fall in line. For example, if those manning an organisation or party are arrogant, conceited, opinionated, manipulative, would a change in organizational structure make any difference? There has been much debate in the past that a democratic centralist organisation fosters dictatorship/ autocracy. In their perception, if we change the structure of the organization and the same type of autocratic people man the new organization the new body should be more democratic? That may be wishful thinking. An autocratic person, let alone in any organization, even in personal interactions will dominate and suppress others freedom/democracy. Basically, unless these values change, particularly of the leadership, there will be no democracy or freedom for others, even in the most democratic of structures. No doubt, any power (and money) tends to generally corrupt, but as this is a major issue, I will deal with it at length a little later.

The very concept of dialectics encompasses democracy and without it there can be no development and growth of ideas. Discussion of conflicting views is the basis of the creation of new thoughts, essential for creative growth. After all, we do know that it is the 'unity and struggle of opposites' that results in development. In the realm of organisation this would entail: starting with a level of unity, then a struggle between conflicting views, finally arriving at a higher level of unity. In the realm of thought it would need an atmosphere of allowing conflicting views to clash and thereby arriving at a higher level on knowledge. Today much of the ossification in parties and organizations is probably due to the lack of such a process in the development of new ideas. In fact, new ideas in Marxist circles are often seen as dangerous, and the person is either labelled, targeted or isolated. This approach does not help

236

growth, particularly at a time when there have been enormous changes in society and most movements for change are either marking time or retreating.

The trouble is, often in a discussion the person does not merely objectively see the view presented, but, more often than not, sees *who* is presenting it and responds on the basis of a bias towards the person. Such an approach leads nowhere, but we all tend to do it, not only in left circles but also in normal life – resulting in either blind acceptance or else blind opposition. One needs to look at views, ignoring the person making them and our likes/dislikes for the individual.

Alienation and Determinism

Much of the reason for this is that as the starting point for freedom is the individual, if he/she themselves are imprisoned within the knots of alienation, they cannot be free. This results in biases and subjectivity. Under such circumstances, quite naturally, there is no question of promoting freedom amongst others. There can be no social, political or economic freedom if the individuals are themselves bound in chains. Greater freedom to the individual must reflect an increasing freedom in the social/political/economic domain. And greater freedom in the latter must create a conducive atmosphere for the flowering of the individuality of the person. There must be a dialectical inter-relationship between the two, as each impacts the other and the individual exists in interaction with his/her social environment and not in isolation.

In addition, much of these knots of alienation from oneself get reflected in the contradiction between our subconscious thoughts, feelings, emotions, desires and our conscious behaviour. Often, the main reason for our lack of freedom is the gap between our new consciousness/ideology and the programming we received in childhood which is deeply imbedded in our subconscious and reflected in our emotions. This results in thousands of knots of alienation and creating what Marx referred to as a 'crippled monstrosity'.

In today's ultra-consumerist world this contradiction has peaked. Alienation has, in today's consumerist society, created such divisions that virtually every individual has become an island unto themselves, competing with all others. This has destroyed family relations, friendships, even love and affection, driving man to extreme levels of isolation and therefore insecurity. In such an individualistic atmosphere only the most unscrupulous can thrive; the sensitive and caring will be seen as weak and tend to get put down.

Take, for example, our education system as it exists today, right from childhood we are trained to compete, we are forced to learn by rote and not use our brains, we develop without a scientific temper where all that is backward is encouraged. And last but not least, the enormous class distinction are being encouraged at all levels – take a child educated at a government school and one at a private or convent school; as we grow older not only have tuitions become a norm, but for the best technical education one has to spend lakhs in either capitation fees, coaching classes or elite universities. The products of this system are either contract labourers or individual monsters ready to do anything to earn a quick buck. It is a heartless system in which, as a rule, only the most ruthless can survive and grow.

Yet again, freedom is the very opposite of determinism. Many a religion propound deterministic views wherein a superior being decides one's fate – everything is pre-ordained and there is nothing like free will. We see such sentiments widespread amongst inmates, where people consider one's release is dependent on 'upper walle' (the One Above). We had this yoga instructor in Jharkhand jail who finally received a life sentence for brutally killing his wife of 18 years; he would always say one cannot go against their destiny, and that it was destiny that had brought him to prison, hence he could do nothing to change that. Very convenient!

Further, mathematical models and biology also tend to introduce deterministic thinking; like the theory that everything is decided by our genes. For example, if we say genes determine behaviour, we do not look for other causes in society; and we would be made to believe that as we cannot change our genes, our behaviour cannot be changed. The same determinism would apply to the theory that who and what we are in 'this' life is due to the deeds in our past lives. Again, if that was so, there is no possibility of change. There is determinism amongst communists as well, like them saying, for example, that 'revolution is inevitable', though it has not come for centuries in India, while worldwide there have been so many major reversals. By repeating by rote that it is 'inevitable' we will never look for the causes for the setbacks. Similarly, if we keep repeating that the proletariat is the vanguard; when in backward countries they are limited, and the nature of the proletariat has, to a large extent, also much changed, at least in India. This determinism was crudely seen among communists in India on the caste issue, which saw only class divisions and the automatic withering away of caste oppression with industrialization and/or revolution.

Factor of a New Set of Values

Finally, real freedom as also happiness must necessarily be linked to the innate goodness in man. The factor of goodness is essential as one's individual freedom should not act to curtail or deprive others/another's freedom. For example, a greedy person may himself be happy (few are), but his/her happiness may come at the cost of causing much pain to others. On the other hand, if linked to good, one's awakening to freedom could have a far-reaching impact and spread joy among many.

Together with this, the goodness within us emanates from the set of values that comprises our outlook. These finer values may take time to evolve, given the rot all around; yet they cannot be imposed or forced down one's throat, they have to grow through a process of self-realization and awareness. Many say that human nature is impossible to change and communists too, when they come to power, will behave much in the same way as others. Unfortunately, that has happened, but it only means there is much more need for activists to give greater attention to our values.

Our consciousness and the world outside are in a dialectical relationship, each acting on and influencing the other. Values do not change in a vacuum, but as reflected in their effect on others. As Marx implied in his *Third Thesis on Feuerbach*: 'Historical materialism helps in understanding the world; proletarian revolution is the means of changing it. In the course of doing so, the proletariat would, in the process of remaking the world, also remake itself. In other words, in the process of remaking society for the better, revolutionaries also remake themselves into better human beings.'

In fact, how the value of love can transform a person is brought out beautifully in the poems of Rumi. For example, in the poem 'I came Alive' Rumi says:

Love transformed me from a
Swaggering
Slave, ass-driver and a lowly thief
Into a generous, selfless being,
A king, a lord, and chief.

240

It ends with:
Move silently on the chessboard,
Your powers by Him prescribed;
Destined to be happy and blissful
Once your vanity and ego have
Died.
(Translated by Farrokh Dhondy)

Subversion by Money and Power

As already mentioned, happiness, freedom/democracy and good values continue to be subverted by money and power. And yet, money is necessary for a decent existence, at least for the present; while power is necessary not only to counter the oppressors but also to prevent anarchy. While money and power are a necessity, they are also subversive. How is this riddle to be solved?

Much like the macrocosm of the 'free' world, inside the microcosm of prison, too, I noticed there was but one God – and that was money. As I've said, in the outside world, that operates on Money, the central factors impinging on Freedom, are Power and Greed. Inside jail, it was only cruder.

Yet, as I said in my very first essay on 'Freedom' in *Mainstream*: 'Without money, in today's world there is no self-respect, there is no recognition, there is no possibility to meet any of our wants and desires.... You are what your money makes you. Yet, it is money that has the power that destroys all freedom, all of natural life, all good, fosters all greed, destroys morals, and wields power over all mankind – the God of Money. The Church/religions wield it to control others, political parties use it to control their cadres, organisations of all types use it to control their flock – it is

241

the one power that subverts the maximum of freedoms.'

In fact, Marx said that Money is 'the power to confuse and invert all human and natural qualities, to bring about fraternisation of incompatibles, the divine power of money resides in its character as the alienated and the self-alienating species life of man. It is the alienated power of humanity.' [Economic and Philosophical Manuscripts]

Even Shakespeare, as far as five centuries back, recognized the negative role of money when he said in *Timon of Athens.*

Who seeks for better of thee, sauce his palate
With thy most operant poison! What is here?
Gold? yellow, glittering, precious gold? No, gods,
I am no idle votarist: roots, you clear heavens!
Thus, much of this, will make black white, foul fair,
Wrong right, base noble, old young, coward valiant.
Ha, you gods! why this? what this, you gods? Why, this
Will lug your priests and servants from your sides,
Pluck stout men's pillows from below their heads:
This yellow slave
Will knit and break religions, bless the accursed,
Make the hoar leprosy adored, place thieves
And give them title, knee and approbation
With senators on the bench: this is it
That makes the wappen'd widow wed again.

There is no doubt that money has this deleterious effect, recognized since centuries. Of course, no longer spoken about these days. Yet, it cannot be wished away. One has to live with it at least as long as it is necessary.

Ironically, while little has been said about the corruption of values by money, much has been said about power corrupting, and absolute power corrupting absolutely. Why, many an anti-communist treatise as well, like say *Animal Farm* brings out the aspect of power corrupting, not money. It is an extremely rare case that power asserts itself without the control over money. The two are different sides of the same coin. What happens in practice is that those who wield control over the finances also exert the power in any structure. Also, it is vice-versa; those who wield power, have, or acquire, control over the finances.

As with money, can we do away with power? For organizations of the oppressed to even suggest that, is to de facto disarm them in the face of brutal rulers. Look at the devastation the US rulers have wrecked all over the world, in just these past three decades. In fact, President Jimmy Carter himself said that in its 242–year history America has enjoyed only 16 years of peace making it the 'most warlike nation in the history of the world'. It has troops deployed in 150 countries and since 2001 has spent $6 trillion on military operations around the world. Before that it was the other colonial powers who exterminated entire populations as in the Americas. A society seeking to be built on justice and freedom cannot ignore these past realities. Besides, power will have to be asserted if not only to sustain the rule of the oppressed but also to prevent anarchy.

Therefore, both money and power will be a necessary evil, at least for some time to come. On the other hand, they will also corrupt. How does one solve this contradiction? Though structural norms can be brought in, to put some controls on the evil influence of money and power, these in themselves will never be sufficient, as there will be limitations to their effectivity. Together with these, the main focus to counter the negative influence of money and power requires continuous education, primarily built around awareness of the need for the correct values and democracy/freedom. If one imbibes the attributes of decent values and continuously strives for them, one can counter the impact that money and power may have on oneself.

First, it is our own awareness of what is good and what is not; next there is the awareness of others, who, if inculcated with the correct values will not encourage negative features in others. If this is coupled with real democracy and freedom in the organisation, or in fact, in any relationship, any incorrigible leader/person could be easy to correct or finally replace. An atmosphere needs to be continuously created of zero tolerance to negative values particularly in those who wield power and influence in any sphere of society. In a country like India this would be much more important than elsewhere, as people acquire a sense of superiority just due to their caste, even without the trappings of money and power. Add money and power to this and one gets an explosive cocktail.

Therefore, to effectively counter the impact of money and power a prerequisite is good values and freedom/democracy with the overall aim of achieving maximum happiness. If this consciousness is there it may reduce the negative impact if not eradicate it totally. There can be no shortcuts. Besides, it is not a one-time affair, it will be a continuous and never-ending struggle within ourselves and without – a thousand cultural revolutions to create the new man which alone can guarantee a just and stable new order. The Utopia one dreams of. As Rumi once said 'be like a tree and let the dead leaves drop'.

~

These were in short, the main points of my reflections in jail, trying to assess my four decades of practice in social and revolutionary work. The essence is that in organizations of the oppressed (as also in social life itself – the two should not be compartmentalized) besides ideology and a dialectical approach one has to introduce, very consciously, the aspects of freedom/democracy and the good values in day-to-day interactions, with the goal of achieving happiness. This alone can be the long-term guarantee against the evils of money and power as also all other negatives cropping up. New generations can draw on these experiences and hopefully build edifices for change which will be more lasting and more humane. Of course, these are my personal reflections which will have the limitations of coming from an individual and not a group, organization or party.

No doubt what has been said here ought to be implemented in the course of all the organizational and political activities that any party does. It must become part of the life of individuals manning organizations/parties and particularly their leadership only then will any revolution/change be not only successful but sustaining as well in the long run. In essence each individual has to start with the new set of values and strongly imbibe these through continuous internal struggles; if this is even partially achieved it must then be reflected in our interactions with others guaranteeing a democratic environment where all can blossom in an atmosphere of freedom. If such methods are adopted happiness for all in the environment should automatically evolve, and if it does not, should be striven for. A movement built on these lines right from the start is less likely to be corrupted by the trappings of power and money.

I had a long time to reflect on all these issues in jail, particularly on the effectiveness of our life-long work. With no real tangible result in hand would there be any regret for my past and the life I led? That too required serious consideration. Should I have instead taken up a professional career? Except perhaps, for journalism, I see no attraction in any other alternative. Greed dominates the atmosphere in the corporate world and that is not something I could have ever lived with. Just making money, without any purpose in life seems a very empty life. And I have no creative talent as a writer, poet, novelist, so that I could have been creative and relevant through these mediums, like many others have been.

Yet, all said and done, under the circumstances it was probably the most fulfilling life possible, in spite of getting little result and experiencing many negative things as well. It was a life filled with rich experiences, meeting many excellent people, unlikely to be encountered in other fields, and experiencing beauty in a very different way. So many people of the Anu variety, not normally seen in ordinary life. Finally, the simplicity and lives of the Dalits we worked with, particularly in Vidarbha, was inspiring, to say the least.

Failures and negative features I would not really treat as failures but experiences on the path towards a new and better society in India and the world. Without these experiences we could never have understood our limitations and failings and could never have learnt how to build anew. It may be too late for people like me at this age, but if we can draw lessons at least new generations may have something concrete to build on.

Having pointed out what our limitations have been, and the changes required to build anew, we need to consider whether the present dispensation which seeks to demonize us, has achieved any success on the basic issues confronting the nation and its people. If not, what then?

Continued Relevance of Radical Change

The tragedy is that even after nearly half a century of work amongst the oppressed, even the basic issues of jal, jungle, jameen, as also jobs, remain as relevant as when we started; if not more so today. On the one hand there would seem apparent failures on our part, on the other, not only are the issues of jal, jungle, jameen and providing jobs more relevant than ever before, but also while communism may not have succeeded, capitalism worldwide has totally failed to answer the needs of the people or, for that matter, the environment. The state of the world economy could not have been worse than what it is today.[1]

While, for the masses, which this time includes much of the middle classes, it is a disaster of unprecedented proportions. Not only is there loss of income source, the isolation due to lockdown and 'social distancing', coupled with fear and insecurity, is resulting in psychological problems on a scale never seen before.

While at the international level the situation is fraught with horrifying dangers the situation in India after 73 years of independence may already be worse than that worldwide before the pandemic.[2]

In reflection, can we just for a moment put ourselves in the shoes of those 46 crore people in our country, who, according to Arundhati Roy, (*Financial Times*, 2 April) live a life in hunger, disease and excruciating poverty; and consider what this would mean in real terms and not merely as a statistic.

Is this, in itself, not ground for serious thought. Why even before the pandemic, Oxfam figures state 'We now know that nine of India's billionaires own as much as the bottom 50% of the country.' Further, the *New Indian Express* reported on 16 April 2020 that the Gini coefficient (which measures wealth inequality in countries) is a high 83, or that India ranked 147th out of the 157 countries by Oxfam's 'Commitment to Reduce Inequality' Index in 2018.

And now together with the lockdown even the RBI as also the IMF expects India's economy to contract this financial year by an unprecedented 10 per cent In fact, the latest IMF data reveals that India's is one of the worst performing economies in the world and over the past five years the decline has led to Bangladesh's per capita GDP overtaking India's from being 40 per cent less in 2015.

It is clear that the present capitalist system as a whole does not provide the answers whether for humans or our environment. It is totally destructive, getting more so with each passing day. Today it is the pandemic forcing isolation as never before seen in history, tomorrow it could be dreadful wars. Things are bound to go from bad to worse as the system has never really been able to recover from the 2008 economic crisis and today, we are seeing levels of contraction never witnessed before. The US economy is estimated to contract 8 per cent in the current financial year; the EU is facing its worst recession ever with the economy expected to contract by over 7 per cent; and the third largest economy, Japan will contract 6 per cent We have another 1929-crash just waiting to happen and after that who knows what is in store for the world?

It is quite apparent that the present system is unable to provide any of the answers to the ills of society, on the contrary, it is aggravating these to the detriment of entire society just for the advantage of a handful. We have already seen this during the pandemic and lockdown. Worse is to come. One is reminded of the famous Malyalam poet, Akkitham Achuthan Namboodthri (he passed away recently at the age of 94), who wrote the long poem 'The World in Ruins' in 1962, and his path-breaking work, 'The Epic of Twentieth Century' a poem that predicted an impending gloom and darkness – disillusioned as he was with the decline of the ideals of the freedom fighters and communist party of which he was a part. Today, the situation is a hundred times bleaker than those days soon after Independence. But it need not be so bad if an alternative agenda is introduced.

For this, there is need for a radical change. What then should be its nature? In the realm of the economy this can only be some derivative of a communist model as that has proven to be more effective than the various forms of capitalism – not only neo-liberalism, but also Keynesianism and state capitalism. But, to be sustainable the alternative must have a human face and be eco-centric.

Though a long-term solution will require detailed discussion, immediate steps to bring the economy on track could be done with the following steps: It should be built on swadeshi, as best propounded by Rajiv Dixit through his extensive videos and lectures through his detailed studies. He has exposed that multinational companies extract from our country in just one year 3 to 5 times that what they invest in total. With extensive data he brings out that it is these 5,000 odd foreign companies that are primarily responsible for our increasing poverty. He repeatedly gives the example of Hindustan Lever (actually the British-Dutch company Unileaver), which came with an investment of ₹33 lakhs 75 years back and has been extracting from our country ₹217 crore every year. He says in 1947 we got rid of one company (the East India Company) but after Independence we have brought in 5,000 such, like the Union Carbide, responsible for the Bhopal holocaust. He is a promotor of Ayurveda and herbs and is said not to have taken a single allopathic tablet in 20 years. Instead of promoting his concepts, it is believed that he was poisoned and killed on 30 November 2010 in Bilaspur at the young age of 43, when he was at the height of his popularity. His body was hastily disposed of without an autopsy. To understand the real cause of our poverty every Indian needs to listen to Rajiv Dixit's lectures, which are freely available on YouTube to understand the extend of the drain of India's wealth abroad, even till this day.

Next there should be a delicate balance between the private and the public sector, with both giving workers permanent employment and disbanding the contract system. Health care and education should be free for all: with the emphasis on prevention and hygiene in healthcare; and inculcating in education a Rudolf Steiner style creative, holistic thinking, with a scientific temper and discarding the existing study-by-rote system. All business should be run by patriots, be professionally run and free from corruption. They should be competitive, curbing monopolies, foreign finance and TNCs while promoting local entrepreneurship. The environment should be protected through afforestation, water harvesting, soil regeneration and encouraging green energy making agriculture sustainable for even the smallest plots of land. Agriculture must avoid the heavy use of foreign seeds, fertilisers and pesticides and rely on indigenous varieties and organic inputs and farmers must be guaranteed a remunerative price for their produce with the annulling of all their debts.

All these steps are merely for a start, basically to undo the damage already caused to society/economy and the environment. If the high levels of corruption are curbed, subsidies to big corporates eradicated, the foreign drain ended and wasteful military and police expenditure reduced to a minimum, there will be ample funds available for these projects. One then does not need to regularly go to foreign shores with the begging bowl. Once peoples' livelihood is restored and the environment healed, one can begin moving step by step towards the utopia of the future that many envisaged. But without such steps we are likely to be entering an age of darkness.

Today, Utopia seems further away for the poor in India and elsewhere. It is a dystopic world in which, at the moment, even the relatively comfortable middle class seem to find themselves.

And yet, while Apocalypse seems to be drawing near, I refuse to believe that the end is near. The seeds of goodness and hope lie embedded in humankind. Some day they will blossom into flowers. Experiences of the past, a history of commitment cannot be totally erased. Future generations may still work towards, create and live in that Utopia whether dreamt by Thomas More or Marx or by millions of women and men whose names we'll never know, who have lived and died in the shadows of history but who will not have lived and died in vain.

Notes

1. While in 2010 a mere 388 billionaires had as much wealth as the bottom 50 per cent, by 2019 this had come down to just 5 billionaires. Can any society be more unjust; and to what extent is this sustainable? Besides, during this pandemic the levels of inequality further skyrocketed. While, in the first three months of the pandemic 1.6 billion people worldwide have lost their source of income, just between March 18 and May 19, the total net worth of the 600-plus US billionaires jumped by $434 billion or 15 per cent. Just the top five US billionaires – Jeff Bezos, Bill Gates, Mark Zuckerberg, Warren Buffett and Oracle's Larry Ellison – saw their wealth grow by a total of $75.5 billion, or 19 per cent. In fact, the pandemic has been a windfall for the digital moguls and pharma companies they could never have imagined. Even in India while millions of migrants and others have been dying of starvation, the share price of Reliance has risen 120 per cent over the four months of the pandemic from ₹883 per share on March 23 to ₹1,934 per share on 13 July – a gain of a massive $81 billion to take its value to $170 billion.

2. According to the latest UNDP's Human Development Index (as reported in 19 March 2020, *Indian Express*), which ranks countries on health, education and income, India ranks an embarrassing 129 out of the 189 countries considered. Imagine this would include all the numerous tiny countries around the world with just a few million population. This is not surprising as India spends the least in the world on public health care (1.4 per cent of GDP compared to EU's 10 per cent). Then again India ranks 103 out of 119 in the Global Hunger Index; the absurdity of the situation is such that while 194 million Indians go hungry, there is $14 billion of wastage of grains taking place every year. The average Indian consumes 2,455 calories per day compared to China's 12,141 calories. Both countries are about

the same size and both achieved independence around the same time and yet the Chinese people are over five times better fed than us. And these are average figures which include the 1 per cent wealthy, the calorie consumption of the rest of the 99 per cent would be well below these figures for both countries. No wonder India has such high levels of malnutrition, stunting and wasting – once again one of the worst in the world. Not only this, things were getting worse even well before the pandemic.

As *The Periodical Labour Force Survey* (PLFS) 2017–2018 showed a drastic drop in women's participation rates in employment, to only 16.5 per cent. In addition, the PLFS notes that 75 per cent of the regular workers earn less than ₹20,000 a month and 60 per cent of the casual workforce earn less than ₹5000 per month. If this is the plight of the 'employed' what would be that of the crores of unemployed, not to mention the plight of our agriculturists who have been committing suicide by the thousands since the last two decades, with over 10,000 taking their lives in 2019 alone – about 40 per cent of which were from Maharashtra.

APPENDIX I
Extracts of Letters from Jail to Gautam Vohra

From the very day of arrest my classmate of the 1963 batch at Doon School has been not only consistently supportive but has also actively campaigned for my release and the injustice of the 10-year confinement. Not only that, he would regularly send me lovely greeting cards which would help lift my spirits. Throughout this book, printing extracts from my letters to him will help give a picture of conditions as they unfolded.

In this appendix I share a few letters to Gautam that reflect some of my thoughts at that time. Those concerning jail conditions I have already interspersed within the main text.

Letter dated 30 December 2010

I have just been reading the two volumes of Chekov from the jail library. He is such a sensitive writer and brings out so well the inner agony of the middle class and declining aristocratic class. He brings out the hollowness in people's lives, both women (mostly young) and men; their frustrations (including sexual), the hypocrisies in relations, et al, of course he can sometimes be quite depressing as most of his short stories/plays end on a negative/hopeless note.

Gorky wrote of Chekov in the foreword: 'No one even understood the tragic nature of life's trifles so clearly and intuitively as Chekov did. Never before has a writer been able to hold up to human beings such a ruthless truthful picture of all that was shameful and pitiable in the dingy chaos of middle-class life.' Of course, he wrote at the end of the 19th century and early 20th century when there was so much turmoil in Russia. The last two decades of ultra-consumerism seems to have killed the sensitivities that existed in the earlier period; but now I think a new sensitivity will grow as a backlash to the tremendous alienation that this culture creates. Unfortunately, the mainline media will not allow it; but cannot control the internet.

16 October 2011

It's nice to hear you have a regular organic farm going, and it seems relatively close to your house to be able to take care. In Mumbai people also have taken such land but it takes 3 to 4 hours to get there. Imagine being able to get organic vegetables – how healthy! Last year I had grown a little dhania here (after that gave it up as the effort was too much) and it had such a strong flavour compared to what was sold to us. We also tried some lassan but it did not grow well. Anyhow the tulsi and neem leaves are a good health food. We have a surfeit now of them. The guava plant I planted last monsoon is also coming up well. Only 5 to 6 of the 12 rose plants may survive.

Regarding the eye, as I finally managed to get to AIIMS, I now feel more confident of reasonable treatment. As, for me, everything is in the eye – reading and writing my main activity. Naturally I got terribly worried when I saw my number increase from 0.75 to 2.5 in just six months. Never in my life has there been much change in my number. And with this, the pain. Now I find that the reason for the pain was that the jail doctor/ DDU had given the wrong number. Having once again changed the lens as per the AIIMS number, the pain is down.

I know that piece I wrote on childhood was terribly dry. One thing I just cannot remember things; second, I feel very embarrassed to write on myself; and thirdly I have been quite an introverted person with little that is particularly exciting. Now, regarding the next phase – Doon School – it will be probably as dry. Regarding my experience there I feel there are two aspects. One was the elite atmosphere. The second and more important aspect was the liberal teaching models with so much focus on sports, P.T., cross-country. It really helped develop an all-round personality. Even the method of educating was never the cramming, learning-by-rote method, which seems to dominate most educational systems. Also, the school taught us some discipline, with strict timings. Overall, I think the entire model was very conducive to the development of an individual and his personality. Then again in our days the general school atmosphere was so different from today – with huge competition, guide/tuition culture and little or no extra-curricular activities (except watching sports, instead of playing it). I do not know why Vikram Seth felt it was negative?

9 April 2012

Gautam, I saw some of the comments in the Rose Bowl. Who wants violence? It is a most abhorrent thing. Particularly for a humanist, who would like to see an end to all suffering. All one would ask for is a genuinely humanist system where people are really free to determine their own lives, in a true democracy. But where are people allowed all these rights and to live peacefully – even RTI activists are killed one after another. Now the IPS officer by the mining mafia. Earlier a missionary in Jharkhand also by the mining mafia. Then the lady in Ramdev's camp. The list is endless. Only a few names reach the newspaper. I am not talking of the 2½ lakh farmers who committed suicide, or the 7,000 who die daily in India due to starvation-related causes; nor the thousands of dowry deaths. Gautam, there is violence all around us. Worse still is the living dead, those who can barely afford one meal a day and for those who have to waste away because they cannot afford medicine. Actually, it is all this violence and much more, that one would want to see ended. It is the economic/political system that perpetuates all this. And the approach paper to the 12th plan is worse that the 11th plan. Of course, what better can be expected from a man (finance minister) who thinks ₹32/day is sufficient to be above the poverty line. Still, one does not want violence, but only if the powers that be allow change in a direction that can bring more humanity in this world. I wish this world could be free of all kinds of violence. I do not expect a utopia, but at least some movement in a positive direction as can be seen in some Latin American countries.

5 June 2012

Thanks also for raising the issue with the EU delegation. Actually, I personally knew some leftist groups/parties in Norway and Belgium (also Germany). They all are close to NGOs and socialists in Parliament and have done much work for human rights in Third World countries – particularly those in Norway and Belgium. In fact, soon after my arrest I was told two/three people from Norway came to see me, but were sent back from the airport. They can do much there as also Maja Daruwala. I am sure neither the EU parliamentarians nor Maja could agree with the Marxist/Maoist ideology, but it is a question of human rights.

25 April 2013

Lately got an interesting book from the Tihar library, *Trial of Socrates*. It gives some insights into the Greek philosophers and a picture of such an advanced democracy as early as the fifth and sixth century BC. Even as we consider the citizens as a restricted lot the level of democratic functioning was probably never repeated in history except for the brief period during the Paris Commune. What struck me was the high sense of responsibility of the citizens, and their sense of fair play. One could not even dream of that today, at least in India. Maybe in Europe it would be possible. At the trial there was a huge jury of 500 and there was a slim majority of just 30 that found him guilty.

The interesting point mentioned was that Socrates himself wanted the death penalty as he had said he did not fancy living in sickness in his old age. He was 70 when he drank the potion of Hemlock. Fantastic reading it was, that book, enlightening. I knew next to nothing of this important period of history. A good diversion from all that is going on in here and at the courts.

10 December 2013

Let us see what change is in store for us. But with a new chief minister, who is also minister for jails, we may hope for some relief; bail for senior citizens for a start. The bulk of the criminals in here, and the staff, are vehemently anti-Kejriwal. As also the Congress. Some dons say that even the Congress is better than AAP. There is no system for inmates to cast their votes in Delhi jails. I do not know why they are disenfranchised. Many have stood as candidates from prison, and several have won. This is all part of the general arbitrariness that harms the system. Of course, many inmates could not be bothered to vote. Most have one aim. To commit a bigger crime on their release and make pots of money. That is the common refrain. For the poorer inmates, life is hell. (Later I wrote of my disillusionment with the new Delhi government as they did nothing for jail reforms; and the only visit of the minister in charge of jails while I was there was a Digambar Jain who came briefly with a totally nude Jain priest – that, of course, was a major attraction as most of the inmates did not know their customs, particularly the Tamilian TSP boys, who were most amused.)

5 September 2014

This jail has a library. Just got a book of short stories by D.H. Lawrence. My problem with Lawrence is that all his characters seem to have a negative twist, and most stories end badly. Don't care for that. And all deal with the man-woman relationship, and all these are morose and sad, nothing joyful enlivens Lawrence's perspective. In Jail 3 I was reading Chekov. He too dealt with distress in human relationships. He seemed far more sensitive. Due to the back pain all I can do is to lie down and read. I better stop D.H. Lawrence; he does nothing to raise one's spirits.

APPENDIX II
Summary of Cases and the Criminal Justice System

Although I was released in October 2019 there are about 10 cases still pending against me. Besides, in the Delhi case the Special Cell have only recently challenged the acquittal in the High Court. In Telangana the police have not filed the charge sheet in six cases so as to keep these cases pending indefinitely.

The problem with the Indian criminal-justice system, as I have described throughout the book, is that the colonial structures continue including the IPC laws and the criminal procedure code. What is worse any amendments only worsen the situation, while, often their own rules/laws are not followed to the detriment of the ordinary citizen. Of course, all know that money and power can bend these laws.

Added to this oppressive criminal-justice system is the massive levels of corruption in the police, in the jails and also said to be in the judiciary. Corruption is a cancer that eats into the vitals of any system, however good. It is generally accompanied by arbitrariness and lack of transparency. It is, de facto, a mechanism against the poor and middle-classes who cannot afford the type of money it entails and is advantageous to the rich.

When I was in Hyderabad jail, I obtained a book entitled *Is it Police* (2014) written by the then DG of prisons, Telangana, Shri Vinoy Kr Singh, IPS, originally from Bhojpur, Bihar, where he outlines two things: corruption in the police force and the high levels of servility to the politicians. The situation must be so bad that even before retirement a top police officer was able to publish such an account. Some of the views presented are an eye-opener as it is from an insider in a top position. I recount a few most relevant ones to the criminal-justice system. The following are quotes taken from the book itself:

> Policemen are great status quoists. Naturally it would be so as we kill all initiative, discourage all change-mongers, and put great value on figures and statistics which can be fudged. Your career can be predicted by your attitude, caste, ability to lobby and having no principles in life... All the honest and sincere ones work for the system to keep it afloat and the smart and unprincipled ones enjoy the fruits without any sweat or plucking hair. This is policing!

It is true I met some very good police in all states except Delhi. Later, he goes on:

> Dishonesty continues; poor people languish in jails; false cases are booked at the behest of the mighty; the laws are bent to subserve political masters and the police look to be meant more for moneyed people. Only commoners have rightly no faith and love for police and they take it more as an enemy... Unfortunately the honest and hard-working policemen protect the dishonest and depraved, and arrogant and

powerful exploiting classes in the name of duty and rule of law... The system likes idealists and moralists but in the shelves and not in the field... In the present system if the powerful man hits, you go to the police and courts. He manages to prolong the case in the courts and ultimately acquittal through good lawyers and good influence. He can purchase or terrorise your witnesses, or you may not get even a single witness against the powerful man.

What the DGP says in this book is something we all witnessed and more, in case after case in the jails. Yet, coming from the mouth of a top IPS officer it is a damning indictment.

I see similar injustice in my cases which has been summarised by a team of lawyers, who have also given suggestions for amendments to the law to prevent the arbitrariness of the police in the future:

Below is a brief account of how the unjust criminal-justice system has been used to incarcerate 72-year-old Kobad Ghandy (KG) for over ten years in spite of being acquitted in case after case. The continuous incarceration, of which nearly seven years were spent in Tihar over a single case [also recognized by a British court as inhuman, as it refused to extradite bookie Sanjay Chawla, only on the grounds that being kept in Tihar could amount to a human rights violation] has destroyed his health and yet no relief was even given by the Supreme Court.

At least he faced no direct torture; others have faced worse. In a real democracy, a starting, minimum prerequisite should be a fair, independent and non-corrupt criminal-judicial system. Take the case of KG:

(i) He was arrested/abducted by the A.P.S.I.B. (AP State Intelligence Bureau) on Sept. 17, 2009, kept in illegal custody for three days, and handed over to the Delhi Special Cell on Sept. 20. The arrest date was shown as Sept. 20 not Sept. 17 and was produced in the Court on Sept. 21.

(ii) Though immediate police custody was refused, later, after 10 days, police custody with the Delhi Special Cell was given, a fake confession was extracted [unsigned by him], on the basis of which he was charged under the anti-terrorist UAPA [Unlawful Activities Prevention Act] sections 10, 13, 18, 20; though there was no concrete incidence on which the FIR was based, except for an alleged fake voter-ID card and supposed medical documents in another name, for which, anyhow, separate 420-related charges were put.

(iii) In early 2010, the A.P. police took him to Karimnagar court and produced him in a case there. This was a general conspiracy case where the police took a day's custody and the next day in the court produced a "confession" statement in Telugu [a language he does not know]. Though KG put on record that he never made the statement, does not even know the language, and has not signed it, this confession statement was made the basis for putting all the other cases in Telangana and Andhra.

(iv) According to the Evidence Act statements made in the police station are not admissible as evidence, even if signed by the accused. Also the main difference between UAPA & TADA was precisely on this point – while in UAPA, statements in police custody cannot be used as evidence, in TADA they could. Yet, courts are conducting trials based on these "confessions".

(v) In Feb. 2010 both Surat police and Patiala police [Punjab] put FIRs on him under UAPA. Though Patiala police began taking him for production the Gujrat police did not. The absurdity of both these cases is that the FIRs were for February 2010 when the accused had already been in jail for the past 4-5 months.

(vi) In the two AP cases (no division then of the state) of Vishakhapatnam and Mahbubnagar the AP High Court had given exactly similar judgements granting bail. The AP police challenged these at the Supreme Court, but not together - one at a time. The Vishaka case went to a Bench that did not accept the AP govt's SLP and threw the case out thereby upholding the bail. They then filed the Mahbubnagar case, and surprisingly it went to another court, which accepted the SLP. After many years the decision was given by a court that rejected the bail and, surprisingly ordered a speedy trial instead (which was impossible because of the imposition of 268 by the Delhi govt.). So, we have two exactly similar cases, and two exactly opposite judgements. Not only that, a judgement that could not be implemented because of 268 which was ignored. Since that time all these cases have been going to this court, of Justice Arun Mishra, which the lawyers say is the norm as once a case goes to a particular court all cases go there; yet two exactly similar judgements by the A.P. High Court went to different benches with opposite results!

(vii) He was produced regularly in the Patiala case [till 268 was clamped] through regular torturous journeys from Delhi, locked in the same cage within the police van used for transport within Delhi. The back-breaking journey was 5 hours there and 5 hours back in a single day. The case was apparently of a supposed incident in Punjab University where two people while taking a morning walk allegedly saw an individual making an inflammatory speech in April 2009 [no specific date was mentioned]. This was not even reported to the police and no FIR was filed. But suddenly, after KG's arrest those two who now filed the case, claimed that the photos in the newspapers they recognized – and so the case. Though he was finally acquitted of all charges in this case in October 2016, the police custody in Feb. 2010, the numerous tortuous trips to Patiala and back from Tihar, and the final 20-day incarceration in Patiala jail took a serious toll on his health.

(viii) In May 2010 the Delhi Lt. Governor at the behest of the Delhi Police/Govt. clamped 268 of the Cr.PC which prevented KG from attending any case outside Delhi until the Delhi case was over. The order de facto infringes the fundamental right to speedy trial and also infringes on the rights of courts in other states. The grounds mentioned for the order was the possibility of escape [at his age and health conditions]. Yet when the order was revoked in Oct. 2015 after the Delhi Court granted him interim bail on health grounds, there was no mention as to why the supposed escape threat no longer existed. The extent the police will go to enact a drama in order to impose 268 can be seen by the front page report that appeared in the Times of India on April 14, 2010 to portray an escape bid: *"…what happened in Allahabad on Sunday evening (i.e 11ᵗʰ Apr) was something the khaki-clad of Sangam city will not forget. A team of seven armed constables from the Delhi Police was escorting Ghandy to Midnapur in West Bengal for a court hearing, when they supposedly received a tip-off that the Naxals were planning to attack the train – and may even hijack it – to free their leader. The escort party is believed to have informed their bosses in Delhi about the threat perception following which the Delhi Police flashed an SOS to the UP police with a contingency plan – to take Ghandy off the train at Allahabad and keep him in heavy police security till alternate arrangements are made. The threat perception sounded real, so the information was taken with all seriousness and the top bosses including the DGP and his deputies – additional DG, ATS Brij Lal, and ADG (railways) got down to arrange a fool proof security blanket for Ghandy who was to reach Allahabad in 45 minutes. In the next one hour almost half the police force of Allahabad district was on its toes as every blue beacon and siren-filled police jeep and van was seen heading towards Allahabad station. Soon the railway station was swarming with the khaki – not only from the district police, but also the PAC, GRP and RPF. As the train rolled into the railway station, a group of 8 armed police got down with a middle-aged man in the Centre. Thereafter everything happened in fast forward mode till, as a stream of police jeeps, buses, vans, PAC & RAF trucks, along with fire tenders and ambulances were seen speeding out of the railway station portico to reach the heavily fortified cantonment PS in Allahabad... Soon the motorcade reached the cantonment PS which had a war-zone like police presence. While the SP city camped at the PS itself, top officials including DIG Allahabad visited the site...*" Thereafter there was no report of any attempt at hijack of that train. Yet, numerous appeals by KG to the NHRC [National Human Rights Commission]to lift 268, putting the real facts before them, fell on deaf ears. What was reported was pure filmi stuff which no wonder became the central theme of the film Chakravyuh.

(ix)   The Delhi case dragged on from Sept. 2009 to June 2016 in spite of the case being in a Fast Track Court, coming before two excellent judges and being argued by one of Delhi's senior advocates. During this entire period all other cases were frozen [because of 268], and came to life only once this was completed, while sitting idle in Tihar. He would see fellow inmates regularly attending court dates outside Delhi and completing 10-15 cases in the time KG finished one.

(x)   After the Delhi case was over (he was acquitted in the main UAPA charges of Maoism, but found guilty of impersonation in the 420-related charges) he was shifted to Hyderabad jail for the 11 cases on him in Telangana. These cases were mostly in places he had never heard of, where his name was merely added to ongoing cases through the "confession". But finally, he was charge sheeted in only ONE, where he was acquitted. In two other cases the charges were so absurd that even the magistrate [JMFC] refused to issue production warrants. The police challenged this in the Sessions Court but this too was dismissed in February 2017.

(xi) In all the other seven cases the police failed to file the charge sheets. It is ridiculous that even after roughly eight years the police are unable to file a charge sheet. Yet the cases do not fall through and only bail is granted; it can be revived at any time at the whims of the police. [lawyers inform that in the Karimnagar case the police has now filed a charge sheet]. Imagine an over 70-year-old person in frail health having to travel from Mumbai to unheard of places like Achampet for some future trial. This too seems like some Damocles sword consciously held over his head for the remaining part of his life.

(xii) The Visakhapatnam case, though bail had been granted long back [upheld by the Supreme Court] it was thought to be completed from jail as the idea of travelling from Mumbai was unthinkable. But here too it seemed that the judge was consciously dragging the case and as his prostrate/urinary problem was getting acute he was forced to take the bail and seek medical treatment.

(xiii) Though finally released from jail on 12 December 2017, he was re-arrested in three days on Dec. 16 while attending the Achampet court. Both the Jharkhand and Surat police had sent production warrants to Tihar while 268 was in force. Though he was never produced the warrants were pending in the file. But after 268 was revoked while all other courts/police sent warrants none were sent from these two places. As a result, in November 2016, KG together with the jail superintendent of Hyderabad jail wrote official letters to the respective courts to take his production. But as there was no response a reminder was once again sent in March 2016. Again, no response. Meanwhile as all his Telangana cases were over, he was sent to Vishaka jail. After news came in of the arrest of a person from Nagpur in the Surat case three more letters were sent by the Vishaka jail superintendent and KG; but again, to no avail. Seeing that all attempts had been made the Vishaka jail authorities released him as no further cases were pending in the records.

(xiv) But before release, fearing precisely the re-arrest that finally took place, KG went to the Supreme Court to prevent arrest in these cases where production warrants were not being served even though requested time and again by the jail authorities, without the intervention of the highest court. Also, evidence of these letters was handed over to the court. An elaborate case was prepared by a team of juniors, vetted by senior advocate Colin Gonsalves and finalized by

India's top most advocate Fali Nariman. Finally, it was argued in the Court by Fali Nariman. In spite of this, and also bringing KG's health and age into account, the bench headed by Arun Mishra was not willing to give relief, so the case was withdrawn.

(xv) Once taken to Jharkhand yet another case was put on him of which there were no earlier records. With new cases being put on in this fashion there could be no end to the incarceration even without being sentenced.

(xvi) Finally, after nearly two years in Jharkhand, as soon as bail was given in April 2019 the Surat police sent the production warrant. If they had sent it earlier both cases could have gone on simultaneously. But no, it was consciously delayed to maximise incarceration. But due to the efficiency of the Gujarat courts and the fact that in that case all the earlier 25 accused had been given bail, KG was finally given bail on 16 October 2019 and achieved freedom.

(xvii) After over 10 years of incarceration in numerous cases in a number of states, he has been found guilty merely of "impersonation" in the Delhi case. Impersonation has often been adopted by investigative journalists [and later openly declared]; besides thousands, nay lakhs of shell companies and benami properties involve impersonation, but one does not hear of a single person being touched for impersonation.

"In other words, the criminal-justice system is able to hound a person without any evidence of any crime - just because he stands up for the poor

- though the person is aged and in ill health; there is no mercy even if it results in death or crippling.

Some questions that arise for a democratic criminal-justice system:

(a)   Why should 'confession' statements made in the police station [and not even signed] be accepted by the courts, and cases conducted on that basis when it is neither allowed by the Evidence Act nor the UAPA. Through this process cases can be put in such unheard of places like – G.K. Veedhi, Achampet, Narayanpet, Tenughat, etc making a mockery of the judicial system.

(b)   While in AP/Telangana cases proceed relatively faster [of course that too depends on the judge and PP] why in the capital city and places like Jharkhand should it be so inefficient. Even in Patiala the case was wrapped up in 20 days.

(c)   268 of the Cr.PC should be treated as unconstitutional for reasons already mentioned.

(d)   Should there not be a time limit for materializing of a FIR or presenting a charge sheet. Should not these become automatically infructuous after say six months. Police inefficiency or government's ill-intentions should not be promoted to play with the lives of individuals and utilized to crush dissent. It is said "let law take its course" – in the case of KG it was doing so, keeping him in jail without any significant conviction for over 10 years! For the elderly and ill it could result in judicial death; but who will take the responsibility?

(e) Though acquitted in the UAPA charges in Delhi, Patiala, Telangana, how can it be put again and again in other states – like say Jharkhand and Surat." Since India is a single nation surely acquittal in one case should be valid everywhere in the country when the charge is the same.

These points were prepared by a team of lawyers for the consideration of human rights organizations and civil liberties groups and also summarise the cases against me.

While summarising the exceedingly unjust criminal-justice system it is necessary to put on record that, on the whole, I faced very fair and sensitive judges in most places. As I have said repeatedly throughout the book, it is not the individuals who are to blame but the system. It was the same, with the police, at the individual level, except for Delhi, in all other places they were considerate and showed no venom. Probably from a certain amount of respect for what I stood for and the integrity of the cause.

If it had not been for the selfless support of all these lawyers and many more, the jail sojourn may have been longer. Yet with all this assistance and not even a single major conviction (except for the impersonation charge in the Delhi case), it took over ten years – so much for the criminal-justice system in India. This resulted in ten years behind bars, in other words encompassing nearly 15 per cent of my entire life.

Acknowledgements

My first and foremost thanks goes out to my relatives and friends who spared no effort to help me when I was in jail and campaign for my release. At the head of this is my sister, Mahrouk, who, at her late age would come all the way from Mumbai to Delhi and even Hazaribagh to assist. Besides, she would regularly bring/send health foods and vitamins which was, probably the main reason why I was able to sustain my health over such a lengthy period and at this late age. Not only that, throughout the ten years she would regularly send magazines (*Outlook*, *Frontline*, etc.) by post which helped keep me updated on events throughout the world and in India and facilitated my writing, as also facilitating my settling down after release. Also, to Reetha Balsavar, my sister-in-law, who not only was the first person to land up at the court after my arrest, (as also Jyoti Punwani) but has consistently helped in numerous ways from beginning to the end and even after release.

Then there were all those who would come and meet me in Tihar in spite of the lengthy, tiring and humiliating procedures. Thanks to my cousin Kamal and her daughter Manisha, not to mention the cheerful Cherryl of Gurgaon who would regularly come and visit me in jail. Particularly

Moushumi was a regular visitor to the jail and she would continuously assist my sister in bringing items needed. Also to Gautam Navlakha who too would come often and in the early phases it was he who brought me the books that helped me write the six-part article 'Freedom'. There were also many others who wanted to come but couldn't as only ten names were allowed on the list.

Particular mention must go to my Doon School classmate, Gautam Vohra, who from day one has campaigned incessantly for my release, not only amongst our classmates but also others. He helped raise money for my cataract operation with contributions from other Doscos like Darshan Singh. Then there were the editors of the two magazines *Parsiana* (Jehangir Patel) and *Rose Bowl* (Valentina – Radhika Trivedi) brought out for Parsis and Doon School Old Boys respectively, who carried numerous articles in my support. Last but not least there were the human rights activists Moushumi Basu, Maja Daruwala, Gautam Navlakha, as also all the lawyers who I will recount later, who were unstinting in their support.

Particular mention must also go to D. Raja, present general secretary of the CPI and earlier a Rajya Sabha member, who not only lobbied for my support and health concerns, but also supported in many other ways. Similarly, thanks also to the local CPI unit in Vishaka and its district secretary for their continuous support, also after release.

Besides these there were the hundreds of others, known and unknown, who lent support in numerous small ways which one can never forget; in confinement even the tiniest support, a word of commiseration, is like nirvana to the hapless.

Next, my thanks go to the vast number of lawyers who mostly fought all my cases pro-bono. Without this help nothing would have been possible as I could never have afforded their fees. These include senior advocate Rebecca

John and her entire team, particularly Bhavook Chauhan, who brilliantly argued the case in Delhi and secured an acquittal in the main charge – UAPA. There were also the other advocates in Delhi who helped out like the Andhra advocates Dashrath and K.D. Rao, Sandeep Vishnu and Priyanka Kakkar, all of whom tirelessly visited me in jail, which was a major source of giving confidence to face the numerous cases, with Sandeep coordinating with all other advocates involved in my cases. In Andhra Pradesh/Telangana there were the dedicated human rights advocates Dashrath, Balla Ravindranath, K.S. Chelam, Appa Rao, K.D. Rao many of whom also assisted in cases in other parts of the country. Particularly Ravi (Ravindranath) helped coordinate my cases all over the country, and Dashrath and K.D. Rao spent a long time in Delhi assisting with the legal work. Dashrath even visited me in Tenughat. Then there was the Punjab case where one of Patalia's senior most advocate, B.S. Sodhi, with the assistance of Chandigarh's two human rights lawyers, Aarti and Ajay, completed my case in a mere 20 days. Particular mention must be made of advocate P.A. Sabastian from CPDR, Mumbai, who not only helped organize lawyers for my defence but also visited me in Tihar. I will never forget their selfless assistance in an alien place. In Jharkhand as well there was the senior advocate Jitendra Singh in the high court without whose assistance nothing would have happened in the courts there. Also, there was advocate Rohit Thakur in the lower court who helped from day one, not only in the case but at a human level getting warm clothes in winter and bringing medicines, health foods, etc. given by my sister. Finally, it was Surat's senior advocate, Panwalla, and his team, who acquired the bail in the case within barely one-and-a-half months, together with the tireless assistance of advocate Atodariya in the magistrate court. Coordination of these lawyers in both Jharkhand and Surat was done by the tireless efforts of advocate Harsheet Dingra of Delhi. Last but not least the list would not be complete without the mention of the senior advocates of the Supreme Court who tried to get relief at that level – Fali Nariman and Colin Gonsalves. Besides these, the Maharashtra lawyers, Surendra Gadling and his Nagpur team (including advocate Nihal Sinh), as also Susan Abraham assisted though there was no case in their state. Lastly, thanks must go to Supreme Court lawyers Prashant Bhushan and advocate Ganesh who agreed to help out in the challenge of the 268, which could not be done. Inspite of this battery of lawyers, mostly fighting free of cost, my cases still took ten years; one can just imagine the plight of an ordinary citizen who does not have access to proper lawyers...

Besides the two magazines already mentioned, particular thanks must go to the journalists of *Indian Express*, particularly Uma Vishnu, and the editor of *Mainstream Weekly*, Sumit Chakravartty for publishing the articles I wrote and bringing my ideas and views from the confines of jail to the light of day. Also, thanks must go to Sunetra Choudhury who wrote a separate chapter on me in her book *Behind Bars*. Also, the many unknown (to me) writers like Sumanta Banerjee, and many others who wrote articles in my support in the media which I came to know of only after my release. The three journalists who met me immediately after release were Sudheendra Kulkarni, Jehangir Patel and Jyoti Punwani who have been a continuous support. What was most touching was that Jyoti and Meenal Baghel (editor of *Mumbai Mirror*) took me for a lunch at the BKC club immediately after release and Sudheendra Kulkarni came with his wife Kamaxshi to my sister's place at Bandra, while Jehangir invited us over for lunch with the family.

Finally, after my release, thanks to the three families that helped me settle back into normal life after so many years of isolation – those of my sister, Sunil/Reetha (Anu's) and Jyoti

Punwani. It was my sister, Mahrouk, who took the final bail in Surat and drove through the night to reach her home at four in the morning. Also to Meenal Madhukar, who received received me at that early hour with flowers, and had twice travelled to Jharkhand to show me methods to work on my energy to remove the fears, guilts, mistrust, frustrations, etc. within myself in order to create positive energies and live more happily and confidently. It was very useful, particularly, when faced with the trauma of long incarceration and frustratingly slow legal processes. And it was Reetha who rendered invaluable help in assisting me settling back into life by helping me getting all my documentation done. Being out of touch for so long I would have never managed on my own. Also, to Anu's mother, Kumud Shanbag, who, in spite of poor health, supported me throughout the incarceration and was regularly in touch.

Major thanks go to Govind and Roshan Shahani for going through the entire manuscript in great detail and giving extremely valuable suggestions. Without the enormous effort they put in to make the original draft readable this book would never have seen the light of day. Also, to Tara Kapur who helped introduce valuable ideas and improvements to the manuscript and did a detailed check of the original manuscript. Also, many thanks to the team of advocates, Xerxes Ranina and Simin Patel, who have been assisting me in every possible way finalizing the manuscript, from giving suggestions on the content, helping with the publishers and also many a technical assistance.

And finally thanks to the entire team of Roli Books for the splendid job done in such difficult Covid time. Particular mention must go to Priya Kapoor for her understanding, perseverance and patience throughout the entire process dealing with a novice like me. Also to Chirag Thakkar who helped initiate the process; and most particularly thanks to the excellent and creative editing done by Priya, Simar Puneet and Neelam Narula. Also thanks to Ahana Singh for her excellent and professional promotion of the book. Most rewarding though has been the warmth in the relationship that evolved between us, even though we have never met.

Index